AF843362

Numanities - Arts and Humanities in Progress

Volume 37

Series Editor

Simona Stano, University of Turin, Turin, Italy

Associate Editor

Alin Olteanu, Institute of Language Sciences, Shanghai International Studies University, Shanghai, China

Editorial Board

Oana Andreica, Gheorghe Dima National Academy of Music, Cluj-Napoca, Romania

Paulo C. Chagas, University of California, Riverside, CA, USA

Teodoro Forcht Dagi, Mayo College of Medicine and Surgery, Newton Center, MA, USA

Kevin Holm-Hudson, School of Music, University of Kentucky, Lexington, USA

Seema Khanwalkar, Faculty of Design, CEPT University, Ahmedabad, Gujarat, India

Ľudmila Lacková Bennett, Palacký University in Olomouc, Olomouc Czech Republic

Dario Martinelli, Kaunas University of Technology, Kaunas, Lithuania

Lina Navickaitė-Martinelli, Department of Musicology, Lithuanian Academy of Music & Theatre, Vilnius, Lithuania

Juha Ojala, Sibelius Academy, University of the Arts Helsinki, Helsinki, Finland

Rima Povilionienė, Department of Musicology, Lithuanian Academy of Music & Theatre, Vilnius, Lithuania

John Tredinnick-Rowe, University of Exeter, Penryn, UK

Jessica Ullrich, University of Fine Arts Münster, Nuremberg, Germany

The book series *Numanities* is a proactive platform in the form of monographs and edited volumes in thematic collections, contributing to new emerging fields within art and humanistic research, i.e. "Numanities" (or New Humanities), which aim at unifying the various approaches and potentials of arts and humanities in the context, dynamics and problems of current societies. Books published in the series discuss the ongoing crisis of the humanities and its possible solutions, in a spirit that is both critical and self-critical.

The series, indexed in Scopus, is aimed at a broad academic audience. Besides publishing work generally deemed as "traditional humanities research", it also publishes texts that meet the demands of societal changes. Such texts include multi/inter/cross/transdisciplinary dialogues between the humanities and social, or natural sciences. Furthermore, the series is interested also in what one may call "humanities in disguise", that is, works that may currently belong to non-humanistic areas, but remain epistemologically rooted in a humanistic vision of the world. It also welcomes less academically conventional forms of research animated by creative and innovative humanities-based approaches, as well as applied humanities. Lastly, this book series is interested in forms of investigations in which the humanities monitor and critically assess their scientific status and social condition.

This series publishes monographs, edited volumes, and commented translations.

Vincenzo De Masi

A Critical Analysis of China's Animation Industry

From the Magic Lantern to Artificial Intelligence

Springer

Vincenzo De Masi
School of Journalism and Communication
Guangdong University of Foreign Studies
Guangzhou, China

ISSN 2510-442X ISSN 2510-4438 (electronic)
Numanities - Arts and Humanities in Progress
ISBN 978-3-032-18655-3 ISBN 978-3-032-18656-0 (eBook)
https://doi.org/10.1007/978-3-032-18656-0

© The Editor(s) (if applicable) and The Author(s), under exclusive license to Springer Nature Switzerland AG 2026

This work is subject to copyright. All rights are solely and exclusively licensed by the Publisher, whether the whole or part of the material is concerned, specifically the rights of translation, reprinting, reuse of illustrations, recitation, broadcasting, reproduction on microfilms or in any other physical way, and transmission or information storage and retrieval, electronic adaptation, computer software, or by similar or dissimilar methodology now known or hereafter developed.
The use of general descriptive names, registered names, trademarks, service marks, etc. in this publication does not imply, even in the absence of a specific statement, that such names are exempt from the relevant protective laws and regulations and therefore free for general use.
The publisher, the authors and the editors are safe to assume that the advice and information in this book are believed to be true and accurate at the date of publication. Neither the publisher nor the authors or the editors give a warranty, expressed or implied, with respect to the material contained herein or for any errors or omissions that may have been made. The publisher remains neutral with regard to jurisdictional claims in published maps and institutional affiliations.

This Springer imprint is published by the registered company Springer Nature Switzerland AG
The registered company address is: Gewerbestrasse 11, 6330 Cham, Switzerland

If disposing of this product, please recycle the paper.

Preface

The present volume represents the culmination of a long research journey devoted to the study of creative industries in China, with a particular focus on animation. My academic interest in this field was shaped during my doctoral years, when I began to investigate how cultural production in China was being reorganized in relation to new state policies, international collaborations, and the emerging global discourse on the creative economy. Within this broad framework, animation quickly revealed itself to be a key site of inquiry. It was at once a cultural expression deeply rooted in China's artistic traditions and a strategic sector promoted by the government as part of its vision for modernization and soft power projection.

In examining the animation industry, I was struck early on by its ability to condense many of the contradictions that define China's creative industries as a whole. On the one hand, animation embodies artistic experimentation, drawing on the visual language of ink painting, paper cutting, and folklore. On the other, it has been tightly embedded in political campaigns, ideological imperatives, and market reforms. This duality continues to mark its development: the same films that celebrate Chinese mythology or experiment with aesthetic innovation are also expected to fulfill political goals and to succeed in highly competitive global markets. Animation thus becomes a privileged vantage point from which to study the broader dynamics of the Chinese cultural economy.

This book brings together years of research that have taken me across archives, universities, festivals, and industry conferences. It revisits historical milestones such as the pioneering work of the Wan brothers in the 1920s and 1930s, the flourishing of the Shanghai Animation Film Studio during the so-called golden age, and the disruptions of the Cultural Revolution. It explores the transformations brought by the market reforms of the 1980s, the entry of foreign media, and the progressive industrialization of animation in the 2000s, when state agencies began to frame it as a pillar of the national creative industries. It also reflects the current global moment of Chinese animation, with films such as *Ne Zha* showing remarkable commercial success and Fengshen-related productions gaining increasing international visibility.

The ambition of this work is not merely descriptive. By adopting a critical approach, I aim to show how Chinese animation reflects the tensions between cultural policy, market logics, and technological innovation. The rise of digital platforms and video-sharing ecosystems has created new modes of circulation and consumption, while also reinforcing mechanisms of control and censorship. At the same time, the emergence of artificial intelligence as a creative tool is reshaping production practices, raising ethical questions, and redefining the very notion of creativity. These are not issues limited to animation alone, but animation provides a particularly sharp and revealing case through which to analyze them.

This research has also been informed by broader comparative perspectives. The development of Chinese animation cannot be fully understood without considering its interactions with Japanese anime, American studios, and regional traditions across East Asia. It has always been part of a dialogue with other aesthetic and industrial models, sometimes through imitation, sometimes through creative adaptation, and increasingly through hybridization. The Chinese animation industry today is both a national project and a global player, simultaneously seeking to assert cultural specificity and to participate in international markets.

The book is addressed to multiple audiences. For scholars in media, film, and cultural studies, it offers a framework to situate Chinese animation within global media history and political economy. For students, it provides a detailed introduction to a cultural form that is at once artistic, industrial, and ideological. For practitioners and policy makers, it sheds light on the institutional contexts, the industrial strategies, and the technological innovations that continue to shape the sector. In this sense, the book speaks to the broader conversation on how creative industries evolve in societies undergoing rapid transformation, and how they negotiate the balance between cultural authenticity, economic viability, and technological change.

Writing this book has been a collective endeavor in many ways. I owe a great debt to the colleagues and mentors who encouraged me to pursue the study of creative industries at a time when animation was rarely considered central to academic debates. I am grateful to the students who, through their curiosity and creativity, have constantly pushed me to refine my ideas and to consider new perspectives. Fieldwork in China has been made possible by the openness of animators, producers, and festival organizers who generously shared their experiences and insights. Archival research, often challenging, was facilitated by librarians, curators, and institutions that safeguarded fragile historical records and made them accessible to researchers.

I would also like to acknowledge the intellectual communities that have sustained this work. Conferences, workshops, and collaborative projects across China, Europe, and North America provided invaluable spaces to test arguments, receive feedback, and remain engaged with ongoing debates. These exchanges have continually reminded me that research is never solitary but always part of a larger dialogue.

Above all, this book is a testimony to the conviction that animation is not a minor art form or a secondary industry. It is a central field through which we can understand how societies imagine themselves, how states articulate their ambitions, and how technology reshapes creativity. To study Chinese animation is therefore to study not only a cultural form but also the transformations of modern China itself.

Guangzhou, China Vincenzo De Masi

Acknowledgments This book owes its existence to the support, friendship, and intellectual generosity of many individuals who accompanied me during the years in which this project gradually took shape.

I would like to begin by expressing my sincere gratitude to Professor Giuseppe Richeri and Professor Michele Sorice, whose guidance and intellectual inspiration encouraged me to pursue the study of media and creative industries with rigor and curiosity. I am also thankful to Professor Cristina Lasagni and Professor Ruth Hungerbühler, who opened my perspective on documentary culture and taught me to appreciate its depth and diversity. Eleonora Benecchi deserves heartfelt thanks for her encouragement during the early phases of my research, while my colleagues Chwen Chwen Chen, Gianluigi Negro, and Gabriele Balbi at the Università della Svizzera Italiana, together with Margrit Tröhler and Veronika Rall of the Universität Zürich, provided an invaluable scholarly environment where many of these ideas were first tested.

My academic path was also enriched by the years spent at the New York Institute of Technology, where I was fortunate to collaborate with William F. Smith, John Smith, and above all my close friend Michael Mallory, whose support and friendship remain deeply meaningful. I warmly thank the colleagues and friends from the "School" community, including Torsten Zenas Burns, Aaron Anderson, Jim Batcho, Carmen Llovet, Erin Bie, Justine Lopez, Gabriel Teo, Zhou Young, and all the students with whom I shared unforgettable experiences and who taught me to see both the challenges and the beauty of China. I would like to express my sincere gratitude to Liu Shunli, Dean Hou Yingzhong, Vice Dean Li Junling, Du Huizhen, and all my colleagues at the School of Journalism and Communication, Guangdong University of Foreign Studies (GDUFS), for their warm welcome, support, and assistance.

The years in Zhuhai were marked by extraordinary friendships that sustained me during the most difficult moments of the Covid-19 period. I am grateful to Ezio Gargantini, Raphael Cooper, Paolo Vincenzo Genovese, Luciano Zubillaga, Holger Briel, Tom Stain, Jocelyn Ford, Brian Clarke, Eduardo Monaco, and Andrew Peat for their companionship and for the sense of solidarity we shared in those demanding years.

I would like to express my sincere gratitude to the Associazione Città Murate del Veneto, and in particular to its President, Claudio Arzenton, who, together with Massimiliano D'Ambra, consistently supports the Italy–China exchange program. I also wish to acknowledge my dear friends from Salento, including Alfonso Riso, Vincenzo Chiarello, Sara Siviero, Daniele e Davide Bleve, Miriam Marzo, Andrea D'Amico, Donato Chiarello, Gino Bleve and many others, who even across distance never ceased to encourage me and to remind me of the importance of perseverance.

Several collaborators have, over time, become trusted friends and indispensable partners in creative and academic projects. I am deeply thankful to Siyi Li, Zhang Bo, Jin Xuetao, Yuhan Song, Qinke Di, Ernestina Xinyi Zhu, Yan Han, Wu Xiaokun, Miroslav Atanasov, Victoria E. Cann, Stuart Burch, Jingwei Piao, Zhan

Zhang, Evelyn Mai, Colin Sparks, Mengjiao Wu, Luo Qing, Bruce Xuanli, Moreno Benigno, Emanuele Asprella, Flavia Pessoa Serafim and Brian Jian, together with many others, for the projects already realized and those that lie ahead.

Finally, my deepest gratitude belongs to my family. To my father and mother, whose love and encouragement have been a constant foundation; to my sisters, Anna and Maria Lucia, whose closeness has always been a guide; to Aiko, Gianluigi, Annachiara, Sofia, Pietro and Renato, whose presence brings joy and hope; to my cousins; and to my aunts and uncles, who have always supported me with generosity and care. To them, as well as to my two dearest companions, Minako and Kai Biagio, I dedicate the warmest and most personal thanks.

Competing Interests The author has no competing interests to declare that are relevant to the content of this manuscript.

Introduction—Reframing Chinese Animation: Critique, Method, and Historical Lens

The trajectory of Chinese animation, from its nascent strokes in the early twentieth century to its current engagement with artificial intelligence, offers a compelling narrative that mirrors and refracts the broader sociopolitical and economic transformations of China. This art form, often relegated to the periphery of cultural studies or viewed simplistically as children's entertainment, demands a more profound and critical examination. This book argues that Chinese animation serves as a crucial lens for analyzing the intricate and often contradictory dynamics of state ambition, market imperatives, evolving cultural identities, and technological disruption in modern and contemporary China. It moves beyond a strictly historical account to critically assess how animation has been instrumentalized as a tool for economic development, a vehicle for ideological dissemination, a contested site of creative expression, and a vanguard in the nation's pursuit of global soft power.

The significance of Chinese animation has undergone a substantial transformation. What began as an artistic endeavor, exemplified by the pioneering works of the Wan brothers (Wan Laiming 万籁鸣, Wan Guchan 万古蟾, Wan Chaochen 万超尘, Wan Dihuan 万涤寰) (Lent 2003), later blossomed into the distinctive "Chinese School" of animation under the Shanghai Animation Film Studio (上海美术电影制片厂, Shànghǎi Měishù Diànyǐng Zhìpiànchǎng, SAFS) (Zhang, H., 2003), often inextricably linked to state ideological agendas. Animation served as a medium for propaganda during times of conflict and political upheaval, reflecting the dominant ideological currents of the moment, particularly during the Anti-Rightist Campaign (反右运动, *Fǎn Yòu Yùndòng*) and the Cultural Revolution (文化大革命, *Wénhuà Dàgémìng*), when artistic expression was largely subordinated to political messaging (Ehrlich 2011; Lent 2001). The subsequent period of reform and opening up (改革开放, *Gǎigé Kāifàng*) allowed for a brief artistic renaissance, which was soon challenged by the influx of foreign animation and the emerging pressures of a market economy.

The dawn of the twenty-first century marked a turning point. The Chinese government began to recognize animation not merely as a cultural product but as a central component of its growing "creative industries" (文化创意产业, wénhuà chuàngyì chǎnyè) and a powerful tool for projecting soft power (软实力, *ruǎn shílì*) on the global stage (Keane 2007; Sun 2010). This top-down industrialization initiative, characterized by generous subsidies, the establishment of animation industrial parks (动漫产业基地, dòngmàn chǎnyè jīdì), and ambitious production targets (Qing 2006; Blue Book of China's Radio, Film and Television 2009), aimed to position China as a global animation powerhouse. Yet this approach has produced a complex and often paradoxical landscape. Although production volume has increased dramatically, questions regarding originality, creative freedom, and lasting cultural impact continue to surface.

The phenomenal success of films such as *Ne Zha* (哪吒之魔童降世, *Nézhā zhī Mótóng jiàngshì*, 2019), which broke box office records and earned acclaim for its reinterpretation of classical mythology through contemporary aesthetics, revealed the growing potential of Chinese animation. This promise was further realized with its sequel, *Ne Zha 2* (哪吒之魔童闹海, *Nézhā zhī Mótóng nào hǎi*, 2025), which not only resonated with domestic audiences but also achieved extraordinary global commercial success, reportedly becoming the highest-grossing animated film worldwide and the first non-English-language title to surpass the two-billion-dollar mark (Xinhua 2025; Reuters 2025a). These milestones, rooted in the creative reinvention of traditional narratives like *Fengshen Yanyi* (封神演义) (Xu, Z., 16th Century), reflect the capacity of Chinese animation to engage audiences on a global scale and to generate valuable intellectual property. The success of the *Ne Zha* franchise, along with the expansion of the "Fengshen Cinematic Universe" (封神宇宙, *Fēngshén Yǔzhòu*), underscores a strategic shift toward leveraging indigenous cultural heritage for economic and symbolic capital.

However, even these landmark successes exist within, and in some cases in tension with, a broader industrial and political framework. This book critically examines the effectiveness and unintended consequences of state intervention in the animation sector. It explores how policies aimed at cultivating national champions have coincided with persistent concerns about a "creativity deficit" in the wider industry, the proliferation of derivative content, and a complex relationship with intellectual property, exemplified by the enduring phenomenon of *shanzhai* (山寨) culture (Keane 2013; Pang 2012). While productions like the *Ne Zha* films have achieved impressive breakthroughs, the industry as a whole continues to grapple with the challenge of producing work that is both innovative and internationally competitive. This study explores how Chinese animation seeks to develop narratives that are simultaneously authentic and globally appealing, negotiating the competing demands of cultural specificity, market accessibility, and ideological alignment. The evolving role of *manhua* (漫画, Chinese comics) as both a creative resource and a contested space for intellectual property and transmedia development (Wong 2002) further illustrates the complexity of this field.

The contemporary landscape is increasingly shaped by the disruptive effects of digital technology. The rise of online video platforms such as Bilibili (哔哩哔哩), Tencent Video (腾讯视频, *Téngxùn Shìpín*), and iQiyi (爱奇艺) has fundamentally transformed patterns of production, distribution, and consumption, offering new opportunities for independent creators while also introducing new mechanisms of control and censorship (Cunningham and Silver 2012; Negro 2011). The proliferation of mobile animation, short-form content, and the active participation of online fan communities has significantly influenced viewer expectations and production trends (Voci 2010). Within this shifting ecosystem, independent works like *Miss Puff* (泡芙小姐, *Pàofú Xiǎojiě*), created by Pi San (邳三), provide meaningful insights into alternative modes of production and creative autonomy.

More recently, the emergence of artificial intelligence (人工智能, *réngōng zhìnéng*) presents both unprecedented opportunities and profound challenges for the Chinese animation sector. As AI tools for scriptwriting, image generation, automated animation, and voice synthesis become increasingly sophisticated, they are poised to reshape production processes. The Chinese government's strategic prioritization of AI development across all industries, including creative sectors, suggests that algorithms will soon play a significant role in shaping animated content. This book extends its critical lens to this evolving "AI Era," investigating its implications for labor, creativity, cultural authenticity, and ethics. It asks whether a uniquely "Chinese style" (中国风格, *Zhōngguó fēnggé*) of animation can emerge in an algorithm-driven creative environment, and what ethical considerations arise when human artistry intersects with machine learning.

To engage with this complex terrain, the study adopts an interdisciplinary approach. It combines historical analysis to track the evolution of Chinese animation within specific sociopolitical contexts, with a critical political economy perspective to assess the influence of state policies, market structures, and institutional frameworks (Richeri 2006; Zhao 2008). Perspectives from cultural studies are employed to examine animation as a medium of meaning-making, identity construction, and cultural negotiation (Caldwell 2008; White 2006). Additionally, insights from Science and Technology Studies (STS) inform the analysis of technological development and its effects on creative practices and industrial trajectories, particularly in relation to digitalization and artificial intelligence (Sismondo 2011). This integrated framework facilitates a nuanced understanding of Chinese animation not merely as a set of texts or market products, but as a cultural formation deeply embedded in China's ongoing transformation.

The book is organized to guide the reader through this critical history and contemporary analysis. Chapters 1 through 4 revisit the formative eras of Chinese animation, tracing its artistic origins (*donghua* 动画, *měishùpiàn* 美术片) and ideological imprint up to the challenges posed by market reforms and globalization in the late twentieth century. Chapters 5 through 7 turn to the present, examining the state-led push for industrialization, the strategic use of soft power, continuing debates around creativity and intellectual property, and the impact of digital distribution platforms. Chapter 7 and the Conclusion explore the algorithmic frontier, evaluating the current and potential role of artificial intelligence in reshaping the Chinese animation landscape and raising critical questions about its long-term implications. A final comparative section in Chap. 8 positions Chinese animation within the global ecosystem, reflecting on its distinct trajectory and the tensions between state priorities, commercial imperatives, cultural authenticity, and technological change. Ultimately, the book argues that the story of Chinese animation is not merely about cartoons, it is a critical narrative about China's past, present, and technologically shaped future.

References

Blue Book 2011. Annual Report on Development of China's Animation Industry. Social Sciences Academic Press.

Caldwell, J. T. 2008. *Production culture: Industrial reflexivity and critical practice in film and television.* Duke University Press.

Cunningham, S., and J. Silver. 2012. *Screen distribution and the new King Kongs of the online world.* Palgrave Macmillan.

Ehrlich, N. 2011. Animated documentaries as masking. *Animation Studies, 6.* https://journal.animationstudies.org/nea-ehrlich-animated-documentaries-as-masking/.

Keane, M. 2013. *China's creative industries: Copyright, piracy, and the state.* Polity.

Lent, J. A. 2001. *Animation in Asia and the Pacific.* Indiana University Press.

Lent J. A. 2003. Asian Animation: Artistic And Commercial Perspectives edited, Vol. 14, No.1, Spring/summer, Asian Cinema Studies Society.

Negro, G. 2011. The video sharing market in China: An overview. *China Media Observatory Newsletter.*

Pang, L. 2012. *The distortion of cultural industries in China.* Routledge.

Qing, L. 2006. *The development of Chinese Animation Industry.* China Radio: Film and Television Press.

Reuters. 2025a, February 18. *Chinese film Ne Zha 2 becomes highest-grossing animated film globally.* https://www.reuters.com/lifestyle/chinese-film-nezha-2-becomes-highest-grossing-animated-film-globally-2025-02-18/.

Sun, W. 2010. Mission Impossible? Soft Power, Communication Capacity, and the Globalization of Chinese Media. International Journal of Communication 4: 54–72.

Voci, P. 2010. *China on video: Smaller-screen realities.* Routledge.

Wong, W. 2002. *Hong Kong comics: A history of manhua.* New York: Princeton Architectural Press.

Xinhua. 2025, June 30. *Ne Zha 2 ends record-breaking China run with 2.13 billion US dollars.* https://english.news.cn/20250630/74574b4e9823406fb2da565b750fa4a7/c.html.

Zhang, H. 2003. Some characteristics of Chinese animation. *Asian Cinema* 14 (1): 70–79.

Contents

Chapter 1
Early Trajectories of Chinese Animation (1900s–1976)

Abstract This chapter traces the emergence and consolidation of Chinese animation from the early twentieth century to the end of the Cultural Revolution in 1976. It begins with theoretical reflections on the definition of animation and its early global origins, including optical devices such as the zoetrope and praxinoscope, before situating the medium in the Chinese context. The pioneering work of the Wan brothers in Shanghai is examined as the foundation of a national industry that sought to integrate indigenous artistic traditions with cinematic innovation. Their milestone film *Princess Iron Fan* (1941) is highlighted as both a landmark of wartime propaganda and a source of inspiration for Japanese animation. The chapter further explores the role of animation in the Republican era, during the Second Sino-Japanese War, and throughout the revolutionary period, emphasizing its function as a medium of ideological communication. With the establishment of the Shanghai Animation Film Studio, animation flourished artistically while increasingly bound to political agendas. The Anti-Rightist Campaign and the Cultural Revolution brought severe repression, reducing animation to a tool of propaganda and silencing creative voices. By 1976, the industry had endured alternating phases of innovation and constraint, laying the groundwork for its later revival under reform policies.

Keywords Wan brothers · Princess Iron Fan · Shanghai Animation Film Studio · Propaganda · Cultural Revolution · Chinese School of animation

1.1 Conceptualizing Animation—From Illusion of Motion to Artistic Medium

The term *animation* within the field of audiovisual media resists a single, universally accepted definition, due to the wide array of theories and interpretations that have attempted to capture its essence. Etymologically, it derives from the Latin *animatio*, meaning "the act of bringing to life," which itself combines the verb *animo* ("to animate" or "to give life to") with the suffix *-atio* indicating action. Over time,

© The Author(s), under exclusive license to Springer Nature Switzerland AG 2026
V. De Masi, *A Critical Analysis of China's Animation Industry*, Numanities - Arts and Humanities in Progress 37, https://doi.org/10.1007/978-3-032-18656-0_1

especially with the development of cinematographic technologies, both the meaning and practice of animation have undergone significant transformations.

Two principal theoretical approaches to film animation have remained particularly influential. The first, grounded in a technical perspective, holds that animation's primary function is to generate the illusion of movement from static images (Vezzoli 2000). This view emphasizes the perceptual process in which a rapid succession of individual images is interpreted by the human eye and brain as continuous motion. The second, expressed with philosophical precision by the pioneering animator Norman McLaren, offers a more conceptual definition: "Animation is not the art of drawings that move but the art of movements that are drawn" (McLaren; LaMarre 2009). McLaren's formulation shifts attention away from the outcome of moving drawings to the artistic process of crafting movement itself, underlining the animator's role as a choreographer of motion who breathes life into inanimate forms through deliberate creative intervention. This perspective resonates strongly with traditions such as the early Chinese *Měishùpiàn*, which often emphasized artistic expression and distinctive stylistic qualities.

The origins of animation as a form of entertainment and visual spectacle predate the invention of cinema. In 1834, British inventor William George Horner created the zoetrope, a device that ingeniously applied the principle of persistence of vision to simulate motion from a series of drawn images (Peruzzi 2010). The cylindrical apparatus, featuring evenly spaced slits through which viewers observed the rotating images on its interior surface, produced a convincing illusion of movement.

A comparable, though more rudimentary, projection device was reportedly invented in China by Ting Huan (丁緩) around 180 AD. Known as *chao hua chich kuan* (昭华之琯, *zhāo huá zhī guǎn*), or "the tube that made fantasies appear," this apparatus, while distinct from Horner's invention, reflects a longstanding fascination with creating and observing animated images across different cultures (Needham 1962).

Further advancements toward modern animation came from the French inventor Charles-Émile Reynaud, who developed the praxinoscope in 1876. This device improved upon the zoetrope by incorporating mirrors to render clearer, less distorted images in motion. Reynaud subsequently introduced the *Théâtre Optique*, which enabled the projection of hand-painted animated sequences onto a screen, a form of entertainment he called *pantomimes lumineuses* (Sangiovanni 2012). Beginning in 1892, Reynaud's public exhibitions at the Musée Grévin in Paris preceded the Lumière brothers' first cinematograph screening by three years. As a result, Reynaud is frequently regarded as the "father of the animated cartoon" (Lupo 2002). His short films, such as *Pauvre Pierrot* (Poor Pierrot), composed of more than 500 individually painted frames, captivated audiences for several minutes at a time and remained popular until celluloid projection technology became dominant at the turn of the century (Lupo 2002). Reynaud's innovations established key principles for animated filmmaking, including frame-by-frame production and public projection, which would serve as the foundation for the subsequent development of film animation.

1.2 Global Beginnings—Animation in the Silent Film Era

The advent of celluloid film rapidly transformed the field of animation, shifting it from optical toys and custom-built projection systems to a more standardized medium suitable for broad distribution. In 1906, James Stuart Blackton, working in the United States, produced *Humorous Phases of Funny Faces*, a short film employing stop-motion techniques to animate chalk drawings, widely regarded as one of the earliest examples of animation on film (Lenburg 2006).

Two years later, in 1908, the French artist Émile Cohl created *Fantasmagorie*. This short film is often recognized by scholars as the first fully animated film, largely due to its cohesive narrative structure, which was achieved through approximately 700 individual drawings, a remarkable undertaking for its brief eighty-second runtime (Crafton 1993). Cohl's whimsical, transformative stick-figure characters demonstrated the expressive possibilities inherent in drawn animation.

The rapidly growing film industry soon recognized the commercial appeal of animated cartoons. The Vitagraph Company of America (later acquired by Warner Bros.) was among the first to capitalize on this potential, producing Blackton's early works, such as *The Enchanted Drawing* (1900), and, more significantly, the films of Winsor McCay. Already a celebrated newspaper cartoonist, McCay brought an exceptional level of artistry and fluidity to early animation. His 1911 short *Winsor McCay, the Famous Cartoonist of the N.Y. Herald and His Moving Comics* (commonly referred to as *Little Nemo*) marked a significant milestone, showcasing sophisticated animation that captivated both audiences and fellow artists (Crafton 1993). Its cultural importance was later acknowledged through its inclusion in the U.S. National Film Registry in 2009 (Library of Congress).

McCay's success stimulated further innovation. In 1914, Raoul Barré and William Nolan established the Barré-Nolan Studio, often regarded as the first studio dedicated exclusively to animated cartoon production. They pioneered a more industrialized, assembly-line approach to meet rising demand (Bendazzi 1999). Barré played a crucial role in developing key animation techniques that streamlined production and improved visual consistency. He introduced the "peg system," which involved perforating drawing paper to ensure precise alignment when overlaying cels, essential for smooth animation. He also developed the "slash system," whereby only moving elements were redrawn on separate cels placed over static backgrounds, significantly reducing the labor required to redraw entire scenes for each frame (Gifford 1990). Series such as *Animated Grouch Chasers* (1915) and *Mutt and Jeff* (1913–1926) were products of this early studio system.

At the same time, John Randolph Bray's Bray Productions Studio, founded around 1913 or 1914 (Corsaro 2002; Browne 2001), played an equally pivotal role. Bray's studio became a training ground for many future leaders of American animation, including Max and Dave Fleischer, who would later create characters like *Popeye* and *Betty Boop* and invent the Rotoscope technique (Simion 2008). Other alumni included Pat Sullivan, credited with *Felix the Cat*, and Walter Lantz, the creator of *Woody Woodpecker*.

Internationally, significant developments were also unfolding. In Argentina, Italian émigré Quirino Cristiani created what is widely considered the world's first feature-length animated film, *El Apóstol* (The Apostle), in 1917. This political satire, produced using cutout animation, ran for 70 min and consisted of 58,000 frames (Bendazzi 1999). Tragically, all known copies were destroyed in a fire. Cristiani also pioneered synchronized sound in animation with *Peludópolis* (1931), which employed a disc-based recording system.

Pat Sullivan Studios, co-founded by Pat Sullivan and Otto Messmer in 1920, achieved international acclaim with *Felix the Cat*, one of the first animated characters to attain worldwide recognition and become a major merchandising phenomenon (Bendazzi 1999).

In Europe, German animators such as Oskar Fischinger, Walter Ruttmann, and Hans Richter experimented with abstract animation, although this avant-garde movement was later suppressed by the Nazi regime, which condemned it as degenerate art. In Germany as well, Lotte Reiniger developed a unique silhouette animation technique inspired by Chinese shadow puppet theatre, culminating in her celebrated feature *The Adventures of Prince Achmed* (1926) (Tortora 2008). Polish animator Władysław Starewicz (also known as Ladislas Starevich) gained recognition for his sophisticated stop-motion animations using insect puppets, with notable works including *The Cameraman's Revenge* (1912).

This rich period of global experimentation and technical innovation laid the foundation for the "Golden Age" of American animation. The rise of studios such as Walt Disney Productions (founded 1923) and Warner Bros. Cartoons (established 1930) would go on to define many of the conventions that shaped cinematic and later television animation for decades. These studios established an industrial and cultural paradigm that would ultimately exert a powerful influence over emerging animation industries worldwide, including that of China.

1.3 Between *Donghua* and *Meishupian*—Defining a Chinese Medium

The historical development of Chinese animation is closely intertwined with the nation's complex political and social transformations throughout the twentieth century. From its earliest artistic expressions to its eventual appropriation as a state instrument, the emerging industry navigated a challenging trajectory, establishing foundational elements that continue to shape its contemporary form.

The very terminology employed in China to designate "animation" or "cartoons" offers significant insight into the cultural perception and historical evolution of the medium. Initially, the predominant term was *Měishùpiàn* (美术片), which literally translates to "art film" or "fine art film." This designation is particularly revealing, as it underscores an early Chinese conceptualization of animation as an artistic practice closely associated with traditional Chinese painting (*guóhuà* 国画) and other fine arts, rather than categorizing it simply as a subgenre of cinema or a form of mass entertainment. The emphasis embedded in *Měishùpiàn* highlighted the aesthetic qualities, craftsmanship, and artistic skill integral to these "painted films," suggesting a cultural valuation that prioritized artistic merit over commercial considerations.

A terminological shift began to take shape, gaining momentum especially during the early 1980s. This period coincided with Deng Xiaoping's era of "Reform and Opening Up" (改革开放, *Gǎigé Kāifàng*), which facilitated a substantial influx of international animated content into the Chinese market. During this time, the term *Donghua* (动画), meaning "moving pictures" or "pictures in motion," began to gain widespread use. *Donghua* became the more common descriptor for animated works in general, particularly for foreign imports. Over time, it gradually supplanted *Měishùpiàn* in both popular and official discourse, although *Měishùpiàn* remains in use, especially in academic contexts, historical retrospectives, or when emphasizing the artistic lineage of specific works.

This linguistic evolution is far more than a simple semantic adjustment; it reflects a broader transformation in the perception and function of animation within China. It marks a shift from an understanding of animation as a fine art valued primarily for its aesthetic and cultural properties, toward recognition of animation as a multifaceted media form encompassing entertainment, commercial enterprise, and, increasingly, a tool for national branding. Yet this transition was not without internal tensions. The foundational ethos of animation as *Měishùpiàn* fostered a distinctive artistic tradition, often referred to as the "Chinese School" (中国学派, *Zhōngguó xuépài*) of animation (Sun 2011; Tan and Yin 2006). Centered around the Shanghai Animation Film Studio, this school was characterized by visual styles drawn from traditional Chinese art forms such as ink-wash painting (*shuǐmòhuà* 水墨画), paper-cutting (*jiǎnzhǐ* 剪纸), and shadow puppetry (*píyǐngxì* 皮影戏). The artistic value ascribed to *Měishùpiàn* allowed Chinese animation to develop unique aesthetic characteristics that were, for a time, recognized internationally and contributed to a distinct global image (Sun 2011).

From its inception, animation in China, as in Western countries and Japan, was recognized for its powerful communicative capacity. Its ability to transcend age and literacy barriers allowed it to reach both children and adults with immediacy unmatched by many other media forms. This communicative power made it an effective tool for transmitting messages, promoting values, and serving as political propaganda, especially during periods of national crisis, warfare, or intense ideological campaigns. However, a significant distinction emerges when comparing its developmental trajectory with that of animation in other major producing nations. In the United States, animation, despite early artistic experimentation, was rapidly industrialized and commercialized, with figures like Walt Disney establishing vast entertainment empires. Similarly, in Japan, animation (*anime,* アニメ) evolved into a large cultural industry with diverse genres targeting multiple demographics (Pelliteri 2002). By contrast, for much of its history, China continued to valorize animation primarily through the lens of art and education, largely under the control of state-managed studios (Tan and Yin 2006). This deeply embedded cultural valuation has left a lasting legacy, influencing production methodologies, thematic choices, and the industry's subsequent challenges in reconciling its artistic heritage with the demands of a market-driven economy and global competitiveness. The legacy of *Měishùpiàn* thus represents both a source of unique cultural capital and a potential obstacle to the full-scale commercialization and industrialization that characterizes other global animation markets.

1.4 The Wan Brothers and the Foundations of Industry

The historical context in which Chinese animation first emerged was marked by profound political upheaval and social transformation. The establishment of the Republic of China (中华民国, *Zhōnghuá Mínguó*) in 1912 brought an end to millennia of imperial rule but ushered in a period of intense internal conflict, including power struggles between warlords and two devastating civil wars that pitted the Nationalists (国民党, *Guómíndǎng*), led by Chiang Kai-shek (蒋介石, *Jiǎng Jièshí*), against the Communists (共产党, *Gòngchǎndǎng*), eventually led by Mao Zedong (毛泽东, *Máo Zédōng*). It was against this turbulent backdrop that the four Wan brothers emerged as the pioneers who would revolutionize and effectively establish the art of animation in China.

Born in Nanjing (南京) between 1899 and 1906, the Wan siblings, Laiming and Guchan, who were twins, along with their younger brothers Chaochen and Dihuan, displayed a strong inclination toward painting and visual arts from an early age. By the 1920s, their artistic skills led them to positions in the art department of the influential Shanghai Commercial Press (商务印书馆, *Shāngwù Yìnshūguǎn*) (based on Quiquemelle's interview). In Shanghai, already a vibrant hub for international cultural exchanges, they encountered American animated cartoons, likely including early works by Disney and other studios. These foreign productions ignited their fascination with the medium.

Their initial efforts, however, were hampered by a scarcity of information on animation techniques and, more critically, limited financial resources, making access to necessary equipment and materials a constant challenge. In an interview with animation scholar Marie-Claire Quiquemelle, one of the Wan brothers recalled how, after finishing their regular workday, the four siblings would retreat to their small attic apartment, which also served as their makeshift studio, where they painstakingly experimented with rudimentary principles of animation (Quiquemelle 1991, as cited in Lent 2003). Their ambition was clear: to create animated works that were distinctly Chinese, drawing from the deep reservoir of Chinese folklore, history, and traditional aesthetics (Drège 2000).

In 1922, working within the confines of their attic studio and using improvised equipment, including household light bulbs for illumination and a malfunctioning camera, they produced their first known animated piece. This was an advertisement titled *Shuzhendong Chinese Typewriter* (舒振东华文打字机, *Shūzhèndōng Huawen Dǎzìjī*,). As its title suggests, this pioneering work was a commercial piece created for a typewriter company. Unfortunately, little else is known about this animation, as the film is considered lost. Despite its commercial nature and subsequent obscurity, it stands as the first instance of animation produced in China.

The Wan brothers continued producing animated advertisements. In 1924, they created *Dog Treat* or *Dog Invites the Guest* (狗請客, *Gǒu Qǐngkè*) for the China Film Company (中华影片公司, *Zhōnghuá Yǐngpiàn Gōngsī*) and *New Year* (過年, *Guònián*) for the Shanghai Tobacco Company (上海菸草公司, *Shànghǎi Yāncǎo Gōngsī*). Although these early works were commercially commissioned, they provided invaluable experience and served as a training ground for refining their animation skills.

More information is available regarding what is considered their fourth animated short, *Uproar in the Studio* (大闹画室, *Dà Nào Huàshì*), produced in 1926. Created while Wan Laiming and Wan Guchan were employed at the Great Wall Film Company (長城畫片公司, *Chángchéng Huàpiàn Gōngsī*), this film reportedly combined live-action footage with animated sequences. While such hybrid techniques were not uncommon globally during this period, it represented a significant step forward for animation in the Chinese context. Unfortunately, this film is also considered lost.

Their 1930 (or 1931, according to varying sources) film *The Paper Man Makes* (纸人捣乱记, *Trouble Zhǐ Rén Dǎoluàn Jì*) likewise incorporated a combination of live-action and animation (Zhang 1999). Reportedly comedic in tone, this short is regarded as an important milestone due to its advancing technical sophistication. The movement was becoming smoother, and the overall production quality was approaching the standards of contemporary Western productions. This film marked the culmination of their initial experimental phase, during which the Wan brothers successfully transitioned from aspiring artists to the acknowledged founders of Chinese animation.

Between 1928 and 1931, the brothers also contributed special effects and animated sequences to a number of live-action films. These included *The Burning of the Red Lotus Temple* (火烧红莲寺, *Huǒshāo Hóngliánsì*), *The Perfumed Skin Beauty* (香革美人, *Xiāng Gé Měirén*), *Scenes of City Life* (都市风光, *Dūshì Fēngguāng*), and *Parents and Children* (父母子女, *Fùmǔ Zǐnǚ*). This body of work allowed them to further refine their skills in integrating animation with live-action footage, developing expertise in hybrid techniques that would prove invaluable for their later, more ambitious productions.

It is important to note, as research by Professor John Lent suggests, that the Wan brothers may not have been entirely alone in their early animation efforts in Shanghai. Lent (2003) indicates that two other animated cartoons, *God Fate* and *Young Boy Adventure*, were reportedly completed in 1925 at the Shanghai South Pacific Film Company by other, as yet unidentified, artists. While the Wan brothers' contributions are far more extensively documented and their influence remains undeniable, this suggests that the impulse to explore animation existed in multiple quarters within Shanghai's vibrant film scene. Nevertheless, it was the sustained effort, artistic vision, and technical perseverance of the Wan brothers that ultimately laid the foundation for the Chinese animation industry.

1.5 Animation, Crisis, and Leftist Ideals (1931–1936)

The period from 1931 to 1936 was marked by escalating tensions between the Republic of China and an increasingly aggressive Imperial Japan. A pivotal event that deeply shaped the political atmosphere and the thematic concerns of Chinese cultural production, including animation, was the Mukden Incident (沈阳事变, *Shěnyáng Shìbiàn*, or 九一八事变, *Jiǔyībā Shìbiàn*) on September 18, 1931. The staged bombing of a Japanese-owned railway in Mukden, Manchuria (then under Japanese control), whose perpetrators remain disputed, was used by Japan as a pretext to accuse Chinese dissidents and launch a full-scale invasion, leading to the annexation of Manchuria. This act of aggression not only violated Chinese sovereignty but also served as a precursor to the broader and bloodier Second Sino-Japanese War (中国抗日战争, *Zhōngguó Kàngrì Zhànzhēng*).

Despite the growing national crisis, Shanghai remained China's most cosmopolitan and economically vibrant city during this period. It was a center of intellectual activity, artistic innovation, and relative openness to Western influences. The city's cultural vitality was evident in events such as the 1930 establishment of new institutions for traditional Chinese opera and the rise of major film studios like the Lianhua Film Company (联华影业公司, *Liánhuá Yǐngyè Gōngsī*). Within this dynamic environment, the Progressive Cinema Movement (进步电影运动, *Jìnbù Diànyǐng Yùndòng*), also known as the Leftist Cinema Movement, took shape. Heavily influenced by leftist intellectuals and often clandestinely supported by the Chinese Communist Party, this movement sought to produce films offering sharp social critiques of the Nationalist government and, importantly, strong anti-imperialist and anti-Japanese narratives.

The nascent field of Chinese animation, largely driven by the Wan brothers, was not immune to these powerful sociopolitical currents. The Wan brothers and their work increasingly aligned with the objectives of this progressive cultural front. Although most Chinese films of the 1930s remained silent, with only limited experimentation in sound synchronization, this period is often referred to as the first "Golden Age" of Chinese cinema, characterized by the emergence of film stars and more sophisticated narrative techniques. The Lianhua Film Company in Shanghai, a central player in this Golden Age, also became a significant platform for the Wan brothers to direct animated films infused with patriotic and anti-Japanese messages.

Scholarly attention to this phase of Chinese animation history has been limited, particularly in Western academic discourse. Even within Chinese scholarship, detailed studies are relatively scarce, often confined to brief mentions or fragmentary filmographies. Yet it was during this period that the foundation of a socially conscious and politically engaged Chinese animation was established. The thematic content and technical developments from these years would exert a lasting, though sometimes overlooked, influence on the future of the medium.

Between 1931 and 1937, the Wan brothers produced a notable body of work marked by patriotic, anti-Japanese, and anti-imperialist themes. Among the earliest and most emblematic of these films was *Compatriots, Hurry to Wake Up!* (同胞速醒,

Tóngbāo Sù Xǐng), released in 1931. The film delivered a clear patriotic appeal against Japanese aggression and called for national unity, reflecting the progressive ideology of the period. Its narrative, designed for broad accessibility, employed striking visual metaphors (Zhang 1999). It reportedly opened with tranquil scenes of the Chinese landscape, showing mountains and lakes, with a large sleeping lion at the center. This peace was shattered by the sudden arrival of Japanese military forces, aircraft and artillery, bombarding the land. The assault awakened the giant lion, which, with a mighty roar, rallied peasants and workers to resist the imperialist invasion (Lin 2002).

A similar approach was taken in *Sincere Unity* or *Solidarity* (精诚团结, *Jīngchéng Tuánjié*), produced in 1932. This black-and-white animation featured a menacing insect, clearly representing Japanese military aggression, encroaching upon Chinese lands from which the people sought to expel it. Both *Compatriots, Hurry to Wake Up!* and *Sincere Unity* or *Solidarity* are now considered lost, and their exact runtimes and further details remain unknown.

In 1932, one of the Wan brothers, Dihuan, left active animation production to establish his own photography studio in Shanghai. While no longer directly involved in the creation of his brothers' animated films, he would later contribute to their major productions in various capacities.

Two other particularly noteworthy films from this period, reflecting the fusion of animation and social critique, were *The Dog Detective* (狗侦探, *Gǒu Zhēntàn*, 1933) and *Blood Money* (血钱, *Xuè Qián*, 1934). Technically, these films adopted a hybrid approach, combining live-action footage with animated environments. *The Dog Detective* followed a singular narrative: a student, played by actress Zhang Minyu (张敏钰), while walking her dog through Shanghai, stumbles upon an opium den. Disturbed by the discovery, she encourages her dog to trace the source of the opium. The trail leads to a foreign military vessel (whether British or French remains unclear), where a large cache of drugs is found. The student then sets fire to the ship, destroying its illicit cargo. The film's message, though allegorical, offered a sharp critique of foreign exploitation and the devastating consequences of imported vices, implicitly advocating for the protection of domestic interests (Baoyan 1984).

Even more explicit in its ideological message was *Blood Money*. The film again featured Zhang Minyu as a student who, after a classroom lesson, imagines a story involving a mysterious man. Through a symbolic blood transfusion, this man acquires a briefcase labeled "Made in China," filled with money. He then uses the funds to purchase airplanes, tanks, and guns, distributing them to the Chinese people to combat and destroy Japanese-manufactured products.

These four films stand as significant examples of progressive animation from the period. Although metaphorical, their narratives were far removed from the realm of children's entertainment. They delivered powerful patriotic messages, advocated for protecting the domestic economy, and voiced strong opposition to Japanese imperialism. Clearly intended for adult audiences, they sought to galvanize public sentiment in support of national resistance.

In 1935, the Wan brothers briefly shifted their focus with the production of a more conventional animated short titled *The Camel's Dance* (骆驼献舞, *Luòtuo Xiàn Wǔ*).

Produced at the Mingxing Film Company (明星影业公司, *Míngxīng Yǐngyè Gōngsī*) in Shanghai, this work targeted a younger audience and contained no overt political content. Notably, it was China's first sound-animated film, with the Wan brothers reportedly employing a synchronized disc system for its audio. Drawing inspiration from Aesop's Fables, the film demonstrated advanced animation techniques and narrative maturity. However, this departure from political themes was brief.

The brothers soon returned to producing progressive films such as *A Tragic History of the Nation* (民族痛史, *Mínzú Tòng Shǐ*) and *New Tide* (新潮, *Xīncháo*), both made in 1936 at the Mingxing Film Company. The former addressed anti-imperialist themes, including depictions of the Opium Wars, while the latter focused on anti-feudalism and the spirit of the May Fourth Movement (五四运动, *Wǔsì Yùndòng*).

A common feature uniting these progressive animated works was their strong moral foundation and accessible narrative style, designed to resonate with a wide audience. These films marked the conclusion of the first phase of politically engaged Chinese animation, a phase that would, unfortunately, be reignited with greater urgency following the full-scale outbreak of the Second Sino-Japanese War in 1937.

1.6 Animation as Propaganda—The Second Sino-Japanese War (1937–1941)

The period from 1937, marked by the outbreak of the Second Sino-Japanese War, until 1941, when China formally aligned with the Allied forces alongside the Soviet Union and the United States, witnessed a profound transformation in the role of Chinese animation. It became almost entirely subsumed within the machinery of wartime propaganda and national resistance. The Marco Polo Bridge Incident (卢沟桥事变, *Lúgōuqiáo Shìbiàn*) on July 7, 1937, is widely recognized as the event that triggered full-scale war. Shanghai, one of the first major cities to fall to Japanese forces, suffered extensive devastation, leading to severe commercial decline and bringing the "First Golden Age" of Chinese cinema to an abrupt and sorrowful end.

The Japanese occupation of Shanghai dealt a devastating blow to the city's film industry. Major studios such as Lianhua, where the Wan brothers and numerous other prominent filmmakers had worked, were forced to shut down, a fate shared by nearly all other production companies in the city. Uniquely, the Xinhua Film Company (新华影业公司, *Xīnhuá Yǐngyè Gōngsī*) managed to continue its operations under Japanese control, a circumstance that invites further critical examination of the political dynamics at play.

Before the complete consolidation of Japanese authority in Shanghai, a significant exodus of artists and intellectuals took place. Many sought refuge in other cities that remained under Chinese control, such as Hong Kong and, most notably, Chongqing (重庆). As the wartime capital of Nationalist China, Chongqing became a symbolic center of resistance, attracting numerous artists, filmmakers, and writers who devoted their talents to supporting the war effort. The Wan brothers initially relocated to Wuhan (武汉), where they joined the China Film Studio (中国电影制片厂, *Zhōngguó Diànyǐng Zhìpiànchǎng*), affiliated with the Chinese Anti-Japanese National Film Association. The war and the imperative of resistance became the dominant themes of animated production during this period. The Wan brothers deliberately harnessed their animation skills to inspire patriotic fervor, disseminate progressive ideologies, and, above all, rally the population against Japanese imperialism.

In 1938, drawing inspiration from American and European serialized animations and newsreel formats, the Wan brothers experimented with episodic animation intended for rapid dissemination and broad public impact. Their first series was titled *War Slogan Series* or *Collection of Anti-Japanese Songs* (抗日歌辑, *Kàngrì Gējí*), reportedly consisting of six short episodes. This was followed by a second series, also titled *Kàngrì Gējí* (possibly distinguished by a different character for *jí* or by numerical sequencing, though sources remain unclear), which comprised seven episodes. These animated shorts functioned essentially as music videos, pairing popular patriotic songs with animated visuals. The soundtracks featured compositions by leading contemporary musicians and composers, including Xian Xinghai (冼星海, Xiǎn Xīnghǎi), Liu Xue'an (刘雪庵, Liú Xuě'ān), Sheng Jialun (盛家伦, Shèng Jiālún, possibly Sneah Kar Loon as a transliteration), and He Luting (贺绿汀, Hè Lǜtīng).

The songs, such as *Fine Horses Gallop* (马儿好, *Mǎ'ér Hǎo*), *Azolla* (满江红, Mǎnjiānghóng), *Heroine* (巾帼英雄, *Jīnguó Yīngxióng*), *Collecting Winter Clothes for Soldiers* (募寒衣, *Mù Hányī*), *May Commemorative Song* (五月纪念歌, *Wǔyuè Jìniàngē*), *Protect Our Homeland* (保家乡, *Bǎo Jiāxiāng*), *Broadswords Chop Off the Devils' Heads!* (大刀向鬼子们头上砍去!, *Dàdāo xiàng guǐzimen tóu shàng kǎn qù!*), *Ballad of the Great Wall* (长城谣, *Chángchéng Yáo*), *To the Frontline* (上前线, *Shàng Qiánxiàn*), and *Fight Back to Our Old Home* (打回老家去, *Dǎ huí lǎojiā qù*), provided a powerful emotional and ideological core to these anti-Japanese animations (Nie 2006).

The strategy of producing animated music videos proved remarkably effective. This format elicited strong emotional responses, captured the attention of diverse audiences, and transcended literacy barriers. The inclusion of music by highly respected composers enhanced both the credibility and the propagandistic power of these films (Nie 2006). These animated shorts became essential tools for boosting morale and reinforcing ideological commitment during the nation's struggle for survival.

In April 1939, Laiming and Guchan Wan returned to Shanghai. During this period, they encountered Walt Disney's *Snow White and the Seven Dwarfs*, which had achieved remarkable commercial success in the city, reportedly remaining in theaters for three years. The impact of this feature-length animated film inspired the Wan brothers to embark on an ambitious project of their own: a full-length animated feature that would incorporate advanced animation techniques while remaining firmly rooted in Chinese cultural traditions. This decision marked a major turning point, reflecting a desire to move beyond short-form propaganda and create works of greater artistic and narrative complexity, even amidst the ongoing war.

It is important to recognize that other animators were also active during this period. Qian Jiajun (钱家骏), like the Wan brothers, dedicated his efforts to producing propaganda animation. His short film *The Happiness of a Peasant Family* (农乐佳, *Nóng Jiā Lè*) conveyed a potent anti-Japanese message, depicting a young girl and her family struggling to expel Japanese forces from their region. Qian Jiajun would later become a significant figure in the animation industry of the People's Republic of China (Lent 2003). The collective efforts of these animators, working under severe constraints and with limited resources, ensured that animation, however modest in scale, played a visible role in China's cultural resistance during the war.

1.7 *Princess Iron Fan*—A Landmark Amid Occupation

During this phase of the Sino-Japanese War, Shanghai was often described as a "Solitary Island" (孤岛, *gūdǎo*), a term reflecting its unique condition as a semi-occupied city. While much of Shanghai fell under Japanese control, the international concessions maintained a degree of autonomy, allowing for a limited yet ongoing continuation of certain cultural and commercial activities. It was within this precarious environment that several film studios, despite immense difficulties, attempted to resume production.

Having witnessed the extraordinary popular and critical success of Walt Disney's *Snow White and the Seven Dwarfs* and other American animated features, the Wan brothers were inspired to pursue a new ambition: to produce China's first feature-length animated film. They fully recognized the severe economic challenges facing Shanghai. Many film studios struggled to re-establish operations, and a large portion of the industry's skilled personnel had either not returned to the city or had dispersed elsewhere. Confronted with these realities, the Wan brothers made a pragmatic decision to temporarily set aside overtly propagandistic projects and concentrate all their energies and resources on this landmark feature. To realize this vision, they invested their personal savings and meticulously assembled a team of artists and technicians, many of whom were also enduring economic hardship.

The Wan brothers' unwavering artistic vision was to create a film deeply rooted in Chinese aesthetic traditions and cultural heritage. For their debut feature, they selected a celebrated episode from the sixteenth-century literary classic *Journey to the West* (西游记, *Xīyóu Jì*), attributed to Wu Cheng'en (吴承恩). This choice was culturally significant, as *Journey to the West* remains one of the most beloved and widely recognized works of Chinese literature, with its characters and stories deeply ingrained in popular culture.

The production conditions for *Princess Iron Fan* were extraordinarily difficult, as vividly described by Marie-Claire Quiquemelle, based on her interviews and research:

> Seventy artists, in two teams, worked without a break for a year and four months, all in the same room, in limited space, in the cold of the winter, and in the atrocious heat of the summer. To assure accuracy of the movement, certain scenes were filmed with actors to serve as a

> guide to the artists. This film, with its many inventions, sparkles with humor, fantasy and poetry. It is a delight to the spectator. But it suits adults and older children better than very young children, who might be frightened by the violence in the fight scenes, underscored as it is by brutal music. Even if, at times, the influence of Disney is still noticeable, we are far from his sweetness and prettiness, far from America and its property. Princess Iron Fan bears witness in its own way to the brutal reality of the daily violence in a country crippled by war, where it would have been impossible for any aware film-maker to produce a film designed purely to amuse. (Quiquemelle 1991, as cited in Lent 2003)

The artistic style developed by the Wan brothers for *Princess Iron Fan* represented a significant maturation. It was profoundly influenced by traditional Chinese painting, particularly in the rendering of backgrounds and landscapes. The visual design drew heavily from the techniques of *shuǐmòhuà* (水墨画, ink-wash painting), giving the film an aesthetic that resonated with established Chinese artistic traditions and elevated it beyond conventional cartooning into the realm of fine art. This fusion of traditional painting methods with modern animation processes marked a seminal moment in Chinese animation, establishing the first feature-length animated film with distinctly Chinese cultural and aesthetic characteristics. It also asserted cultural identity within a medium that had been largely dominated by Western styles.

The production of *Princess Iron Fan* spanned approximately three years and involved a large team, estimated at around 237 Chinese artists, draftsmen, and technicians (Clements 2010). The total production cost reached 350,000 yuan, a considerable sum for the time. Midway through production, the Wan brothers faced a severe financial crisis, as they lacked sufficient capital to pay their staff. This led to a temporary suspension of work, and at one point, the project nearly collapsed. The film was ultimately saved through the intervention of producer Zhang Shankun (张善琨), a major figure in the Shanghai film industry.

Following the production model established by Disney, leading actors and actresses of the period provided voice performances for the film's principal characters. These included popular stars such as Bai Hong (白虹), Yan Yueling (严月玲), Jiang Ming (姜明), Han Langen (韩兰根), and Yin Xiucen (殷秀岑), contributing to the film's prestige and enhancing its public appeal.

Technically, the film had a runtime of one hour and twenty minutes and was produced in black and white. The film reel measured approximately 23,000 m and comprised nearly 200,000 hand-drawn cels, animated using the single-frame exposure technique.

Upon its release in 1941, *Princess Iron Fan* received an overwhelmingly positive reception from audiences in Shanghai and across China. It became one of the most widely viewed films of its time. Lijun Sun (孙立军), director and vice-director of the Beijing Film Academy, in his *Research on the History of China's Animation*, attributed the film's popularity partly to the emotional climate and escapist needs of wartime audiences:

> Cartoons will give the audience a rich space for fantasy; because of the current political situation and the unrest generated by the war, many Chinese want to find a vision for the future, also thanks to cartoons. From children to adults, they keep their eyes fixed on the cinema. (Sun 2011, p. 34)

Princess Iron Fan achieved several historic firsts. It was not only China's first feature-length animated film but also the first produced in all of Asia. It is also considered, by some estimates, the twelfth animated feature film globally and the ninth among those still surviving. Ironically, it was one of the first Chinese films to be screened in wartime Japan.

The film's influence extended beyond China, playing a crucial role in shaping the future of Japanese animation. It is well documented that a young Osamu Tezuka (手塚治虫), who would later become the "God of Manga" and a foundational figure in the anime industry, was profoundly inspired after viewing *Princess Iron Fan* (Pellitteri 2008). Tezuka himself acknowledged that the film was a decisive factor in his decision to pursue a career in manga and animation, abandoning his medical studies (Hu 2010). The film's arrival in Japan was somewhat fortuitous; following the attack on Pearl Harbor and the subsequent American embargo, U.S. films ceased to enter Japanese cinemas for a time. This created an opportunity for *Princess Iron Fan* to fill that void, inadvertently planting the seeds that would contribute to the rise of Japan's own powerful animation industry (Sun 2011). This cross-cultural impact underscores both the artistic merit and the historical significance of the Wan brothers' achievement, a testament to their resilience and vision in the face of immense adversity.

1.8 Voices of Transition—Animation Across War, Occupation, and Revolution (1941–1950)

The years from 1941 to 1950 marked a period of profound and continuous turmoil for China. The nation faced the dual challenges of the ongoing War of Resistance against Japanese imperialism, which concluded in 1945, and the subsequent Chinese Civil War (国共内战, *Guó-Gòng Nèizhàn*) between the Nationalists and the Communists. This prolonged era of conflict created an extremely precarious environment for all forms of cultural production, including cinema and the still-developing animation sector. Film production slowed dramatically, resources were scarce, and artistic endeavors were frequently overshadowed by the immediate demands of war and political instability.

Following Japan's defeat in 1945 and the restoration of occupied territories to Chinese control, the internal political situation remained highly unstable as the Civil War intensified. Confronted with economic uncertainties and the rapidly shifting political landscape, the Wan brothers were among those who temporarily relocated, moving to Hong Kong for a period.

Despite these adverse circumstances and the general slowdown in production, this period was not entirely dormant for Chinese animation. New figures and emerging directors entered the scene, and although their contributions may not have achieved the same level of recognition as those of the Wan brothers, they played important roles in sustaining the art form and laying the groundwork for its future development.

After the success of *Princess Iron Fan*, the Wan brothers harbored ambitions to create another feature-length animated film, this time employing advanced animation techniques and, notably, color. Their intended protagonist was Sun Wukong (孙悟空), the Monkey King, who had already played a prominent role in their previous feature. As one of the most iconic figures in Chinese cultural tradition, Sun Wukong was an ideal subject for their evolving cinematic vision. This new film, tentatively titled *Monkey King*, was likely the conceptual foundation for what would later become *Havoc in Heaven*.

Zhang Shankun (张善琨), the producer at the Xinhua Film Company who had previously supported *Princess Iron Fan*, initially expressed willingness to back the Wan brothers' new project, recognizing the commercial potential of animated film. However, the Japanese occupation authorities, who exercised strict control over cultural production in Shanghai, reportedly denied the necessary permits for new film projects, forcing Xinhua to withdraw its support (Wu 1995).

Undeterred, the Wan brothers sought alternative financing and managed to initiate preliminary work on *Monkey King*. Yet, once again, their efforts were thwarted when their new financial backers unexpectedly reneged on their contractual obligations. Production was halted, and the Wan brothers, facing insurmountable obstacles, made the decision to postpone the project, awaiting more favorable conditions (Hui 2005). In 1948, they relocated to Hong Kong. It would not be until their return to mainland China under a new political regime that their vision of adapting the Monkey King narrative into a full-color animated feature would finally be realized.

Historical documentation and scholarly analysis of Chinese animation between 1941 and 1947 are limited, indicating a significant decline in animation production during the height of the war and its immediate aftermath. Nevertheless, some animators and studios continued to work within the constraints of the era. One particularly noteworthy figure who emerged during this period was Chen Boer (陈波儿, also known as Chan Bo Yee). Originally a prominent film actress, Chen Boer transitioned into directing, becoming the first known female animation director in China. She directed *Huángdì Mèng* (皇帝梦, *The Emperor's Dream*), produced by the Northeast Film Studio (东北电影制片厂, *Dōngběi Diànyǐng Zhìpiànchǎng*) in 1947. This pioneering work employed stop-motion animation with marionettes, a relatively uncommon technique in Chinese animation at the time. The film's narrative was overtly political, reportedly satirizing the corruption of the Kuomintang government through an allegorical tale set in ancient China. Chen Boer's contribution holds particular significance not only for her pioneering role as a female animation director but also for her involvement in the founding of the Institute of Performing Arts, which later evolved into the prestigious Beijing Film Academy (北京电影学院, *Běijīng Diànyǐng Xuéyuàn*). Her promising career was tragically cut short by her sudden death from a heart attack at the age of forty-four.

The Northeast Film Studio, where *The Emperor's Dream* was produced, became an increasingly influential filmmaking center during this period. Operating under the auspices of the Chinese Communist Party, the studio actively supported films aligned with the party's ideological and political objectives (Tan and Yin 2006). As a result, much of its output, including animation, conveyed overt propaganda messages.

A notable example of such propaganda animation from the studio is *Turtle Caught in a Jar*, also translated as *Go After an Easy Prey* (瓮中捉鳖, *Wèng Zhōng Zhuō Biē*), released in 1948. This film was directed by Mochinaga Tadahito (持永只仁), a Japanese animator working in China under the name Fang Ming (方明). The film offered a pointed critique of Nationalist leader Chiang Kai-shek, who was supported by the United States during the Civil War, while also targeting American imperialist policies. In the film, Chiang Kai-shek was allegorically portrayed as a turtle trapped inside its shell.

Stop-motion animation with puppets was also employed in *Prince of the Woods* (大树王子ĭ, *Dà Shù Wángz*), directed by Tan Xinfeng (谭新风) in 1950. Although produced within the politically charged environment of the late Civil War period, this film reportedly contained fewer overt propaganda elements, instead adopting a more fantastical narrative approach. Despite the difficult circumstances under which these varied productions were created, they reflect the continued vitality of animation in China during one of the nation's most turbulent historical junctures, ultimately setting the stage for its systematic development under the People's Republic.

1.9 The Shanghai Animation Film Studio—Forging a National Style

The conclusion of the Chinese Civil War in 1949 and the proclamation of the People's Republic of China (中华人民共和国, *Zhōnghuá Rénmín Gònghéguó*) under Mao Zedong marked the beginning of a new era, bringing sweeping reforms that dramatically altered the nation's social, political, and cultural fabric. The film industry, including animation, was profoundly reshaped by these transformations. Films originating from or produced in the United States and Hong Kong were quickly banned. For the new Communist government, cinema was not simply a form of entertainment, but a powerful instrument for ideological education and propaganda, capable of molding public opinion and disseminating Party doctrine. Under the principles of socialist realism, film narratives were expected to focus on the lives of workers, peasants, and soldiers, with all scripts and productions subject to stringent Party oversight. Within this framework, animation was conceived as a medium to educate both children and adults, instilling the values and ideals of the new socialist China.

Despite the initial hardships of the postwar years, artists and animators slowly resumed their work, experimenting with new styles and narratives that resonated with the ideological climate. A critical institutional development during this period was the establishment of the Shanghai Animation Film Studio (SAFS). Officially founded in April 1957, SAFS's origins can be traced to the early 1950s, with several films already crediting its name prior to its formal founding (Zhang Huilin 2002).

The studio was created through the consolidation of talent from various entities, including the animation department of the Northeast Film Studio, artists from the Central Academy of Fine Arts (中央美术学院, *Zhōngyāng Měishù Xuéyuàn*), the Art Institute of Suzhou (苏州美术专科学校, *Sūzhōu Měishù Zhuānkē Xuéxiào*), the returning Wan brothers, and numerous other animators who would become key figures in the development of Chinese animation.

Even before its formal inauguration, SAFS and its precursor units produced several notable works that foreshadowed the direction of post-revolutionary animation. *Thank You, Little Kitty* (谢谢小花猫, *Xièxie Xiǎohuā Māo*), released in 1950, was directed by Japanese animator Mochinaga Tadahito, working under the name Fang Ming. Aimed at young children, the film presented a simple narrative about a diligent cat defending its community from mice, subtly reinforcing themes of vigilance, community solidarity, and collective action. The visual design, while simple, already revealed an effort to integrate Chinese cultural elements into the animation style.

In 1951, Te Wei (特伟), who would emerge as one of the most influential figures in Chinese animation and a primary architect of the so-called "Chinese School," collaborated with Mochinaga Tadahito on *Little Iron Pillar* (小铁柱, *Xiǎo Tiě Zhù*). This production brought together several artists who would go on to define the future trajectory of Chinese animation. Mochinaga Tadahito continued to contribute prolifically to SAFS's early output, moving from overtly propagandistic works to more general children's entertainment. Nevertheless, his Chinese productions consistently reflected a conscious effort to adopt Chinese cultural aesthetics, avoiding the dominant stylistic influence of contemporary Japanese anime. For instance, his 1952 film *The Little Cat Fishing* (小猫钓鱼, *Xiǎo Māo Diàoyú*), scripted by Jin Xi (靳夕), depicted kittens learning to fish under the guidance of their mother, framed in traditional Chinese attire and environments.

Te Wei emerged as the most representative figure of this era and a principal founder of the celebrated "Chinese School" of animation. Originally a graphic designer and illustrator for publications such as *Great Evening News* (大晚报, *Dà Wǎnbào*) and *Shanghai Sketch* (上海漫画, *Shànghǎi Mànhuà*) in the 1930s, Te Wei had also produced anti-Japanese propaganda cartoons during the war for outlets like *Resistance War Cartoons* (抗战漫画, *Kàngzhàn Mànhuà*). Prior to becoming the first director of SAFS, he worked intermittently between Shanghai and Hong Kong, creating comic series. In 1950, the Party tasked him with organizing a dedicated animation production center in Shanghai. Te Wei successfully recruited many of China's most talented animation artists to this mission, united by a shared goal of creating films reflecting a distinctly Chinese "National Style" (民族风格, *mínzú fēnggé*) (Zhang 1999). While the term would later be co-opted for propaganda purposes, its initial conception represented a sincere artistic aspiration to produce animations rooted in Chinese cultural traditions.

Even before its official founding, SAFS had become a center of creativity under Te Wei's leadership. In 1953, he directed *Picking Mushrooms* (采蘑菇, *Cǎi Mógu*). The following year, in 1954, SAFS produced its first color puppet animation, *The Little Hero* (小小英雄, *Xiǎo Xiǎo Yīngxióng*), directed by Jin Xi (靳夕). Jin Xi, who specialized in puppet animation, would remain active at SAFS until the 1980s. That same year, Te Wei directed *Good Friends* (好朋友, *Hǎo Péngyǒu*), a simple narrative that, unlike his later works, did not heavily incorporate traditional Chinese aesthetics but focused instead on universal themes of friendship.

A significant early achievement for SAFS came with *The Magic Brush* (神笔, *Shén Bǐ*) or *Ma Liang and His Magic Brush* (神笔马良, *Shén Bǐ Mǎ Liáng*), a stop-motion puppet animation directed by Jin Xi and released in 1955.

The film received international acclaim, earning awards at festivals in Warsaw, Venice (First Prize in the children's section), and Belgrade. Jin Xi's mastery of stop-motion was evident in the film's naturalistic character movements and rich visual detail. The narrative, based on a well-known Chinese folktale, told the story of a poor boy, Ma Liang, who receives a magical brush that brings his drawings to life. Ma Liang uses his gift to help the needy while outwitting corrupt officials who attempt to exploit the brush for selfish gain. This tale of justice, ingenuity, and virtue resonated powerfully with both domestic and international audiences.

SAFS also ventured into color cel animation with *Why Is the Crow Black-Coated ?* (乌鸦为什么是黑的, *Wūyā Wèishéme Shì Hēi De*), directed by Wan Laiming and Wan Guchan following their return from Hong Kong. Sponsored directly by Mao's government, the film offered a moral fable about a beautiful but lazy bird whose negligence leads to its transformation into a black crow. The film was screened at the 8th Venice Film Festival, marking China's reemergence on the international animation stage.

This formative period reached a milestone with the release of *The Proud General* (驕傲的將軍, *Jiāo'ào de Jiāngjūn*) in 1956. Directed by Te Wei, with key contributions from Duchun Fu (杜春甫), Tang Cheng (唐澄), Pu Jiaxiang (浦家祥), and Duan Jun (段浚), and music composed by Chen Gexin (陈歌辛), the film was the first major animation to adopt stylistic principles drawn from Beijing Opera (京剧, *Jīngjù*). The characters wore traditional costumes, and the narrative was accompanied by a musical score that reflected Beijing Opera traditions. The story, a cautionary tale of a victorious general undone by his arrogance, carried both moral and artistic significance. Visually, it marked a groundbreaking application of ink-wash painting (水墨画, *shuǐmòhuà*) techniques to color animation, fully realizing the "National Style" that SAFS had been striving to achieve.

The establishment and early productions of SAFS represented a critical turning point. The studio consolidated artistic talent, fostered experimentation, and defined a uniquely Chinese approach to animation that sought to harmonize indigenous cultural traditions with the cinematic medium. This foundation would lead directly into what is now remembered as the "Golden Age" of Chinese animation, while remaining deeply embedded within the ideological framework of the People's Republic.

1.10 Artistic Zenith and Institutional Power—The SAFS Golden Age

The official establishment of the Shanghai Animation Film Studio (SAFS) in April 1957, although it had already been operating effectively for several years, signaled the beginning of what is widely regarded as the "Golden Age" of Chinese animation. This era, which extended until the eve of the Cultural Revolution in the mid-1960s, witnessed an extraordinary flowering of artistic innovation, technical sophistication, and the production of works that would come to define the so-called "Chinese School" (中国学派, *Zhōngguó xuépài*), earning considerable international acclaim. SAFS became a vibrant hub of creative talent, employing approximately 200 individuals organized into around 20 creative teams, each dedicated to the development of original projects. Functioning as the national center for animation experimentation and production, SAFS served as a de facto state institution for artistic development (Rosen and Zhu 2010).

While operating within the ideological framework of the Communist Party, animators at SAFS during the late 1950s and early 1960s experienced a surprising degree of artistic freedom, which allowed them to explore diverse styles and narrative approaches rarely seen elsewhere in global animation at that time. This period was characterized by a collective spirit of experimentation, with artists collaborating to push the boundaries of the medium through the development of new narrative languages and visual aesthetics. Though many of their works reflected or aligned with socialist ideals, they often incorporated rich national and folkloric elements, contributing to their broad appeal both domestically and internationally.

The Chinese School that matured at SAFS emphasized aesthetic excellence, drawing heavily from the country's vast heritage of myths, legends, folktales, and traditional art forms. These cultural elements were interwoven with the socio-political ideals of the post-1949 era, creating a unique synthesis of mythology, traditional Chinese narratives, and contemporary socialist values. This formula resonated deeply with Chinese audiences and attracted increasing attention from international critics, who were captivated by the exoticism, visual beauty, and distinct cultural character of these films (Zhang 1999).

Many of the animations produced during this period also conveyed philosophical undertones derived from Confucian, Daoist, or Buddhist traditions, often expressed through simple, engaging, and humorous narratives accessible to audiences of all ages. To enhance aesthetic authenticity, animators employed traditional Chinese art tools and techniques, such as ink-wash painting (*shuǐmòhuà* 水墨画) executed with calligraphic brushes. These visual compositions were frequently accompanied by scores featuring traditional Chinese music, which played a crucial role in establishing atmosphere and narrative rhythm, often evoking themes of natural harmony and philosophical reflection.

During its first decade of formal operation, SAFS was remarkably prolific, producing approximately 188 films across a range of animation techniques. This included about 40 puppet animations, 25 paper-cut animations (*jiǎnzhǐ dònghuà*

剪纸动画), and 28 cel animations, among others (SAFS production data). At its peak, before the Cultural Revolution, the studio employed as many as 380 people. The films created during these years represent the zenith of artistic accomplishment in Chinese animation and remain foundational works within China's modern visual culture.

Several productions from this period stand out as masterpieces of the Chinese School. *Pigsy Eats Watermelon* (猪八戒吃西瓜, *Zhū Bājiè Chī Xīguā*), directed by Wan Laiming and Wan Guchan in 1958, was a landmark work in paper-cut animation. While the technique lacked the fluidity of cel animation, it was developed at SAFS into an expressive and distinctive style, with *Pigsy Eats Watermelon* serving as a pioneering example of its application in longer narrative form.

The Zhuang Tapestry (一幅僮锦, *Yī Fú Zhuàngjǐn*), directed by Qian Jiajun (钱家骏) in 1959, exemplified the influence of traditional Chinese landscape painting. Its ethereal mountains and stylized trees recalled classical scroll paintings, giving the film a visual language steeped in Chinese artistic heritage.

That same year, the Wan brothers, along with Xu Jingda (许经达, also known as A Da 阿达), who would later emerge as a major director himself, created *The Radish Returns* (萝卜回来了, *Luóbo Huíláile*). Aimed at children, this heartwarming tale about animal friends sharing a giant radish was presented with wit and visual charm.

Wan Guchan continued refining the paper-cut animation technique with his 1959 work *Yú Tóng* (渔童, *The Fishing Child*), notable for its increasingly naturalistic character movement and exquisite detail in its landscapes, demonstrating growing mastery over the medium.

Perhaps the most internationally celebrated innovation from SAFS during this Golden Age was the development of ink-wash animation (*shuǐmò dònghuà* 水墨动画), spearheaded by Te Wei. His 1960 animated short *Little Tadpoles Look for Mama (小蝌蚪找妈妈, Xiǎo Kēdǒu Zhǎo Māma*), realized in collaboration with Qian Jiazhen, attained wide international recognition as a seminal work of Chinese ink-wash animation. Drawing on pictorial conventions developed by masters of Chinese ink painting, in particular Qi Baishi (齐白石), the film translates this fragile and contemplative visual idiom into continuous, fluid movement. From a technical perspective, the animation dispenses with conventional contour lines, rejecting the standard "ink and paint" procedure in which characters are first outlined and then filled with color. Instead, animators applied washes of ink directly onto multiple layers of celluloid, modulating density and tonal value to construct form and motion simultaneously. This procedure demanded extremely precise control of timing and brushwork in order to sustain, frame by frame, the illusion of ink diffusing organically across the surface. The resulting labor-intensive process differentiated the studio's artisanal practice from the more standardized, assembly-line production models prevalent in contemporaneous Western animation. Each frame resembled a living ink painting, resulting in a poetic and visually stunning work deeply rooted in Chinese aesthetics. The film received numerous international awards, including recognition at Locarno (1961), Cannes (1964), Zagreb, and the Pompidou Centre, firmly establishing the Chinese School on the world stage.

In parallel, SAFS also explored *origami animation* (折纸动画, *zhézhǐ dònghuà*), a technique involving the animation of folded paper figures. Yu Zheguang (虞哲光) pioneered this approach with his short *The Smart Little Ducks* (聪明的鸭子, *Cōngmíng de Yāzi*) in 1960. While technically innovative, this work targeted a young audience and did not heavily emphasize Chinese cultural motifs.

The early 1960s continued this trajectory of artistic and technical excellence. The Wan brothers finally realized their long-anticipated project, *Havoc in Heaven* (大闹天宫, *Dà Nào Tiāngōng*), also known as *The Monkey King*.

Released in two parts (Part 1 in 1961 and Part 2 in 1964, though some sources list 1965 for the second part), this Technicolor cel animation is widely considered the crowning achievement of the Golden Age and one of the masterpieces of world animation. Based on episodes from *Journey to the West*, it featured the iconic character of Sun Wukong, whose design and persona became deeply embedded in Chinese visual culture. Google later honored Wan Laiming's 112th birthday with a Doodle featuring the Monkey King.

Havoc in Heaven represented a monumental artistic undertaking. Its visual style, character animation, and musical score drew heavily from the traditions of Beijing Opera. Sun Wukong's character design became iconic. The film was the culmination of years of preparation, initially conceived by the Wan brothers following their earlier work on *Princess Iron Fan*. After nearly two decades of interruptions and delays, their vision was fully realized. The film achieved enormous success in China and garnered significant international attention, being broadcast in numerous countries. Technically, it was a tour de force, with a runtime of 117 min and a film length of approximately 3140 m.

Amid this creative flourishing, however, early signs of shifting political winds began to emerge. An unexpected propaganda animation, *The Asian People Angrily Expel the Plague God* (亚洲人民怒逐瘟疫, *Yàzhōu Rénmín Nù Zhú Wēnyì*), was reportedly produced by *Changchun Film Studio* (长春电影制片厂, *Zhǎngchūn Diànyǐng Zhìpiànchǎng*) in 1961 (Zhang Huilin 2002). Little is known about the film or its creators, but its emergence presaged the increasing political pressures that would soon affect the entire industry.

The paper-cut technique continued to evolve through directors like Hu Xionghua (胡雄华), whose *Waiting for Tomorrow* (等明天, *Děng Míngtiān*) appeared in 1962. Hu would go on to become a master of the genre, producing numerous paper-cut animations through 1981.

The Golden Age also witnessed the creation of China's first feature-length puppet animation, *The Peacock Princess* (孔雀公主, *Kǒngquè Gōngzhǔ*), directed by Jin Xi in 1963. This 80-min film was adapted from a traditional folktale of the Dai ethnic minority.

That same year, Te Wei and Qian Jiajun collaborated on another ink-wash masterpiece, *The Cowherd's Flute* (牧笛, *Mùdí*), also known as *The Buffalo Boy and His Flute*. Distinguished by its lyrical beauty and complete absence of dialogue, relying solely on its visuals and a haunting flute score, this work is regarded as one of the pinnacles of Chinese animation. It too earned international accolades, including at the Odense International Film Festival in 1979.

This extraordinary period of artistic achievement at SAFS firmly established a distinctive and internationally recognized Chinese School of animation. The studio successfully merged indigenous artistic traditions with modern animation technologies, producing works of lasting beauty and cultural significance. However, as the political climate in China grew increasingly rigid, this Golden Age approached its end, soon to be eclipsed by the ideological upheaval of the Cultural Revolution.

1.11 The Anti-Rightist Campaign and Ideological Encroachment

Despite the extraordinary artistic achievements of the Shanghai Animation Film Studio (SAFS) during its Golden Age, the broader political climate in China was becoming increasingly precarious. After a decade of relative creative flourishing within state-controlled frameworks, the animation sector, like all cultural industries, found itself increasingly entangled in the escalating political campaigns launched by the Chinese Communist Party (CCP) under Mao Zedong. These campaigns sought to consolidate Party authority and suppress any perceived deviation from socialist orthodoxy. Among the most consequential of these movements was the Anti-Rightist Campaign (反右运动, *Fǎn Yòu Yùndòng*).

Initially launched in 1957 under the pretext of encouraging intellectual debate through the *Hundred Flowers Campaign* (百花齐放, 百家争鸣, *Bǎihuā Qífàng, Bǎijiā Zhēngmíng*), the Anti-Rightist Campaign rapidly transformed into a systematic purge of individuals labeled as "rightists" for expressing dissent, criticizing Party policies, or simply holding views deemed bourgeois or counter-revolutionary. Though officially targeting a narrow political category, the campaign's scope expanded widely, deeply affecting intellectuals, artists, writers, and academics. A second, though less formally designated, wave of political tightening unfolded in the early 1960s, further restricting independent thought and creative freedom. Millions were subjected to public denunciations, demotions, imprisonment, or forced relocation to labor camps (劳动改造, *láodòng gǎizào*), where they endured physical hardship and ideological re-education.

Media sectors, including film and animation, came under particularly intense scrutiny. While SAFS animators had previously benefited from a period of remarkable artistic latitude during the 1950s, the onset of the Anti-Rightist Campaign dramatically altered the creative atmosphere. Artists and studio leaders were now required to exercise extreme caution, ensuring that their works adhered strictly to Party ideology, with any deviation carrying the risk of severe political repercussions. The creative freedom that had characterized the Golden Age steadily eroded under mounting ideological pressure.

By 1964, the impact of these political shifts had become starkly visible. Several animated films that had completed production and received initial approval were abruptly blocked from release or withdrawn by Party censors. One illustrative case was *Red Army Bridge* (红军桥, *Hóngjūn Qiáo*), a paper-cut animation directed by Qian Yunda (钱运达). Though initially deemed ideologically appropriate for its revolutionary themes upon release in 1964, the film was later criticized and its distribution halted in 1965 (Qing 2006). This reversal reflected the increasingly arbitrary and unpredictable nature of censorship decisions during the period.

Even highly celebrated productions were not immune. The Wan brothers' *Havoc in Heaven* (大闹天宫, *Dà Nào Tiāngōng*), despite its cultural and artistic significance, came under political scrutiny. Its central figure, the rebellious Monkey King who defies celestial authority, was viewed by some Party ideologues as a potentially subversive symbol of resistance to established power, a dangerous suggestion within the prevailing political context (Ehrlich 2011).

Similarly, Te Wei's *The Cowherd's Flute* (牧笛, *Mùdí*), though praised for its artistic mastery, was condemned by Party leaders for failing to promote class struggle and was censored for fourteen years, labeled as a work that could "numb the consciousness of the masses" (Lent 2001a, b).

As ideological orthodoxy tightened, only those animated films that directly served the propaganda objectives of the CCP or strictly adhered to approved socialist themes were permitted for production and distribution. Although scholarship on these politically constrained works remains limited, this period is critical to understanding the extent to which political intervention stifled the creative development of Chinese animation.

Production figures for 1964 vary slightly, but it is estimated that 13–15 animated films were produced that year, including the second part of *Havoc in Heaven* and *Red Army Bridge*. Among the works considered ideologically acceptable were *Two Heroic Sisters of the Grassland* (草原英雄小姐妹, *Cǎoyuán Yīngxióng Xiǎojiěmèi*), directed by Qian Yunda and Tang Cheng (唐澄), and *The Cock Crows at Midnight* (半夜鸡叫, *Bànyè Jī Jiào*), directed by You Lei (尤磊). The former recounted the story of two young sisters from Inner Mongolia who heroically safeguard their collective's flock during a blizzard, exemplifying self-sacrifice for the socialist collective. The latter depicted a greedy landlord who tricks his laborers into working extra hours by manipulating his rooster to crow before dawn, only to have his scheme thwarted by the ingenuity of a peasant child.

While these works were not overtly propagandistic in the extreme sense of earlier wartime animations, their narratives clearly reflected Party priorities, emphasizing class struggle, rural idealism, and the heroism of ordinary citizens, particularly youth, in service of socialist values. The glorification of rural settings and the portrayal of children as revolutionary exemplars became common motifs in the Party-approved cinema of the time.

One production that adopted a slightly distinct yet still ideologically compliant approach was *Xiaolin's Diary* (小林日记, *Xiǎolín Rìjì*), 1965, directed by Hu Jinqing (胡进庆). Like its contemporaries, this film centered on themes of class struggle and rural life.

As China's foreign policy took an increasingly antagonistic stance toward the United States in the early 1960s, anti-American sentiment permeated creative production. Animated films began to reflect this political orientation, giving rise to a subgenre of anti-American propaganda animation. Notable examples included:

- *Support the Dominican People's Anti-US Armed Struggle* (支持多米尼加人民反美武装斗争, *Zhīchí Duōmǐníjiā Rénmín Fǎn Měi Wǔzhuāng Dòuzhēng*), also cited in alternative form as *Support Dominica Against US Armed Aggression* (支持多米尼加反对美国武装侵略, *Zhīchí Duōmǐníjiā Fǎnduì Měiguó Wǔzhuāng Qīnlüè*). Produced at SAFS, this film's direction is often attributed to collective studio authorship.
- *Support the Vietnamese People to Defeat the US Aggressors* (支持越南人民打倒美国侵略者, *Zhīchí Yuènán Rénmín Dǎdǎo Měiguó Qīnlüèzhě*), also produced at SAFS, though little is known about its specific content.
- *Expose the US Imperialist Peace Talk Fraud* (揭穿美帝和谈骗局, *Jiēchuān Měi Dì Hétán Piànjú*), a paper-cut animation portraying the suffering of the Vietnamese people under American bombings and their courageous resistance, ultimately rejecting deceptive American peace offers in favor of continued armed struggle.
- *The Red Scarf* (红领巾, *Hónglǐngjīn*), a paper-cut animation distinguished by backgrounds rendered in a refined Chinese aesthetic. The plot followed a patriotic girl who identifies American spies disguised as PLA soldiers, leaving her red scarf—a symbol of the Young Pioneers—as a clue to alert authorities, leading to their capture.
- *Southern Boy* (南方少年, *Nánfāng Shàonián*), which depicted a young Vietnamese boy assisting his community in resisting American forces.

Many of these animated propaganda films were later adapted into comic books (*liánhuánhuà* 连环画), often reproducing scenes directly from the films. Some of these comics were even translated and published internationally, as exemplified by the Italian collection *I Fumetti di Mao* (*Mao's Comics*), edited by Umberto Eco and Jean Chesneaux in 1971, with translations by Gino Nebiolo (Chesneaux 1971).

The period spanning the Anti-Rightist Campaign through the early 1960s represents a decisive constriction of creative space in Chinese animation. While technical mastery remained, the capacity for artistic innovation and critical exploration was sharply curtailed, replaced by a growing emphasis on works that functioned primarily as political instruments. This increasingly restrictive climate set the stage for the even more severe disruptions that would follow during the Cultural Revolution.

1.12 Shadows of the Cultural Revolution (1966–1976)

The Great Proletarian Cultural Revolution (无产阶级文化大革命, *Wúchǎnjiējí Wénhuà Dàgémìng*), launched by Mao Zedong in 1966 and lasting until his death in 1976, stands as one of the most tumultuous and destructive periods in modern

Chinese history. Its devastating consequences for China's cultural and artistic landscape extended deeply into the animation sector, resulting in a near-complete cessation of creative production and widespread persecution of artists. The movement's stated goal was the eradication of bourgeois elements, capitalist tendencies, and feudal cultural remnants to safeguard the purity of communist ideology. In practice, however, the Cultural Revolution quickly devolved into violent factional struggles, mass persecution, and profound national trauma.

The animation industry was particularly vulnerable to these upheavals. The artistic accomplishments of the Golden Age were now viewed with suspicion, often condemned as manifestations of "old culture" or deemed insufficiently revolutionary. The few films that were produced during this period were stripped of the artistic nuance and cultural richness that had previously characterized Chinese animation, replaced almost entirely by rigid political propaganda. Protagonists were often depicted as idealized children portrayed with adult-like seriousness, embodying revolutionary fervor and participating in class struggle or anti-imperialist campaigns. Narrative formulas became inflexible and heavily didactic, functioning more as vehicles for adult political indoctrination than as imaginative storytelling for children. The unique capacity of animation to address audiences across generations was subordinated to its role as a blunt tool for ideological messaging.

Central to the Cultural Revolution was the campaign to eradicate the "Four Olds" (破四旧, *Pò Sìjiù*): Old Ideas (旧思想, *jiù sīxiǎng*), Old Culture (旧文化, *jiù wénhuà*), Old Customs (旧习惯, *jiù xíguàn*), and Old Habits (旧风俗, *jiù fēngsú*). This initiative resulted in the widespread destruction of cultural artifacts, historical sites, and religious institutions. Temples were shuttered or desecrated, libraries and archives were looted, and much of China's historical heritage was eradicated. The slogan "Without destruction, there can be no construction" (不破不立, *bù pò bù lì*) chillingly encapsulated the radical iconoclasm that swept across the country.

Intellectuals, educators, and artists became principal targets of persecution. Professors and teachers were publicly denounced, beaten by students often organized into militant Red Guard (红卫兵, *Hóngwèibīng*) factions, and imprisoned or exiled to remote rural areas for ideological re-education through hard labor. The Red Guards, empowered by Party directives, carried out violent campaigns against anyone suspected of harboring counter-revolutionary tendencies or engaging in ideologically impure practices.

As in other totalitarian regimes of the twentieth century, such as Fascist Italy and Nazi Germany, cinema was entirely subsumed under state propaganda. The Shanghai Animation Film Studio (SAFS), the heart of Chinese animation, was forced to suspend almost all creative activity from approximately 1966 to 1972. Many of its most talented artists and animators suffered immense personal and professional hardship. Some were publicly humiliated, beaten, and subjected to political denunciation. Others were compelled to create strictly orthodox propaganda films under extreme political pressure, where failure to conform could be life-threatening.

The Wan brothers and Te Wei, foundational figures in Chinese animation, were among those severely persecuted. Forced to leave their families, they were dispatched to remote areas for re-education through grueling physical labor. Their tasks included hauling grain, tending livestock, and digging ditches, while at night they engaged in self-criticism sessions and were required to compose confessional writings renouncing their supposed ideological errors. John Lent's research into Asian animation documents the suffering of artists such as Lin Wenxiao (林文肖) and Yan Dingxian (严定宪), who were compelled to leave their six-month-old child in the care of relatives when they were sent from Shanghai into exile (Lent 2001a, b). Some animators later reflected on this period as a time of brutal hardship but also of personal introspection and stripped-down existential confrontation.

Documentation on animation production during the most intense years of the Cultural Revolution (1966–1972) is extremely limited. Official SAFS records reflect a near-total void in output. Nevertheless, sporadic production, almost exclusively dedicated to overt propaganda, did continue, often outside the original studio system or in restructured production units. Films attributed to this period include:

- *Shanghai Arts and Crafts* (上海工艺美术, *Shànghǎi Gōngyì Měishù*), though little is known of its contents.
- *New Seedlings in the Mountain Village* (山村新苗, *Shāncūn Xīn Miáo*), 1966, accompanied by music from Wu Yingju (吴应炬), depicting rural children forming a revolutionary brigade under Party guidance.
- *The Great Statement* (伟大的声明, *Wěidà de Shēngmíng*), for which few details are available.
- *Fruit* (果实, *Guǒshí*), 1967, reportedly aimed at very young children, though production details remain unclear.

The years from 1967 to 1972 constituted a particularly barren period for Chinese animation. Only in 1972, as the most extreme phase of the Cultural Revolution began to subside, did SAFS tentatively resume activity. Returning artists faced mandatory periods of intense ideological re-education before being allowed to work again. Even then, production was narrowly focused on Party-sanctioned propaganda themes.

The first SAFS animation produced after this reopening was *Battle Song of the Ten-Thousand-Ton Hydraulic Press* (万吨水压机战歌, *Wàn Dūn Shuǐyājī Zhàngē*), directed by Hu Jinqing and Wu Qiang (吴强) using paper-cut animation. The narrative celebrated the *Great Leap Forward* (大跃进, *Dà Yuèjìn*), portraying Shanghai workers overcoming technological obstacles by relying on Maoist philosophical guidance to construct a massive hydraulic press, thereby advancing industrial and agricultural production.

Another post-reopening production was *Fàngxué Yǐhòu* (放学以后, *After School*), directed by Yan Dingxian using traditional cel animation. This story followed members of the Little Red Guards (小红卫兵, *Xiǎo Hóngwèibīng*), who exposed a reactionary soldier disseminating "bad songs" within their school. With the assistance of a teacher, student Li Guohua (李国华) uncovered the soldier's true identity as a notorious criminal. Similarly, *Bù Chā Bànfēn Háo* (不差半分毫, *Not a Fraction of a Penny Off*), a paper-cut animation directed by Lian Di (廉迪) and Yanping Xiao (肖念萍) from Xi'an Yaping Studio (西安亚平工作室), remained fully aligned with Party orthodoxy. For many of these productions, only propaganda comic book adaptations (*liánhuánhuà* 连环画) remain, limiting access to the original animated versions.

Two SAFS veterans, Wang Shuchen (王树忱) and Yan Dingxian (严定宪), directed *The Little Trumpeter* (小号手, *Xiǎo Hào Shǒu*), which became a model for subsequent propaganda animations. Its young peasant protagonist learns trumpet to aid the Red Army against Nationalist forces. After being wounded, he discovers an enemy hideout, alerts the army with his trumpet, is captured and rescued, and finally forces the enemy leader to his death. Despite its rigid ideology, the film demonstrated more sophisticated animation and a comparatively modern narrative structure.

Little Sentinel of the East China Sea (东海小哨兵, *Dōnghǎi Xiǎo Shàobīng*), another paper-cut animation, echoed themes found in *The Red Scarf* (红领巾, *Hónglǐngjīn*), 1965, with improved animation quality and more naturalistic movement. Puppet animation reappeared with films like *The Resounding Bow and Arrow* (带响的弓箭, *Dài Xiǎng de Gōngjiàn*), also known as *Little Eighth Route Army Soldier*, depicting young resistance fighters during the Second Sino-Japanese War. A recurring visual convention in these films was the stylized depiction of child protagonists bearing adult-like expressions and revolutionary solemnity, reflecting the era's emphasis on early ideological maturation.

Even Te Wei (特伟), after enduring severe persecution, returned to direct *The Golden Wild Goose* (金色的大雁, *Jīnsè de Dàyàn*) in 1976. The film depicted Tibetan children, guided by the Party, confronting reactionary forces. While still adhering to propaganda constraints, Te Wei sought to introduce subtle variations in artistic style, distinguishing the work slightly from the most rigid aesthetics of the Cultural Revolution.

Following Mao Zedong's (毛泽东) death in September 1976, the Cultural Revolution officially ended. Nevertheless, its ideological shadow continued to influence animation for some time. Animated films continued to promote revolutionary themes and pay tribute to the late leader. One of the last notable propaganda films from this immediate post-Mao period was *The Fiery Red Rock Standard* (火红的岩标, *Huǒhóng de Yán Biāo*), portraying Tibetan villagers mourning Mao's death and erecting a monument in his honor, reaffirming their devotion to the Communist Party (Wang 2005).

Throughout the late 1970s, Chinese animation remained heavily marked by Maoist ideology and political imperatives, only gradually beginning to rediscover artistic innovation as China entered a period of profound reform.

References

Bendazzi, G. 1999. *Cartoons: Cento anni di cinema d'animazione*. Marsilio.
BlueBook of China's Radio. 2009. *Film and television*. Beijing: Social Sciences Academic Press.
Browne, P., and R.B. Browne. 2001. *The guide to United States popular culture*. Popular Press.
Caldwell, J.T. 2008. *Production culture: Industrial reflexivity and critical practice in film and television*. Duke University Press.
Chen, J., and J. Zou. 2005. *Centennial Chinese movie collection*. China Social Sciences Press.

Chesneaux, J., Eco, U., and Nebiolo, G. 1971. I fumetti di Mao. Laterza.

Clements, J. 2010. *Tactics: Volume 2*. A-Net Digital LLC.

Corsaro, S. 2002. *The flash animator*. New Riders.

Crafton, D. 1993. *Before Mickey*. University of Chicago Press.

Cunningham, S., and J. Silver. 2012. *Screen distribution and the new King Kongs of the online world*. Palgrave Macmillan.

Drège, J.P. 2000. *Shanghai commercial press, 1897–1949*. Shanghai Commercial Press.

Ehrlich, N. 2011. Animated documentaries as masking. *Animation Studies, 6*. https://journal.animationstudies.org/nea-ehrlich-animated-documentaries-as-masking/.

Gifford, D. 1990. *American animated films: The silent era, 1897–1929*. McFarland & Company.

Hu, T.-Y.G. 2010. *Frames of anime: Culture and image-building*. Hong Kong University Press.

Huangxian, W. 2002. *Last night starlight: 20th century Chinese film history*. Hunan People's Publishing House.

Hui, Y. 2005. *Film di storia / secolo cinese Film Studies libro della serie di animazione della Cina*. China Film Press.

Keane, M. 2007. *Created in China: The great new leap forward*. Routledge.

Keane, M. 2013. *Creativity and its discontents: China's creative industries and creative industries in China: Art, design and media*. John Wiley & Sons.

LaMarre, T. 2009. The Anime Machine: A Media Theory of Animation. University of Minnesota Press.

Lent, J. A. 2001a. *Animation in Asia and the Pacific*. Indiana University Press.

Lent, J. A. 2001b. *Illustrating Asia: Comics, humor magazines, and picture books*. Indiana University Press.

Lent, J.A. 2003. Asian animation: Artistic and commercial perspectives. *Asian Cinema* 14 (1).

Lenburg, J. 2006. *Who's who in animated cartoons: An international guide to film & television's award-winning and legendary animators*. Hal Leonard Corporation.

Lidào, X. 2004. *Storia del cinema cinese 1937–1945*. Capital Normal University Press.

Lin, Z.H. 2002. *20th century, storia dell'arte del animazione Cinese*. Shaanxi People's Fine Arts Publishing House.

Liu, P., and X. Yang. 2012. *Progettazione character animation*. Esphere Media: Jiangxi Fine Arts Publishing House.

Lupo, G. 2002. *Poesia come pittura: De Libero e la cultura romana, 1930–1940*. Vita e Pensiero.

Mai, L.H. 2006. *Illustrated Chinese comics*. Lingnan Art Publishing House.

Needham, J. 1962. *Science and civilisation in China, Volume 4: Physics and physical technology*. Cambridge University Press.

Negro, G. 2011. The video sharing market in China: An overview. *China Media Observatory Newsletter*.

Nie, X.R. 2006. *Cartoon*. Fudan University Press.

Pang, L. 2012. *Intellectual property rights offenses*. Duke University Press.

Pelliteri, M. 2002. *Anatomia di Pokémon: Cultura di massa ed estetica dell'effimero fra pedagogia e globalizzazione*. SEAM.

Pellitteri, M. 2008. Il drago e la saetta. Modelli, strategie e identità dell'immaginario giapponese. Tunué.

Peruzzi, G. 2010. *Vortici e colori: Alle origini dell'opera di James Clerk Maxwell*. Edizioni Dedalo.

Qing, X. 2006. An Economic Research of China's Animation Industry (中国动画片的产业经济研究). China Market Press.

Quiquemelle, M. C. 1991. The Wan Brothers and sixty years of animated film in China. In *Perspectives on Chinese cinema*, ed. C. Berry, 175–186. British Film Institute.

Richeri, G. 2012, Economia politica dei media, Laterza.

Rosen, S., and Zhu, Y., eds. 2010. Art, Politics, and Commerce in Chinese Cinema. Hong Kong University Press.

Sangiovanni, A. 2012. *Le parole e le figure: Storia dei media in Italia dall'età liberale alla Seconda Guerra mondiale*. Donzelli Editore.

Simion, D. V. 2008. Il Dizionario dei Cartoni Animati. Anton Edizioni.
Sismondo, S. 2010. *An introduction to science and technology studies*, 2nd ed. Wiley-Blackwell.
Sun, W. 2010. Mission impossible? Soft power, communication capacity, and the globalization of Chinese media. *International Journal of Communication* 4: 54–72.
Sun, L. 2011. Research on the History of China's Animation (中国动画史研究). Commercial Press.
Tan, L, and Yin, J. 2006. Animation industry (动漫产业 / 21世纪文化产业前沿丛书). Sichuan University Press.
Tiānchāo dòushì. 2006. *Explorers thrilling life*. Hyweb Technology Co.
Tortora, M. 2008. *Viaggi nell'animazione: Interventi e testimonianze sul mondo animato da Émile Reynaud a Second Life*. Tunué.
Vezzoli, P.G. 2000. *Dizionario dei termini cinematografici: Italiano-inglese*. Hoepli Editore.
Voci, P. 2010. *China on video: Smaller-screen realities*. Routledge.
Wang, D. 2005. Confusion in the Chinese animation industry (困惑中的中国动漫业). Guǎnggào Dàguān [广告大观], (8).
Wang, D., and F. Zheng. 1990. *Twentieth century dictionary of the Chinese patriotic celebrities*. Jilin University Press.
Wong, W.S. 2002. *Hong Kong comics: A history of manhua*. Princeton Architectural Press.
Wu, Z. 1995. *Racconto del cinema della Repubblica Cinese*. Henan University Press.
Ying, S.H. 2002. *Goose cold shock: Hunan Hengyang "Cultural Revolution" historical events*. Publisher unknown.
Zhang Y. 1999. Shanghai Film Collection (上海电影志/上海市专志系列丛刊), Shanghai Academy of Social Sciences Press.
Zhang, H. 2002. Chinese Animation Art History in 20th Century. Shaanxi People's Fine Arts Publishing House.
Zhang, H. 2003. Some characteristics of Chinese animation. *Asian Cinema* 14 (1): 70–79.
Zhu, G. 2005. *Most of Chinese art*. Shanghai Bookstore Publishing House.

Chapter 2
Reform, Marketization, and Global Integration: Chinese Animation from the 1970s to the 2010s

Abstract This chapter examines the transformation of Chinese animation from the late 1970s to the early 2010s, highlighting the impact of economic reform, marketization, and globalization. Following the Cultural Revolution, animators returned to the Shanghai Animation Film Studio and other institutions, reviving creativity through productions such as *Nezha Conquers the Dragon King* (1979). Television became a central platform for animation, expanding audiences and shaping a second golden age. However, as foreign content, especially Japanese anime and American cartoons, entered China, domestic studios faced new competition. Many animators moved into outsourcing for international companies, particularly in Shenzhen and other Special Economic Zones, altering the structure of the industry. The 1990s and 2000s brought technological modernization, with digital tools, 3D animation, and co-productions emerging as significant trends. The state increasingly treated animation as part of the creative industries, establishing subsidies, festivals, and industrial parks to encourage growth. Despite increased production and market expansion, challenges persisted, including limited originality, uneven quality, and dependence on service work for global studios. The chapter concludes that this period was both transitional and contradictory, combining remarkable industrial growth with structural fragilities that would shape the future of Chinese animation.

Keywords Nezha Conquers the Dragon King · Marketization · Outsourcing · Shenzhen · Television animation · Creative industries

2.1 Artistic Renewal in the Post-Mao Thaw

The death of Mao Zedong in September 1976, followed one month later by the arrest of the "Gang of Four" (四人帮, *Sìrénbāng*),[1] signaled the formal end of the Cultural Revolution. This pivotal political shift ushered in the gradual reemergence

[1] The "Gang of Four" (四人帮, *Sìrénbāng*) refers to a political faction composed of Jiang Qing (江青, Mao Zedong's last wife), Zhang Chunqiao (张春桥), Yao Wenyuan (姚文元), and Wang Hongwen (王洪文). They were highly influential figures during the Cultural Revolution. Their arrest in October 1976, one month after Mao Zedong's death, is widely considered to mark the

© The Author(s), under exclusive license to Springer Nature Switzerland AG 2026
V. De Masi, *A Critical Analysis of China's Animation Industry*, Numanities - Arts and Humanities in Progress 37, https://doi.org/10.1007/978-3-032-18656-0_2

of artistic and cultural activities throughout China. For the animation industry, which had suffered severe repression and creative paralysis during the preceding decade, this period, often referred to as "the thaw", offered a fragile but genuine prospect for creative recovery. Artists and animators who had been silenced, exiled, or forced into menial labor cautiously returned to institutions such as the Shanghai Animation Film Studio (SAFS). In the immediate aftermath of the political transition, approximately seventeen animated films were produced within a relatively brief timeframe, marking a deliberate, though tentative, break from the rigid propagandistic formulas of the Cultural Revolution and an initial attempt to reconnect with the artistic vitality that had characterized the earlier Golden Age.

Within the artistic community, the dominant sentiment was one of profound relief tempered by persistent apprehension, rooted in years of political instability and repression. Yan Dingxian (严定宪), a leading director at SAFS, later articulated the deep frustration and anger felt by many animators. He described how the Cultural Revolution had extinguished a full decade of artistic growth, suppressed emerging creative energies, and halted promising experimental projects at what should have been SAFS's most dynamic period of development. In a 1992 interview with David Ehrlich, Yan spoke of the enduring bitterness experienced by artists who were forced to comply with the Party's ideological dictates, unable to express their creative visions or challenge official narratives (Ehrlich, as cited in Lent 2001). Even during the early return of artists to SAFS in the 1970s, prior to Mao's death, a climate of surveillance and political caution persisted, compelling them to remain guarded in both content and process. As Yan Dingxian, who would later assume SAFS's directorship, observed, a genuinely stable and creatively supportive environment did not fully materialize until the 1980s (Lent 2001). It was during this period that he, alongside Wang Shuchen and the esteemed Te Wei, co-directed the highly acclaimed feature *Nezha Conquers the Dragon King* (哪吒闹海, *Nǎzhā Nào Hǎi*, 1979), a film that emphatically reasserted SAFS's artistic ambition and technical mastery.

Te Wei, the former director of SAFS and one of the principal figures of the pre-Cultural Revolution Golden Age, had endured particularly brutal persecution. Publicly humiliated, he was forced to write endless self-criticisms, confined for long periods, and ultimately assigned to factory work for two years. When political persecution escalated further, he was imprisoned in a small room for another two years, sleeping on the floor under constant Red Guard surveillance. During this confinement, Te Wei was subjected to beatings that resulted in the loss of several teeth (Lent 2001). Ironically, Te Wei later reflected that a relative sense of "freedom" only arrived when he was sent to a rural re-education camp. Although subjected to arduous labor, cleaning manure, digging irrigation ditches, and performing agricultural tasks, he was reunited with fellow persecuted artists, including Xu Jingda (许经达, also known as A Da 阿达), who had similarly been prohibited from practicing his craft. Their shared hardships, which for Te Wei included the demeaning task of transporting pigs

formal end of the Cultural Revolution. The term "Gang of Four" itself was popularized after their downfall.

by hand, lasted approximately one year and fostered a powerful sense of solidarity among SAFS's surviving artists (Lent 2001).

Upon his return to SAFS, Te Wei was initially relegated to the role of librarian. However, following the collapse of the Gang of Four and the political shift in 1976, he was reinstated as studio director. His principal objective upon resuming leadership was unequivocal: to restore SAFS's pursuit of a distinctly Chinese "National Style" (民族风格, *mínzú fēnggé*) in animation, recovering the creative vision and artistic spirit that had been suppressed during the Cultural Revolution. Among the SAFS artists, there was a collective determination to reignite experimentation, rediscover creative freedom, and reclaim the studio's preeminent status.

One of the first significant works to emerge from this rejuvenated environment was *A Night in the Art Gallery* (画廊一夜, *Huàláng Yīyè*), directed by Xu Jingda (A Da) and released in 1978. This film offered a symbolic and indirect critique of the Gang of Four and the Cultural Revolution's cultural vandalism. It portrayed grey, oppressive figures, caricatures embodying the forces of censorship and iconoclasm, systematically defacing and destroying works of Chinese cultural heritage inside a museum. The narrative climaxed when the figures within the paintings came to life, rose up against the vandals, and expelled them from the gallery (Ehrlich 2011). *A Night in the Art Gallery* served as both a metaphor for the end of the Cultural Revolution's most extreme censorship and a cautiously defiant affirmation of artistic resilience. It represented an early attempt by SAFS artists to begin processing the traumas of the preceding decade and to reassert the value of cultural legacy, even while operating within the evolving ideological parameters of the post-Mao Communist Party.

This fragile artistic revival unfolded within a rapidly transforming global animation landscape. By the late 1970s, American animation had secured its global dominance across both cinema and television markets. Simultaneously, Japanese animation (*anime*) was embarking on its own ascent toward international influence. Television series such as *Barbapapa* (バーバパパ, 1974), a Japanese-Dutch co-production that began airing in Italy in 1976, were soon followed by landmark productions like *Heidi, Girl of the Alps* (アルプスの少女ハイジ, *Arupusu no Shōjo Haiji*, 1974) and *UFO Robot Grendizer* (UFOロボグレンダイザー, *UFO Robo Gurendaizā*, 1975), captivating audiences across Europe and other regions. These early cultural exports foreshadowed the global rise of Japanese animation that would reshape international perceptions of the medium and generate new global markets.

In contrast, China's domestic television infrastructure remained relatively underdeveloped during the late 1970s. Although roughly a dozen stations had achieved national reach, actual television penetration was limited, with estimates suggesting that only one television set existed for every one hundred people (Hazelbarth 1997). The need for both technological expansion and content production was urgent. In 1978, a major institutional development occurred when Beijing Television (北京电视台, *Běijīng Diànshìtái*) was reorganized and renamed China Central Television (中国中央电视台, *Zhōngguó Zhōngyāng Diànshìtái*, CCTV). New regional broadcasters, such as Shanghai Television (上海电视台, *Shànghǎi Diànshìtái*), also emerged during this period, generating increased demand for broadcast content, including animated programming suitable for television. This evolving media landscape opened new opportunities for SAFS and the broader Chinese animation sector, providing an expanded platform for artists to revive their creative ambitions.

The production and release of *Nezha Conquers the Dragon King* (*Nǎzhā Nào Hǎi*, 1979) ultimately became emblematic of this rebirth. The film demonstrated not only the restoration of technical excellence but also the renewed artistic confidence of Chinese animators. It signaled that after years of repression, Chinese animation had reentered the cultural arena with both creative vitality and national pride, setting the stage for the next chapter in its ongoing evolution.

2.2 Television's Ascent and the Reconfiguration of Animation's Golden Age

The period following the release of *Nezha Conquers the Dragon King* is often identified as a "Second Golden Age" for Chinese animation. While it may not have recaptured the same pioneering fervor or international novelty that had characterized the first Golden Age (circa 1957–1965), this era witnessed a renewed flourishing of artistic expression, technical refinement, and a deliberate expansion into diverse narrative forms and aesthetic styles. A defining factor in this resurgence was the growing influence of television as a dominant medium for distributing animated content to a broader domestic audience. Animators at the Shanghai Animation Film Studio (SAFS), alongside emerging production units, actively seized the opportunities presented by this changing media landscape to develop new works that extended the legacy of the "Chinese School" while adapting to evolving technological and cultural contexts.

One of the leading figures contributing to this creative revival was Qu Jianfang (瞿建方). He pioneered a new form of puppet animation specifically designed for television with the episodic series *The Story of Afanti* (阿凡提的故事, *Āfántí de Gùshi*), which aired from 1979 to 1988. This series was distinctive not only for its technical sophistication but also for its narrative setting. Its protagonist, *Afanti*, based on the folkloric figure Nasreddin Khoja from Turkic and Central Asian cultural traditions, was situated within the Xinjiang Uyghur Autonomous Region, one of China's Muslim-majority territories. This geographical and cultural departure was significant, as it showcased narratives and visual styles drawn from China's ethnic diversity, breaking with the predominantly Han-centric narratives that had previously dominated Chinese animation. In a 2012 interview, Qu Jianfang emphasized that SAFS animators during this period were actively seeking fresh thematic material and culturally diverse storytelling approaches, aiming to reflect the full spectrum of China's cultural tapestry while remaining firmly rooted in national traditions. Qu immersed himself in Xinjiang's local culture, spending months studying the physiognomy and customs of its people to ensure accurate and respectful representation in his puppet characters. The resulting series was widely praised for its detailed craftsmanship and sensitive portrayal of regional culture (Ni 2006; interview with Qu Jianfang). In addition to its popular entertainment value, *The Story of Afanti* implicitly broadened the cultural awareness of national audiences.

A decisive milestone of this period arrived with the release of *Three Monks* (三个和尚, *Sān Gè Héshang*) in 1980, directed by Xu Jingda (A Da). This film introduced a remarkably fresh animation style that was minimalist yet highly expressive. Characters were drawn with elegant simplicity, while backgrounds remained sparse, focusing attention on the monks' subtle interactions. The hill, the temple, and a solitary tree served as the primary visual elements, rendered with refined economy. Notably, the film contained no dialogue; its narrative was conveyed entirely through gesture, facial expression, and meticulously composed sound design. Aesthetically, *Three Monks* combined traditional brush-stroke sensibilities (shuǐmò 水墨-like simplicity, though not strictly ink-wash animation) with modern comedic narrative. Its universal themes of cooperation and its refined execution earned widespread acclaim both domestically and internationally. The film was awarded the Silver Bear for Short Film at the 1982 Berlin International Film Festival, becoming one of the most internationally recognized and decorated Chinese animated works.

Xu Jingda continued his stylistic explorations with the 1980 release of *Snow Child* (雪孩子, *Xuě Háizi*), also known as *Snow Kid*, revisiting the rabbit character previously seen in *The Radish Returns* (萝卜回来了, *Luóbo Huíláile*). In this story, a snowman brought to life by a young rabbit forms a poignant friendship with his creator. Although aimed at young audiences, *Snow Child* was equally appreciated by adults for its emotional resonance and artistic quality, earning the "Prize for the Best Film" from the Chinese Ministry of Culture in 1980.

Puppet animation techniques also matured significantly during this period, as demonstrated in *The Taoist Priest of Laoshan* (崂山道士, *Láoshān Dàoshi*), released in 1981. This film skillfully blended traditional puppet animation with backgrounds evoking classical Chinese painting, crafting a fairy-tale atmosphere that resonated with audiences. The protagonist became widely recognizable in China and was still celebrated decades later as one of the nation's most beloved animated characters (Niu 2014). Throughout the 1980s, SAFS remained committed to diversifying its animation styles and drawing inspiration from China's rich artistic heritage, even as new technologies began to emerge. The studio revisited and refined established techniques, attaining greater precision and expressive fluidity. Notably, the ink-wash animation style (水墨动画, *shuǐmò dònghuà*) underwent further development, becoming increasingly delicate and sophisticated. A leading example of this refined technique was *The Deer's Bell* (鹿铃, *Lù Líng*), also known as *Bell on a Deer*, released in 1982. Visually inspired by the "Six Masters of the early Qing period" (清六家, *Qīng Liù Jiā*), renowned for their elegant landscape paintings, *The Deer's Bell* successfully translated these aesthetic qualities into lyrical, animated form.

In 1981, another major figure of Chinese popular culture entered the animated realm: *Old Master Q* (老夫子, *Lǎo Fūzǐ*). Created in 1962 by Hong Kong-based cartoonist Alfonso Wong (王家禧, *Wáng Jiāxǐ*), this iconic character had previously appeared in numerous live-action films. His transition to animation further cemented his place as one of China's most enduring comic figures. Animated adaptations from this period, including *Old Master Q Water Margin* (老夫子水虎傳, *Lǎofūzǐ Shuǐ Hǔ Zhuàn*, 1981 or 1982 depending on sources) and *Old Master Q & "San-T"* (山T老夫子, *Shān T Lǎofūzǐ*, 1983), successfully introduced his humor and satirical wit to younger audiences through animated storytelling.

A particularly noteworthy contribution of the Second Golden Age was *Legend of the Sealed Book* or *Secrets of the Heavenly Book* (天书奇谭, *Tiānshū Qítán*), released in 1983. This feature-length production displayed strikingly stylized character designs and background art. Its bold color palette and elaborate scenic compositions evoked visual aesthetics reminiscent of Qing Dynasty (清朝, *Qīng Cháo*) paintings. The character designs appeared inspired by historical portraiture of the period, creating a uniquely immersive world that blended narrative fantasy with visual artistry.

The character of Sanmao (三毛), created by Zhang Leping (张乐平) in 1935, also reappeared on screen in the animated adaptation *The Wanderings of Sanmao* (三毛流浪記, *Sān Máo Liúlàng Jì*), released in 1984. This adaptation, rich in references to modern Chinese society, reintroduced the iconic "three-haired" orphan to new generations, reaffirming his position as one of China's most enduring and culturally significant animated figures (Yan 2014).

The Second Golden Age thus emerged as a dynamic period defined by artistic renewal, a deepened engagement with China's cultural heritage, and the strategic adaptation to television's growing role as a mass distribution platform. Although shaped by political and economic conditions distinct from those of the first Golden Age, this period nonetheless produced a substantial body of work that expanded the canon of Chinese animation and demonstrated the medium's continued potential as both a vehicle of cultural expression and a site for artistic innovation.

2.3 The Digital Turn—Outsourcing, Labor, and Industrial Realignments

As the 1980s transitioned into the 1990s, the Chinese animation industry confronted the transformative forces of digitalization, which promised new efficiencies but also introduced complex challenges that significantly reshaped its institutional and creative structures. This period coincided with the acceleration of economic globalization, positioning China as an increasingly important hub for international animation outsourcing. Attracted by lower labor costs, foreign animation studios, particularly from Japan, the United States, and Europe, began to rely heavily on Chinese production facilities for labor-intensive aspects of animation, profoundly altering domestic workflows and patterns of talent allocation. The Japanese animation industry, already a global leader, spearheaded the integration of digital tools into its production pipelines. In parallel, China's deepening economic reforms encouraged foreign investment and the establishment of joint ventures, enabling Japanese studios to open branch offices or engage in substantial partnerships with Chinese firms. These collaborations primarily sought to capitalize on China's comparatively inexpensive, skilled labor for demanding production stages such as in-betweening and coloring, effectively incorporating Chinese studios into the global animation supply chain. Facing mounting technological and market pressures, the domestic Chinese animation sector cautiously initiated its own transition toward computer-based production techniques. The State Administration of Radio, Film, and Television (SARFT) acknowledged this impending transformation, acquiring its first computer systems for experimental graphics programs as early as 1988. However, it was not until the early 1990s that Chinese digital animation began to produce concrete results. While the Shanghai Animation Film Studio (SAFS) remained a vital institution, its historical dominance began to be challenged by newer private or joint-venture studios that proved more agile in adopting digital production methodologies.

This technological evolution unfolded within the context of profound socio-economic changes in China. Deng Xiaoping's "Southern Tour" (南巡, *Nánxún*) of 1992 reaffirmed the country's commitment to market-oriented reforms and international economic integration. For the domestic film and television industries, these reforms offered expanded opportunities for collaboration and technological acquisition but also intensified the influx of foreign media products. The animation sector was particularly affected, as American cartoons and Japanese anime rapidly gained dominance on Chinese television screens. These imported works, featuring established characters, complex storylines, and powerful merchandising strategies, captivated young Chinese audiences and posed formidable competition to domestic productions.

One consequence of these developments was a marked "talent drain" from state-run studios like SAFS toward better-funded private and foreign-invested outsourcing companies. Many experienced animators, colorists, and technicians were drawn to studios such as Jade Animation (深圳翡翠动画设计有限公司, *Shēnzhèn Fěicuì Dònghuà Shèjì Yǒuxiàn Gōngsī*), based in Shenzhen, a rapidly developing Special Economic Zone. Jade Animation emerged as one of the leading outsourcing studios, providing large-scale production services to major international clients from North America, Japan, and Europe (specific case studies are addressed in the following chapter). While this migration facilitated skill development and provided employment, it also weakened the creative core of original Chinese animation, as much of the domestic talent became engaged primarily in fulfilling foreign production mandates rather than developing indigenous narratives and styles. Despite these commercial pressures, efforts to sustain original Chinese animation persisted, though on a more limited scale and often with reduced financial resources. SAFS attempted to navigate this shifting environment through diversification strategies. In 1986, the studio initiated co-production projects with Japan's Toei Animation, one of the industry's global leaders. Further co-productions followed in 1987 with partners in Canada, France, the United States, and Germany. Domestically, SAFS sought to solidify distribution networks by forming strategic partnerships with major television broadcasters in cities such as Beijing, Shanghai, Nanjing, and Fujian (Huilin 2002). The geographical landscape of Chinese animation production also began to shift. While Shanghai retained symbolic and historical significance, Shenzhen rapidly emerged as the new center of mass animation production, primarily driven by outsourcing contracts. Other cities, including Suzhou, Nanjing, Hangzhou, and Wuxi, developed significant animation clusters, often specializing in service work for foreign clients. Production schedules were highly intensive, with many studios operating continuous shifts to meet demanding international deadlines.

In an effort to bolster domestic creative capacity and encourage international recognition, SAFS and other institutions actively participated in global animation festivals and initiated academic exchanges with foreign partners. The Chinese animation sector entered a phase of dynamic experimentation, simultaneously negotiating the opportunities and disruptions posed by digitalization and globalization. Several original works emerged during this transitional period, demonstrating both the continuity of established artistic traditions and the exploration of new narratives and technical approaches. While some productions retained elements of state-sanctioned themes, including adaptations of *The Little Trumpeter* (小号手, *Xiǎo Hào Shǒu*), other works expanded the aesthetic and narrative repertoire of Chinese animation. The year 1988 witnessed an increase in animated television and film production that combined diverse artistic techniques with high production values. A particularly distinguished example was *The Eight Immortals and the Flea* (八仙与跳蚤, *Bāxiān Yǔ Tiàozǎo*), directed by Zhan Tong (詹同). The film employed an exquisite paper-cut animation technique, rendered primarily in monochromatic tones, and featured character designs inspired by traditional Chinese shadow puppetry. The musical score incorporated subtle references to Beijing Opera, while the narrative offered humor and sophistication. *The Eight Immortals and the Flea* demonstrated a conscious blending of classical techniques with emergent computer-assisted processes for tasks such as background rendering and movement plotting (Ni 2006).

Another work reflecting artistic innovation was *The Fish Dish* (鱼盘, *Yú Pán*), 1988, directed by Fang Runnan (方润南). This animation drew visual inspiration from Chinese blue-and-white porcelain (青花瓷, *qīnghuācí*), creatively addressing emerging environmental concerns, a theme increasingly recognized in global discourse (Bin 2005).

In one of the earliest direct engagements with Western narrative traditions, directors He Yumen (何玉门) and Jin Qingmin (靳庆敏) adapted the medieval French fable *Roman de Renart* into *Húlí Liènà* (狐狸列那, *Reynard the Fox*, 1989). Co-produced with Germany's ZDF, this project marked an early Chinese foray into European co-productions, following a strategy similar to Japanese anime studios that had successfully adapted Western literary classics for international markets.

The Cow's Injustice (牛冤, *Niú Yuān*), 1989, directed by Zhong Quan (钟泉), represented an even more radical departure, drawing stylistic influences from European Expressionism and modernist painters such as Henri Matisse and Pablo Picasso. This production exemplified the widening creative horizon of Chinese animators during this period, who increasingly integrated international artistic vocabularies into their work.

The early 1990s saw the emergence of China's first computer-generated animated series for television. *Son of the Sun* (太阳之子, *Tàiyáng Zhīzǐ*), 1990, consisting of 52 episodes, was produced by the Beijing Brilliant Animation Company (北京辉煌

动画公司, *Běijīng Huīhuáng Dònghuà Gōngsī*), which maintained close ties with CCTV. Director Jia Fou (贾否), trained at the Xi'an Academy of Fine Arts and the Beijing Film Academy, introduced a distinctive painterly sensibility to her work. Her 1991 film *Square-Faced Grandpa and Round-Faced Grandma* (方脸爷爷和圆脸奶奶, *Fāngliǎn Yéye hé Yuánliǎn Nǎinai*) featured innovative designs and narrative structures that distinguished it from more conventional productions.

The adoption of computer animation offered the potential for vibrant color palettes, real-time editing, and sophisticated visual effects. However, initial implementation was uneven, requiring steep investments in hardware and expertise, while early outputs often reflected the industry's learning curve.

Despite the accelerating shift toward digital tools, SAFS continued to produce traditionally animated films of considerable artistic merit. Notable works from this period include *Liánhuā Gōngzhǔ* (蓮花公主, *The Lotus Princess*, 1991), *Shí'èr Zhī Wénzi hé Wǔ Gèrén* (十二只蚊子和五个人, *Twelve Mosquitoes and Five People*, 1992), *Shuí Shì Guànjūn* (谁是冠军, *Who Is the Champion?*, 1992), and *Mófāng Dàshà* (魔方大厦, *Rubik's Cube Mansion*, 1994), which attracted a dedicated following for its distinctive visual style and unconventional storytelling.

In contrast, television-oriented productions increasingly adopted simplified designs and formulaic narratives influenced by global children's programming conventions. An example of this commercial turn was *Lán Pí Shǔ hé Dà Liǎn Māo* (蓝皮鼠和大脸猫, *The Blue Mouse and the Big-Faced Cat*, 1993–1994), which prioritized easily recognizable characters and episodic storytelling.

During this period, a new genre known as "edu-tainment" (教育娱乐, *jiàoyù yúlè*) gained prominence. Actively promoted and funded by the government, these programs aimed to combine educational content with entertainment, instilling scientific knowledge, civic values, and ideological tenets in young audiences. Among the most successful was *Hǎi'ěr Xiōngdì* (海尔兄弟, *Haier Brothers*), which premiered in 1995 (with some sources noting 1996). Produced with the support of the Haier Group, this series combined global adventure narratives with scientific and cultural instruction. Its educational approach contrasted sharply with the action-oriented fare of contemporary Western children's programming and even reached American audiences (People's Daily 2001).

Toward the end of the decade, *3000 Whys of Blue Cat* (蓝猫淘气3000问, *Lán Māo Táoqì Sānqiān Wèn*), which began airing in 1999, epitomized the rise of "Knowledge Animation" (知识动画, *zhīshì dònghuà*). Produced by the Beijing Sunchime Happy Culture Company (北京三辰影库声像出版社, *Běijīng Sānchén Yǐngkù Shēngxiàng Chūbǎnshè*), *Blue Cat* reached unparalleled levels of popularity, reportedly attracting 80 million daily viewers and airing on over 700 television stations nationwide. Over 3100 episodes were produced, totaling more than 70,000 min of content, making it one of the longest-running educational animation series worldwide (Liping 2007).

The decade closed with the ambitious SAFS production *Lotus Lantern* (宝莲灯, *Bǎo Lián Dēng*, 1999), an adaptation of a traditional Chinese legend. While rooted in classical mythology, the film's musical score, narrative pacing, and production scale bore unmistakable influence from contemporary Disney features. Its production engaged over 300 creative staff, generated 150,000 painted cels, and cost

21 million RMB. Accompanied by an extensive merchandising campaign, *Lotus Lantern* signaled the Chinese industry's growing awareness of intellectual property's commercial potential beyond ticket sales. In many respects, it marked the transition toward a more industrially-oriented Chinese animation sector, poised to confront the demands and possibilities of the twenty-first century.

2.4 State Intervention and Industrial Ambitions in the New Millennium

The early years of the twenty-first century marked a decisive turning point for the Chinese animation industry, as the state launched a comprehensive set of policy initiatives aimed at transforming the sector into a central component of the national creative economy. This period coincided with the proliferation of personal computers, the growing accessibility of animation software, and the maturation of digital production technologies, all of which provided a technical foundation for renewed expansion. Yet it was the systematic intervention by the Chinese government, motivated by economic, cultural, and geopolitical considerations, that most fundamentally shaped the industry's trajectory, with ambitions not only to stimulate domestic production but also to enhance China's global cultural influence.

Throughout the 1990s and the early 2000s, Chinese television screens and cinema theaters remained heavily dominated by foreign animated productions, particularly Japanese anime and American cartoons. This foreign dominance extended beyond content consumption to control over ancillary markets such as merchandise licensing, character branding, and related consumer products. The Chinese government, increasingly concerned by both the economic implications and the perceived cultural encroachment posed by this situation, began implementing a series of targeted policy interventions designed to support indigenous animation studios and intellectual property development. While state support for animation had existed in previous decades, the interventions launched from approximately 2000 onward were unprecedented in scale, strategic coherence, and explicit ambition to cultivate domestic champions capable of contesting both domestic and international markets (Qing 2006).

A major regulatory inflection point occurred in 2000, when the State Administration of Radio, Film, and Television (国家广播电影电视总局, *Guójiā Guǎngbō Diànyǐng Diànshì Zǒngjú*, SARFT) introduced a directive that profoundly altered the broadcasting environment for animated programming. This regulation required that all animated content, whether domestic or imported, receive official SARFT approval prior to broadcast. Crucially, it mandated that domestic productions receive equal or greater airtime than foreign works, effectively curbing the previously overwhelming dominance of Japanese anime on Chinese television. These protections were intended not merely to regulate content but to provide critical market space for emerging domestic animation studios.

The inclusion of animation as a strategic development sector in China's Tenth Five-Year Plan for Economic and Social Development (国民经济和社会发展第十个五年计划纲要, *Guómín Jīngjì hé Shèhuì Fāzhǎn Dì Shí Ge Wǔnián Jìhuà Gāngyào*) for 2001–2005 further institutionalized state support for the industry. In 2002, SARFT issued additional directives encouraging the creation of dedicated children's television channels that would prioritize the broadcast of domestically produced animation. By August 2003, SARFT had expanded its strategy by calling on provincial and municipal governments to actively develop local animation industries, establish production hubs, and formulate regionally specific policy frameworks to support industrial growth. This multi-level governance approach represented a deliberate attempt to integrate the animation sector into China's broader agenda of national economic development and cultural revitalization.

These initial policies produced measurable outcomes, at least in terms of production volume. By 2004, the annual growth rate for the domestic animation sector had reached 15%, marking a significant increase. However, the structural challenges posed by foreign competition remained formidable. That year, Japanese anime still accounted for approximately 70% of the animated content broadcast on Chinese television, translating to roughly 50,000 min of airtime. By comparison, total domestic production amounted to approximately 23,800 min. Given that government sources estimated total domestic demand for animated content at around 260,000 min annually, the gap between supply and demand remained stark, underscoring both the scale of the domestic opportunity and the urgency driving government intervention.

The Shanghai Animation Film Studio (SAFS), while no longer the sole center of gravity in China's increasingly diversified animation landscape, continued to produce major works while experimenting with new technologies and narrative formats. Building on the modest commercial success of *Lotus Lantern* (宝莲灯, *Bǎo Lián Dēng*, 1999), SAFS released *Keke's Magic Umbrella* (可可的魔伞, *Kěkě de Mó Sǎn*) in 2000. This project represented an ambitious attempt to integrate 2D and 3D animation techniques with live-action elements. The decision to pursue such a technologically complex production was driven in part by the relative market validation *Lotus Lantern* had achieved, demonstrating a domestic appetite for more sophisticated, visually rich animated features (Blue Book of Animation 2013a, b).

Other productions from this era revealed a growing diversification of themes and aesthetic strategies, often reflecting conscious efforts to adapt global trends for domestic audiences. The television series *Dàzhàn Qiānnián Chóng* (大战千年虫, *Wars of the Millennium Bug*, 2001), jointly produced by several studios including Beijing Green Olives Animation, Beijing Chang'an Animation, and Shanghai Red Dragonfly Animation, was broadcast nationally on CCTV. Thematically, the series addressed the Y2K computer bug, a highly contemporary global anxiety at the time. Visually, it adopted an internationalized cartoon aesthetic more reminiscent of American animated sitcoms such as *The Simpsons* or *Futurama* than the classical "Chinese School" tradition.

Similarly, *Music Up*, or *Crazy for the Song* (我为歌狂, *Wǒ Wèi Gē Kuáng*, 2001) marked a significant thematic and stylistic shift for Chinese animation. The series centered on pop star aspirations and youth culture, directly engaging with global media trends that had captivated younger audiences worldwide. Visually, the series was heavily influenced by Japanese anime conventions, particularly in its character designs, narrative structures, and dynamic visual language. This 52-episode co-production between SAFS and Shanghai Television represented one of China's earliest large-scale commercial experiments in youth-oriented animation. Its reported production budget of 18 million RMB (approximately 2 million Euros) was substantial for the time. Although *Music Up* achieved only moderate success in terms of television ratings, it proved more successful in generating sustained merchandising revenues, highlighting an emerging awareness within the Chinese animation sector of the long-term value of ancillary markets.

The global success of American 3D animation studios such as Pixar and DreamWorks provided an additional impetus for Chinese producers to invest in 3D technologies, though early results were uneven. *Urban Platoon* (城市野战排, *Chéngshì Yězhàn Pái*), a 26-episode 3D animated series broadcast on CCTV, demonstrated the technical and financial challenges associated with the transition to digital production. Despite significant capital investments in hardware and training, early Chinese 3D productions often suffered from low-quality rendering, unnatural character movement, and weak visual appeal when compared to global benchmarks, resulting in limited commercial success.

By contrast, *Zetrix* (2002; some sources cite 2004 for its broader release), a high-quality 3D series produced by Imagi Animation Studios, a Hong Kong-based company with extensive transnational partnerships, demonstrated what could be achieved when technical proficiency and international narrative conventions were prioritized. Emphasizing mecha-action narratives and deliberately eschewing overt Chinese cultural elements, *Zetrix* successfully penetrated markets in Japan, Germany, and the United States, indicating that productions emerging from the Chinese-speaking world could compete globally under certain industrial and aesthetic conditions.

The early 2000s thus constituted a critical formative phase in which state intervention took on an increasingly strategic and institutionalized role in reshaping China's animation sector. While the government's objective of building a globally competitive domestic industry was clearly articulated, significant obstacles remained. These included the entrenched dominance of foreign content, the steep technological learning curve required to compete in 3D animation, and the still-evolving challenge of creating original intellectual properties that could resonate both domestically and internationally. Nevertheless, the policies adopted during this period laid an essential institutional and industrial foundation that would enable more intensive state involvement and accelerated sectoral development in the years ahead.

2.5 The 3D Imperative and Expanding State Support

While the Chinese animation industry had made notable strides in the early 2000s, its overall development remained relatively sluggish compared to the rapid progress and sustained global dominance of established animation powerhouses such as Japan and the United States. The domestic market continued to be saturated with foreign content, while original Chinese productions struggled to gain substantial visibility or commercial viability. Aware of these limitations and motivated by the ambition to cultivate a globally competitive creative industry, the Chinese government significantly escalated its intervention in the animation sector from 2004 onward. This new phase of state-driven development was characterized by comprehensive financial incentives, stringent regulatory protections for domestic content, and an increasingly explicit policy emphasis on adopting 3D animation technologies as a pathway to industrial modernization and global competitiveness.

Central to this intensified state involvement was a growing awareness that, despite China's abundant pool of trained artists and its growing role as a major outsourcing hub for foreign studios, the country remained weak in generating original intellectual property and in capturing the high-value segments of the global animation value chain. The government's approach thus shifted towards a far more proactive and interventionist model. A critical catalyst came in February 2004, with the release of the influential policy document *Several Opinions on Further Strengthening and Improving the Ideological and Moral Construction of Minors* (中共中央国务院关于进一步加强和改进未成年人思想道德建设的若干意见, *Zhōnggòng Zhōngyāng Guówùyuàn Guānyú Jìnyībù Jiāqiáng hé Gǎijìn Wèichéngniánrén Sīxiǎng Dàodé Jiànshè de Ruògān Yìjiàn*), jointly issued by the Central Committee of the Communist Party of China and the State Council. Though broad in scope, this document identified the animation sector as a crucial instrument for constructing a national cultural identity suited to the ideological education of minors. It articulated a clear dual mandate: to foster a distinct national cultural character and to ensure that animated content served the pedagogical and moral development of young audiences.

This high-level guidance was rapidly operationalized through concrete regulatory measures by SARFT. On September 20, 2004, SARFT issued the *Regulations on the Review of Television Dramas* (电视剧审查管理规定, *Diànshìjù Shěnchá Guǎnlǐ Guīdìng*), which, while primarily addressing live-action television, extended its oversight to include animated productions. The regulations imposed strict pre-production censorship procedures, requiring producers to submit detailed synopses, storyboards, full scripts with dialogues, subtitles, and theme songs for official review before production could commence. This system effectively embedded SARFT's ideological oversight into the creative process itself, ensuring that both form and content conformed to Party-approved narratives and moral frameworks.

The policy momentum accelerated further in October 2004, when the central government approved a directive formally designating animation and video game development as a "special and strategic task" within China's broader national development strategy. The Ministry of Culture (文化部, *Wénhuà Bù*) was subsequently charged with overseeing the technical quality and industrial upgrading of these sectors. This marked a decisive shift in government emphasis—from merely encouraging production volume to actively enhancing technical sophistication, with particular focus on digital production pipelines and 3D technologies.

Complementing these policies, SARFT introduced additional protective measures for domestic animation producers. One key directive mandated that no less than 60% of animated programming aired during children's prime-time viewing hours must consist of domestically produced content (Cooper-Chen 2010). At the same time, new advertising restrictions were imposed on children's programming, limiting the number of commercial breaks allowed within animated shows exceeding 60 min. These measures sought to both limit the market penetration of foreign animated imports and create a stable, protected space for Chinese animation to develop its own audiences.

Between 2005 and 2006, these policies crystallized into the creation of regional industrial clusters. Several major cities—including Chengdu, Guangzhou, Shanghai, and Beijing—were designated as *National Animation Industry Development Bases* (国家动画产业基地, *Guójiā Dòngmàn Chǎnyè Jīdì*) or *National Game and Animation Industry Revitalization Bases* (国家动漫游戏产业振兴基地, *Guójiā Dòngmàn Yóuxì Chǎnyè Zhènxīng Jīdì*). These designations came with highly favorable financing, tax incentives, and infrastructure development programs aimed at encouraging the clustering of creative enterprises, including both animation studios and associated service providers.

On January 20, 2005, SARFT enacted another critical regulation: the *Provisions on the Implementation of the Licensing System for the Issuance of Domestically Produced Television Cartoons* (国产电视动画片发行许可证管理办法, *Guóchǎn Diànshì Dònghuàpiàn Fāxíng Xǔkězhèng Guǎnlǐ Bànfǎ*), which came into full effect on July 1, 2005. This licensing system required that all domestically produced animated television programs obtain formal approval from SARFT prior to distribution. Even previously aired programs were required to reapply for licenses if rebroadcast. This regulation granted SARFT an unprecedented level of control not only over content but also over market access and circulation, reinforcing ideological conformity while further incentivizing producers to align with state priorities (Tan 2006).

The cumulative effect of these overlapping policies was the creation of a highly structured, though at times restrictive, industrial ecosystem. While officially justified as measures to protect youth audiences and promote indigenous culture, the new regulatory regime also served to consolidate state oversight over an increasingly strategic sector of cultural production. The policy emphasis on 3D animation was particularly noteworthy. While conceived as a modernization strategy to close the technological gap with global leaders such as Pixar and DreamWorks, the industry's rapid investment in 3D technology often outpaced its creative and technical readiness to fully exploit these new tools.

Despite the uneven quality of many early 3D productions, the sheer volume of domestic animation output grew substantially during this period. Numerous high-profile projects emerged, often benefiting from state support or originating within the newly established national industrial bases. One of the most significant early examples of 3D feature film production was *DragonBlade: The Legend of Lang* (龙刀奇缘, *Lóng Dāo Qíyuán*), 2005, a co-production with Hong Kong studios whose greater technological expertise compensated for production gaps in mainland facilities. The film was distributed in Cantonese, Mandarin, and English, reflecting early ambitions to secure international market penetration.

Privately funded projects also gained prominence. *Little Soldier Zhang Ga* (小兵张嘎, *Xiǎobīng Zhāng Gā*), 2005, directed by Sun Lijun (孙立军) of the Beijing Film Academy, adapted a well-known revolutionary narrative for an animated format intended to appeal to younger audiences.

Released to coincide with the 60th anniversary of Japan's surrender in World War II, the film softened many of the ideological tropes of earlier revolutionary cinema, blending patriotic themes with accessible family entertainment. Produced at an estimated cost of 1.2 million euros, the project reflected an emerging model in which educational institutions collaborated with industry to train students while producing commercially viable films (Jiu 2008). In the television sector, producers experimented with themes drawn from contemporary youth culture and adapted popular *manhua* into animated series. *The Dreaming Girl* (梦里人, *Mèng Lǐ Rén*), 2005, co-produced by CCTV and Beijing Golden Pinasters Animation Company, represented one of the first major Chinese efforts to emulate Japanese anime's cross-media strategy of adapting successful comic properties for television. Its visual style, thematic content, and even occasional meta-references to Japanese anime culture revealed the complex intertextual influences shaping this period of Chinese animation.

Ambitious co-productions with Western partners also continued. *Thru the Moebius Strip* (魔比斯环, *Mó Bǐ Sī Huán*), 2005, produced in Shenzhen in partnership with American studios, marked one of the first fully 3D animated features created primarily within China. Despite its technical achievements, the film's complex narrative structure reportedly failed to connect with audiences, limiting its commercial impact. Nonetheless, its realization demonstrated China's growing capacity to execute technically sophisticated 3D productions.

As state subsidies and favorable broadcasting opportunities via CCTV expanded, an industrial production chain for television animation began to take form. *Century Sonny: The Adventure of the Extra-Galactic Prince* (精灵世纪, *Jīnglíng Shìjì*), a 105-episode 3D series, epitomized this new industrial scale. Reportedly costing approximately 150 million euros, the series achieved broad exposure, initially airing on major networks such as CCTV, Beijing TV, and Shanghai TV, before ultimately reaching over 500 channels across China. The production was further supported by a comprehensive merchandising strategy that extended its commercial reach (Xinmin Weekly 2006).

Other projects continued to build on this momentum, including *SkyEye* (天眼, *Tiānyǎn*), 2005, a massive 500-episode 3D series jointly produced by CCTV, the

Central Academy of Drama, and the Beijing Film Academy. Meanwhile, *Tortoise Hanba's Stories* (憨八龟的故事, *Hān Bā Guī de Gùshi*), 2006, a 500-episode series produced by Shenzhen Toonring Animation, achieved broad distribution but largely eschewed overt Chinese cultural references in favor of a more generic international cartoon aesthetic.

Yet paradoxically, the most successful and culturally resonant production to emerge during this state-driven push for industrial-scale 3D development was a modest 2D Flash-animated series: *Pleasant Goat and Big Big Wolf* (喜羊羊与灰太狼, *Xǐ Yáng Yáng yǔ Huī Tài Láng*), 2005. Created by Huang Weiming (黄伟明), the series—built around simple character designs, repetitive but engaging storylines, and broad comedic appeal—became a cultural phenomenon among Chinese children. Generating billions of yuan in box office receipts, merchandising revenues, and theme park developments, *Pleasant Goat* demonstrated that commercial success was not necessarily contingent on cutting-edge technology. Rather, it revealed the enduring commercial viability of simple, well-conceived characters and accessible narratives rooted in cultural familiarity and emotional resonance.

This period thus closed on a revealing paradox: while immense government resources had been mobilized to advance 3D technological capabilities, many of the industry's most commercially and culturally successful productions remained rooted in simpler 2D techniques and domestic narrative sensibilities. The industry stood at a transitional juncture, balancing state-directed ambitions for industrial modernization with market-tested preferences for locally resonant storytelling.

2.6 Building Scale: Intensified State Commitment

The year 2006 marked a decisive turning point in the Chinese government's commitment to developing a robust domestic animation industry. Building upon the regulatory and financial frameworks established in the early 2000s, this period witnessed an unprecedented intensification of state intervention, characterized by expanded financial subsidies, stricter regulatory controls, and the formal designation of animation as a strategic sector within China's broader national development agenda. The overarching objectives remained consistent: to reduce dependence on imported animated content, to foster original Chinese intellectual property, to stimulate economic growth within the creative industries, and to project China's cultural influence both domestically and abroad.

The clearest articulation of this heightened policy commitment appeared in April 2006 with the release of *Several Opinions on Promoting the Development of China's Animation Industry* (国务院办公厅关于推动我国动漫产业发展的若干意见, *Guówùyuàn Bàngōngtīng Guānyú Tuīdòng Wǒguó Dòngmàn Chǎnyè Fāzhǎn de Ruògān Yìjiàn*), issued by the General Office of the State Council and widely referred to as Document No. 32. This directive instructed the Ministry of Finance and other relevant agencies to actively support the animation industry, mandating the allocation of dedicated central government funds for its development. Simultaneously, the Ministry of Culture was tasked with formulating comprehensive cultural development plans for the sector, placing particular emphasis on the role of animation in the ideological and moral education of minors. For the first time, animation was formally identified at the highest policy level as a "pillar" of China's emerging knowledge-based economy and national cultural system.

The policy rationale behind this escalation was multifaceted. Animation, with its inherent appeal to younger audiences, was seen as a potent vehicle for state-directed ideological education and the dissemination of officially sanctioned cultural values. Moreover, the government expressed growing concern over the pervasive influence of foreign cultural products on Chinese youth, particularly Japanese anime and American cartoons. To counteract this, policymakers sought to create a protected domestic market capable of sustaining homegrown alternatives. In August 2006, SARFT issued a particularly consequential directive: effective from September 1, 2006, all Chinese television broadcasters were prohibited from airing foreign-produced animated content between 17:00 and 20:00, the critical after-school viewing window. This regulation effectively reserved primetime exclusively for domestic productions.

Document No. 32 also established ambitious quantitative targets. Within five to ten years, China was to emerge as a global leader in animation production. This goal was to be achieved through an integrated suite of policies encompassing scientific research, industrial support, creative development, and the robust enforcement of intellectual property protections.

The promise of substantial state subsidies, tax incentives, and regulatory protections triggered what has been described as an "animation gold rush" (淘金潮, *táojīn cháo*). Entrepreneurs, often with little prior experience in animation production, rapidly entered the sector, motivated as much by policy-driven financial opportunities as by creative ambitions. While this influx of capital and entrepreneurial activity succeeded in expanding the sector's production capacity, it also led to a proliferation of substandard content, exposing weaknesses in both technical expertise and creative development. The initial allocation of public funds, often awarded without rigorous merit-based assessments, exacerbated quality-control challenges that would persist throughout the subsequent decade.

To further stimulate domestic production, several local governments introduced direct financial incentives for animated content broadcast on state and provincial networks. Reports from the period suggest that producers could earn approximately 230 euros (around 2000 RMB) per broadcast minute for content aired on CCTV, while provincial broadcasters offered approximately 120 euros (1000 RMB) per minute (Tan 2006). These generous incentives contributed to a rapid expansion in production volume.

By 2006, official statistics from the State Administration for Industry and Commerce (国家工商行政管理总局, *Guójiā Gōngshāng Xíngzhèng Guǎnlǐ Zǒngjú*) and SARFT indicated explosive growth: more than 5000 registered animation studios were operating across China, while 447 universities offered specialized animation programs and 1230 additional universities had established animation-related curricula. Television production volumes soared to 81,000 min of domestic animation in 2006, nearly doubling the previous year's output of 42,000 min.

Several notable productions emerged from this phase of intensified state support, though many of the projects released in 2006 reflected development timelines initiated under earlier policy frameworks. *Rainbow Cat & Blue Rabbit: Legend of the Seven Martial Arts Masters* (虹猫蓝兔七侠传, *Hóng Māo Lán Tù Qī Xiá Zhuàn*), 2006, a 108-episode martial arts series aired on CCTV and numerous local networks, achieved broad popularity but subsequently faced temporary suspension due to parental complaints about its allegedly violent content. Despite this controversy, the series generated substantial commercial revenues through spin-off media, including video games, comic books, novels, and music albums. The studio behind the production, Hunan Greatdreams Communications Co., reportedly earned over 2 million euros (16 million RMB) from book sales alone prior to the broadcast suspension (Changchun Film Studio 2007).

In the cinematic realm, *Monkey King vs. Er Lang Shen* (孙悟空大战二郎神, *Sūn Wùkōng Dàzhàn Èrlángshén*), 2007, directed by Liang Hansen and produced by Yuan Cheng, represented an attempt to creatively reinterpret *Journey to the West* using a hybrid aesthetic blending 3D digital techniques with puppet-inspired animation. Produced on a relatively modest budget of 800,000 euros, the film demonstrated technical ambition, though its box office performance fell short of expectations (China Film Press 2009).

Among the most significant 3D animated series of this period was *The Legend of Qin* (秦时明月, *Qín Shí Míng Yuè*, first season 2007), based on the novel by Wen Shiren. This wuxia-themed epic distinguished itself through its fusion of martial arts action and historical fantasy, pioneering a new narrative direction for Chinese animation. *The Legend of Qin* was eventually translated into seven languages and distributed in thirty-seven countries, marking a rare international success for a domestically produced Chinese animated series.

Revolutionary narratives remained prominent within the state-backed animation canon. *Sparkling Red Star: The Children's Sky* (闪闪的红星孩子的天空, *Shǎnshǎn de Hóngxīng: Háizi de Tiānkōng*), 2007, directed by Hong Kong filmmaker Dante Lam and produced by Puzzle Animation Studio in Shenzhen, revisited familiar "Red Culture" themes through updated storytelling techniques.

Similarly, *Little Soldier Zhang Ga*, previously adapted as a feature film, reflected an ongoing effort to modernize revolutionary narratives for contemporary animated formats.

By 2008, government support for animation had become deeply institutionalized. According to the *Blue Book of China's Culture* (2008), China operated more than 2000 provincial and municipal television stations, 25 dedicated children's channels, and 289 additional networks offering children's programming blocks. Simultaneously, the rise of digital platforms created new distribution opportunities: China boasted 123 million internet users and 430 million mobile phone subscribers, opening vast new channels for animated content dissemination.

Regulatory protections for domestic animation continued to expand. In May 2008, foreign animated content was further restricted, with all imported animation banned from airing between 17:00 and 21:00. In 2009, the Ministry of Culture announced five tax relief measures for qualified animation companies, including VAT exemptions. Later that year, SARFT extended protected broadcast hours for domestic animation to 22:00. In November 2009, Jiangsu Television received official approval to launch the national satellite children's network Cady TV (优漫卡通卫视, *Yōu Màn Kǎtōng Wèishì*), further strengthening national distribution infrastructure for domestic animation. By early 2009, the number of dedicated children's channels had increased to 34.

Production volume continued its rapid ascent. In 2009, Chinese studios produced 322 titles, totaling approximately 170,000 min of animation, a 31% increase over the previous year. Yet despite these quantitative gains, concerns persisted regarding the generally uneven quality of many productions, which often failed to meet either broadcast standards or audience expectations. Nonetheless, some projects demonstrated more sophisticated integration of narrative, merchandising, and cross-platform revenue models.

Among the more prominent feature films of this period was *Storm Rider: Clash of Evils* (风云决, *Fēngyún Jué*, 2008), directed by Dante Lam and produced by Puzzle Animation Studio in collaboration with Shanghai Media Group. Based on the Hong Kong manhua *Fung Wan* (风云) by Ma Wing-shing (马荣成), the film utilized a hybrid production pipeline combining 2D character animation with 3D environments and special effects. Despite a lengthy five-year production cycle, a budget of approximately 7 million euros, and box office receipts totaling 3.6 million euros (33 million RMB), the film struggled to recoup its production costs, highlighting ongoing challenges in achieving commercial viability even for high-profile projects (Popular Film Magazine 2008).

On a smaller scale, the independent series *Ming Kee* (茗记, *Míng Jì*, 2006–2010), produced by L-Key Studio, demonstrated the potential of web-based distribution for niche animated content. With its intimate portrayal of youth life in 1990s China and its stylistic affinities to Japanese slice-of-life anime, *Ming Kee* won multiple domestic and international awards, including recognition from Japan's Digicon6 competition. Its online popularity, particularly on platforms like Youku, positioned it as one of the most critically acclaimed original Chinese web animations of its time.

The rapid expansion of internet-based distribution prompted additional state regulation. In April 2009, SARFT introduced new licensing requirements for websites distributing animated content, extending regulatory control to digital platforms.

By 2012, China's animation sector had become geographically concentrated across several major production hubs, including Suzhou, Guangzhou, Dongguan, Fuzhou, Hangzhou, Hefei, Wuxi, Shenzhen, Ningbo, and Beijing. While these aggressive state policies succeeded in establishing China as the world's largest producer of animation by volume, the enduring challenge of translating production scale into consistent creative quality and sustained international competitiveness remained the central dilemma confronting Chinese animation as it entered the next phase of its development.

2.7 Toward Industrial Maturity—Balancing Quality, Creativity, and Market Pressures

The period spanning from approximately 2010 to the mid-2010s reflected the cumulative outcomes of nearly a decade of intensive state-driven efforts to foster a domestic animation industry in China. Production volumes had reached unprecedented levels, briefly allowing China to claim the distinction of being the world's largest producer of animated content in terms of total minutes. Aesthetic diversity was gradually expanding, technical competencies, particularly in 3D animation, continued to improve, and the overall industrial infrastructure had grown considerably. Nevertheless, the quantitative growth did not consistently translate into corresponding qualitative advancements, nor into the sustained creation of globally resonant intellectual properties. Despite clear progress, the Chinese animation sector continued to confront substantial obstacles on its trajectory towards full industrial maturity, particularly in the domains of creative originality, sustainable commercial models, and international competitiveness.

Simultaneously, consumption patterns were undergoing profound transformation, driven by the explosive growth of internet penetration and mobile device usage. Increasingly, younger audiences accessed animated content on demand through personal computers, smartphones, and tablets, often via online streaming platforms. This shift introduced both new opportunities and complex challenges, as expanded distribution channels also intensified market competition and highlighted persistent deficiencies in content appeal. Animation, with its strong visual characteristics and versatile narrative forms, proved highly adaptable to these multi-platform environments, though the industry's ability to capitalize on these trends varied considerably across individual projects.

Despite the extensive state investment and regulatory support, many domestic and international analysts continued to highlight a persistent "creativity deficit" in much of China's animated output (Qing 2006; Lu 2012). While technical execution was increasingly competent, critics often identified weaknesses in storytelling, character development, and narrative originality. Numerous productions appeared to imitate or superficially adapt formulas previously successful in foreign markets, particularly those from Japan and the United States. The difficulties of developing durable value chains beyond simple broadcast revenues further exacerbated these challenges.

Nevertheless, several productions emerging during this period demonstrated growing artistic ambition and industrial sophistication. *The Legend of a Rabbit*, released in July 2011, represented one of the highest-profile 3D animated features of the era. Produced by Tianjin Film Studio in collaboration with the Beijing Film Academy, the film was widely interpreted as a domestic response to the enormous success of DreamWorks Animation's *Kung Fu Panda* (2008), which had deeply resonated with Chinese audiences and set new domestic box office records for foreign animated features. *The Legend of a Rabbit* was a major investment, reportedly requiring a budget of approximately 12 million USD (circa 8.7 million Euros at the prevailing exchange rate) and three years of production. While it did not replicate the international success of its American counterpart, it achieved modest overseas distribution, with Cartoon Network acquiring broadcasting rights in Australia, New Zealand, India, and Taiwan. Sun Lijun (孙立军), the film's director and dean of the animation school at the Beijing Film Academy, characterized the film as a partial success but emphasized that the Chinese animation industry still faced a "long road ahead."

The television series *Sweetheart Princess* (甜心格格, *Tiánxīn Gégé*, 2011) exemplified a hybrid stylistic approach that blended Japanese anime aesthetics, particularly the "kawaii" (かわいい) visual style, with narrative elements rooted in Chinese imperial history and courtly life. This deliberate stylistic fusion aimed to present culturally specific themes to younger Chinese viewers who were increasingly accustomed to international animation formats. Produced by Puzzle Animation Studio and broadcast across CCTV and multiple regional networks, the 104-episode series illustrated ongoing efforts to render Chinese cultural content more accessible to a youth audience heavily influenced by foreign animation.

Another example of growing narrative and visual ambition was *Rainbow Sea* or *Star Travels* (星游记, *Xīng Yóujì*, 2011), produced by KAKU TV, a leading children's broadcaster. This high-quality 2D animated series incorporated 3D elements and adopted a more complex action-adventure structure, targeting an older youth demographic than many of its domestic contemporaries. Its dynamic visual style, heavily influenced by Japanese action-adventure anime, and its relatively mature thematic content were praised for advancing both artistic standards and audience expectations within the Chinese animation sector (Shenzhen Yearbook 2009).

KAKU TV also produced *Steel Flying Dragon*, or *Dragon Force* (钢铁飞龙, *Gāngtiě Fēilóng*, 2012), a 3D animated science fiction series depicting a special police unit combating extraterrestrial threats with advanced robotic armor. Targeting a pre-teen and adolescent audience, the series aired on CCTV and was subsequently made available online via CNTV, demonstrating state broadcasters' commitment to expanding animated content offerings across multiple platforms.

While Chinese television animation diversified in narrative and stylistic approaches, often drawing heavily from global trends, cinematic animation remained dominated by attempts to emulate the global 3D production standards set by Disney, Pixar, and DreamWorks. Nevertheless, the high financial and technical demands of high-quality 3D production continued to challenge many domestic studios.

An exception to this prevailing trend, and one of the period's most artistically distinctive cinematic productions, was *Kuiba* (魁拔, *Kuíbá*). The first installment, *Kuiba: The Ten Thousand Urgent Cases* (魁拔之十万火急, *Kuíbá Zhī Shíwàn Huǒjí*), 2011, produced by Vasson Animation (北京青青树动漫科技有限公司, *Běijīng Qīngqīng Shù Dòngmàn Kējì Yǒuxiàn Gōngsī*), deliberately adopted aesthetic and narrative conventions drawn from Japanese anime fantasy epics while incorporating distinctly Chinese cultural references. Although the first *Kuiba* film underperformed domestically and was not widely exported, it attracted a dedicated fan base and critical praise for its artistic ambition and sophisticated world-building.

Its sequel, *Kuiba II: The Great War Against the Yuan Yang World* (魁拔II:大战元泱界, *Kuíbá Èr: Dàzhàn Yuányāng Jiè*), 2013, achieved significantly greater box office success, entering China's Top Ten films during its release window in June 2013 and indicating a growing domestic audience appetite for locally produced fantasy animation.

The summer of 2013 saw additional domestic animated features perform competitively at the box office. *Qiántǐng Zǒngdòngyuán Sān: 3D Cǎihóng Yú Chuánshuō* (潜艇总动员3-3D彩虹鱼传说, *Submarine Story 3: 3D Legend of the Rainbow Fish*), directed by American filmmaker Anthony LaMolinara, reflected ongoing international collaboration in Chinese animated filmmaking. Similarly, *Xīnbādá Lìxiǎn Jì* (辛巴达历险记, *The Adventures of Sinbad*) expanded the variety of cinematic content available to domestic audiences.

The intensifying competition with foreign animation blockbusters remained a defining feature of this period. In 2013, DreamWorks Animation's *The Croods* was unexpectedly pulled from Chinese cinemas approximately two weeks ahead of schedule, despite strong box office performance that threatened to surpass the record previously set by *Kung Fu Panda*. While no official explanation was provided, industry analysts widely speculated that SARFT intervened to favor the concurrent release of domestic productions such as *Submarine Story 3* and *Kuiba II* (Hollywood Reporter 2013). This episode underscored the continued willingness of Chinese authorities to engage in direct market intervention to bolster domestic animation, raising ongoing debates regarding fair competition and consumer choice.

Meanwhile, franchises such as *Pleasant Goat and Big Big*, *Kuiba*, and *SEER* (赛尔号, *Sàiěr Hào*) demonstrated increasing commercial viability through sequel films, merchandise, and cross-platform extensions, indicating that the Chinese animation industry was beginning to establish a foundational portfolio of marketable intellectual properties. This represented a crucial step toward the construction of self-sustaining value chains within the domestic animation sector.

In summary, the early 2010s constituted a period of significant output growth and emerging commercial successes for Chinese animation, particularly for established domestic franchises and productions that skillfully blended local cultural elements with internationally familiar animation aesthetics. Nonetheless, the sector continued to face considerable obstacles in achieving consistent creative originality, developing robust transmedia business models, and securing sustainable international market penetration. The underlying "creativity deficit" remained a persistent concern, with many productions still perceived as derivative or lacking narrative depth. The ongoing pursuit of a genuinely mature and globally competitive Chinese animation industry, one capable of producing works that were both culturally authentic and universally compelling, remained an active and evolving endeavor.

References

Bin, Z. 2005. *The digital transition in Chinese animation*. China Film Press.
Blue Book of Animation. 2013a. *The evolution of Chinese animation in the 1980s*. Social Sciences Academic Press.
Blue Book of Animation. 2013b. *The impact of state policies on Chinese animation*. Social Sciences Academic Press.
Blue Book of China's Culture. 2008. *The growth of Chinese Animation*. Social Sciences Academic Press.
Changchun Film Studio. 2007. *The commercial success of Rainbow Cat & Blue Rabbit*. China Film Press.
China Film Press. 2009. *The challenges of 3D animation in China*. China Film Press.
Cooper-Chen, A. 2010. *The regulatory framework for Chinese animation*. Routledge.
Ehrlich, D. 2011. *Chinese animation: A history and analysis*. University Press of Mississippi.
Hazelbarth, S. 1997. *The development of Chinese television*. China Radio: Film and Television Press.
Hollywood Reporter. 2013. *The removal of the Croods from Chinese Cinemas*. Hollywood Reporter.
Huilin, Z. 2002. *The history of the Shanghai Animation Film Studio*. China Film Press.
Jiu, L. 2008. *The production of Little Soldier Zhang Ga*. China Film Press.
Lent, J. A. 2001. *Animation in Asia and the Pacific*. Indiana University Press.
Liping, Z. 2007. *The success of Blue Cat and the Chinese Animation Market*. China Film Press.
Lu, X. 2012. *The creativity deficit in Chinese Animation*. China Radio: Film and Television Press.
Ni, Z. 2006. *The second golden age of Chinese Animation*. China Film Press.
Niu, L. 2014. *The Taoist Priest of Laoshan and its cultural impact*. China Film Press.
People's Daily. 2001. *The rise of Chinese Educational Animation*. China Daily.
Popular Film Magazine. 2008. *The box office performance of Storm Rider: Clash of Evils*. China Film Press.
Qing, L. 2006. *The development of Chinese Animation Industry*. China Radio: Film and Television Press.
Shenzhen Yearbook. 2009. *The evolution of Chinese Animation in the 2000s*. Shenzhen Publishing House.
South China Morning Post. 2025. *Plan to improve the quality of television and animation in China*. South China Morning Post.
Tan, H. 2006. *Chinese animation: A historical and contemporary perspective*. China Radio: Film and Television Press.
Xinmin Weekly. 2006. *The commercial success of Century Sonny*. China Film Press.
Yan, L. 2014. *The Wanderings of Sanmao and Its Legacy*. China Film Press.

Chapter 3
Creativity and the Shanzhai Paradigm

Abstract This chapter investigates the notion of creativity in Chinese animation through the lens of the shanzhai paradigm, a cultural and industrial logic characterized by imitation, replication, and reinvention. It begins with a comparative overview of global aesthetic frameworks, contrasting the narrative and stylistic models of American studios, the innovations of Japanese anime, and the hybrid adaptations that informed Chinese practices. Within this context, Chinese animation is analyzed as both a receiver and producer of cross-cultural influences, blending indigenous artistic traditions with external visual languages. The chapter then addresses creativity under constraint, exploring how market pressures, outsourcing, and weak screenwriting infrastructures limited originality while also generating forms of adaptive innovation. The concept of shanzhai is introduced as a broader cultural phenomenon in China, rooted in manufacturing and extended into media, where copying functions as both economic strategy and creative reinterpretation. Case studies such as *Astro Plan*, *Crystal Warrior*, and *Dinosaur Baby* illustrate how shanzhai practices operate on screen, sometimes blurring the boundary between piracy and grassroots innovation. The chapter concludes that shanzhai reveals the contradictions of China's creative industries: it undermines intellectual property while simultaneously fueling cultural diffusion, industrial resilience, and new models of exchange in global animation.

Keywords Shanzhai · Astro Plan · Crystal Warrior · Dinosaur Baby · Creativity · Imitation · Shenzhen

3.1 Global Styles and Aesthetic Frameworks in Animation

Animation is a complex language that encompasses a variety of genres and techniques, many of which draw inspiration from the stylistic canons of painting, cinema, theater, and, more recently, video games. Over the years, the visual and narrative conventions of animation have incorporated multiple cultural influences, adapting to different screens, audiences, and aesthetic paradigms. These canons have continually evolved, adopting new rules and conventions that have altered their original

© The Author(s), under exclusive license to Springer Nature Switzerland AG 2026

V. De Masi, *A Critical Analysis of China's Animation Industry*, Numanities - Arts and Humanities in Progress 37, https://doi.org/10.1007/978-3-032-18656-0_3

meanings to the point of becoming easily recognizable by global audiences (Bitatti 2011).

This section offers a comparative analysis of Western and Eastern animation canons, with particular attention to the dominance of American studios on one side and Japanese anime (アニメ) on the other. Both traditions have profoundly influenced the development of global animation aesthetics, serving as reference points for new markets and emerging industries.

China has played a crucial historical role in shaping Japanese animation. Numerous Japanese and American productions have drawn upon Chinese mythology, visual motifs, and cultural symbols for creative inspiration. Yet, China's position today is not limited to being a source of motifs: the country is actively striving to develop a new hybrid style that merges two elements. The first is the heritage of traditional Chinese drawing and brush-painting techniques, which reflect the long history of Chinese artistic and animated practices. The second is the incorporation of stylistic conventions from American and Japanese studios, adapted to local production logics and audience sensibilities.

The analysis of selected Chinese animated series reveals that their success depends not only on government support and cultural policy but also on audience demand for original narratives and innovative visual contexts. The market increasingly rewards productions that combine cultural specificity with modernized storytelling formats.

In the American context, the study will focus on the classic Disney tradition alongside newer schools such as DreamWorks Animation, Blue Sky Studios, and Illumination Entertainment. These studios have reshaped global animation by diversifying narrative strategies, aesthetics, and production models.

From the Japanese perspective, the most influential creative traditions are represented by Tezuka Productions, Studio Ghibli, Sunrise, and Gainax, each of which contributed to the consolidation of anime as a globally recognizable form. Their distinctive approaches, ranging from Tezuka's limited animation and serialized storytelling to Studio Ghibli's philosophical humanism and Gainax's postmodern experimentation, reveal the diversity of Japan's contributions to world animation.

Ultimately, this comparative approach sheds light on how China navigates between global influences and indigenous aspirations. By combining elements from both American and Japanese traditions while grounding them in its own artistic legacy, Chinese animation seeks to assert a distinctive creative identity capable of competing on a global scale.

3.1.1 Disney's Legacy—Narratives of Music and Myth

When discussing animation, Disney immediately comes to mind as the most renowned creator in the history of the medium and the only studio that has never faced financial crisis since its founding in 1923. From a stylistic and narrative perspective, Disney developed a cinematic language close to that of musicals, rooted in popular tales and myths. Its narratives consistently position characters in moments of difficulty, usually caused by antagonists, and redemption is sought through friendship and moral virtue. Although recent productions have experimented with new narrative frameworks, the underlying structure remains anchored in a fairy-tale model reinterpreted for modern sensibilities (Ceruso 2013).

The aesthetic of the so-called Disney Classic era privileged naturalism, yet this naturalism was not a mere imitation of reality. Technically, it was mediated through rounded forms, delicate shading, and the illusion of three-dimensionality made possible by the technique of full animation at twenty-four frames per second. This technique, emblematic of Disney's commitment to perfection, distinguished its productions from many competitors. Today, computer-based animation technologies can generate the same frame rate automatically, but the visual continuity with Disney's hand-drawn tradition persists (Benecchi 2005). In contrast, many contemporary 3D animations tend to privilege spectacle, dynamic editing, and visual excess, often at the expense of narrative cohesion.

The success of Disney lay not only in artistic innovation but also in the industrialization of creativity. Early films were at times demanding for young viewers, but the company soon expanded its audience to include the entire family. This expansion was supported by a production pipeline organized into specialized departments that managed every stage of development, from the initial idea to storyboards and scripts. Such a model reveals the tension between collective labor and the mythology of the "authorial genius" embodied in Walt Disney himself. While Disney has been celebrated as a creative visionary, the studio's achievements depended on an elaborate system of division of labor, standardized procedures, and constant market research attentive to audience preferences.

This dual nature, between the romanticized figure of the auteur and the realities of industrial organization, constitutes one of the main contradictions of Disney's legacy. On the one hand, the studio produced works that defined the emotional memory of generations, shaping global imaginaries of childhood. On the other, it exemplified the commodification of storytelling, where narratives were carefully calibrated to secure commercial success. By 2012, Disney's revenue reached 32 billion euros, consolidating its status as the world's leading brand in media and entertainment. What had begun with the invention of a mouse, Mickey Mouse, had grown into a global empire that combined cultural hegemony, economic power, and a form of soft power that continues to influence the global animation industry.

3.1.2 Hollywood's New Wave—DreamWorks, Illumination, and Blue Sky Studios

Since the late 1990s American studios such as DreamWorks Animation and Illumination Entertainment have embraced CGI (computer-generated imagery) as the principal technology to produce feature-length 3D animation. DreamWorks Animation, founded in 1997, challenged Disney's hegemony not simply by adopting superior technical tools but by gradually reshaping narrative expectations. Early works like *The Prince of Egypt* (1998), *Joseph: King of Dreams* (2000), and *Sinbad: Legend of the Seven Seas* (2003) reflected classical narrative forms reminiscent of Disney. Over time, however, DreamWorks pioneered stories imbued with parody, ironic undertones, and meta-humour, with *Shrek* (2001) being especially significant for its subversion of fairy-tale tropes, even in its aesthetic references (for instance, the visual inspiration drawn from the French wrestler Maurice Tillet) while still retaining echoes of canonical Disney figures like Snow White or Peter Pan (Biagi 2013).

Illumination Entertainment, founded in 2007 by Chris Meledandri, also leveraged 3D CGI to reach a global audience at lower cost and risk than the more ornate productions typical of Disney or DreamWorks. Its success rests on stylised character design, simplicity of visual form, strong brand identities (Minions), and soundtracks aligned with popular music tastes. The studio's model reveals tensions between commercial imperatives and creative experimentation: narrative complexity is often secondary to recognizability and marketability.

Blue Sky Studios, which became known for *Ice Age* (2002) and its sequels, followed a similar path of CGI technical mastery plus light, family-oriented humour. But unlike DreamWorks or Illumination, Blue Sky no longer operates independently; Disney closed Blue Sky in 2021, absorbing or shelving much of its production capacity. Its legacy illustrates how mid-level studios face pressures from cost escalation, consolidation, and the dominance of conglomerates.

In 2025 the landscape reflects greater uniformity in technique: full CGI 3D animation is now standard among major American studios. Visual spectacle, dynamic editing, trendy music scores, and stories designed for global box office appeal dominate. Audience targeting remains mixed: Disney and Pixar often attempt to preserve a balance, combining family friendly content with artistic or thematic risk. DreamWorks and Illumination lean more heavily toward globally palatable narratives and spectacle, though there are occasional ventures into more mature or unconventional themes.

These developments highlight contradictions. Advanced technology enables ever more polished imagery yet may lead to homogenization of style. The commercial success of animation strengthens soft power, exporting American cultural norms about humor, friendship, heroism, and moral structure. At the same time the consolidation of studio ownership reduces the diversity of creative voices. In some cases, studios that once experimented with more daring forms (in terms of theme, style or ideology) revert to safer formulas to guarantee returns (Table 3.1).

Table 3.1 Top ten highest-grossing animated films worldwide (as of 2025) *Source* The-numbers.com (accessed 29/08/2025)

Rank	Released	Movie	Worldwide Box Office
1	2025	*Ne Zha 2 (哪吒之魔童闹海)*	$2,000,814,256
2	2024	*Inside Out 2*	$1,698,831,782
3	2019	*Frozen II*	$1,451,653,316
4	2013	*Frozen*	$1,269,758,653
5	2015	*Minions*	$1,157,271,759
6	2023	*The Super Mario Bros. Movie*	$1,359,146,628
7	2017	*Despicable Me 3*	$1,032,809,657
8	2019	*Ne Zha (哪吒之魔童降世)*	$742,718,496
9	2012	*Ice Age: Continental Drift*	$879,765,137
10	2009	*Ice Age: Dawn of the Dinosaurs*	$886,686,817

3.1.3 The Birth of Anime—Japan's Emergent Visual Language

Japanese animation began to emerge in the early twentieth century, when a number of artists experimented with techniques borrowed from Western pioneers. Unsurprisingly, Japanese animators were also influenced by Disney's visual innovations and by American narrative models. Yet the foundations of Japanese visual culture were already deeply rooted in the Edo period (1603–1868), when manga (漫画), literally "whimsical images," had taken shape as a popular art form. This genealogy reveals that the formal language of Japanese animation did not arise in isolation but combined imported cinematic techniques with a long indigenous tradition of graphic storytelling.

Early manga artists such as Katsushika Hokusai (葛飾北斎) and Rakuten Kitazawa (北澤楽天, Beizé Letian) illustrate the continuity between Edo-period visual culture and the illustrated narratives of the early twentieth century. Their works established the interplay of sequential art, caricature, and dynamic gesture that would later become central to anime. In Japan, animated film was initially described with terms such as dōga eiga (動画映画, animated film) or manga eiga (漫画映画, comic film), expressions that reflected a linguistic connection to both moving images and printed comics. Over time the abbreviated form anime (アニメ), derived from the English word "animation," became the dominant term, still used today both domestically and internationally (Benecchi 2008).

The decisive turning point in defining modern anime aesthetics was the work of Osamu Tezuka (手塚治虫), who combined Japanese and Western influences to develop a distinctive style. His use of large expressive eyes, adapted from American models such as *Betty Boop* and *Bambi*, became emblematic of Japanese animation's emotional intensity (Patten 2004). Tezuka himself acknowledged the impact of Chinese animation, particularly the Wan brothers' *Princess Iron Fan* (万氏兄弟,

1941). After watching the film he abandoned his medical studies to dedicate his life to manga and animation, a decision he later described as transformative (Tze-Yue G. Hu 2010). This transnational interplay of influences, American character design, Chinese narrative innovation, and Japanese visual culture, illustrates how anime developed as both a national art form and a global hybrid.

The official birth of anime is often associated with the first broadcast of *Astro Boy* (鉄腕アトム, Tetsuwan Atomu) on 1 January 1963 by Fuji TV. Confronted with severe budget constraints, Tezuka and his Mushi Production studio created an innovative cinematic language that relied on limited animation techniques, narrative economy, and serial storytelling. His creative manifesto was unambiguous: "I am convinced that comics should not only make people laugh. That is why in my stories you will find tears, anger, hatred, pain, and endings that are not always happy." This statement positioned anime as a cultural form capable of expressing the full range of human emotion, transcending the perception of animation as mere children's entertainment (Table 3.2).

From this moment onward anime developed into a system of genres and subgenres designed for diverse audiences, from children to adults and even niche communities, some of which are unique to Japan (Pellitteri 2002). The international breakthrough came when *Astro Boy* was broadcast in the United States between 1963 and 1966, opening the way for Japanese animation to gain recognition far beyond national borders. Its success demonstrated that anime could serve both as a vehicle of cultural identity and as a tool of soft power, a dual role that continues to define the global perception of Japanese animation today.

3.1.4 Japanese Animation—Global Reach and Local Identity

Japanese animation has achieved a reputation for high quality despite comparatively low production costs, largely because it developed a distinct visual language and a set of innovative technical devices. For many years television series relied on what became known as "limited animation," often produced with as few as five frames per second. The lack of fluidity was compensated through cinematic framing, the illusion of three-dimensionality, the use of multiplane techniques, and unusual perspectives that created a dynamic visual experience. In order to save on drawing while maximizing expressive impact, Japanese animators emphasized the eyes of characters as mirrors of their emotions and perceptions (Schodt 2003). Codified expressions quickly emerged: stars in the eyes to indicate joy, wide eyes to communicate pain or shock, red coloring of the face to signify anger, and a drop of sweat to represent embarrassment. Body language and gestures were likewise systematized, establishing a rich semiotic code unique to anime.

Another strategy to reduce production costs while enhancing expressive power was the creative use of camera movements and editing techniques. By shifting focus from the number of drawings to the dynamics of framing, anime developed a narrative rhythm that encouraged viewers' imagination to fill the gaps. This approach stood

Table 3.2 Main genres of Japanese anime

Genre	Japanese term	Description	Primary Audience
Shōnen	少年	Action, adventure, rivalry, friendship, perseverance	Young male teens (12–18) but widely consumed
Shōjo	少女	Romance, interpersonal relationships, emotion, visual elegance	Young female teens (12–18)
Seinen	青年	Mature themes such as politics, crime, sexuality, psychological depth	Adult men (18+)
Josei	女性	Realistic romance, daily life, women's challenges in society	Adult women (18+)
Mecha	メカ	Robots, technology, and futuristic battles with philosophical undertones	Broad, mixed audiences
Isekai	異世界	"Other world" adventures, often RPG-inspired fantasy universes	Young audiences, male and female
Kodomo	子供	Educational and moral stories for children	Children under 12
Sports	スポーツ	Competition, teamwork, discipline, national identity	Predominantly young male audiences
Horror	ホラー	Psychological and supernatural fear, trauma, anxiety	Mature audiences
Slice of Life	スライス・オブ・ライフ	Everyday realism, subtle emotions, social interaction	Young adults and adults
Hentai / Seijin	変態 / 成人向け	Explicit pornographic works; "hentai" used mainly abroad, "seijin" used domestically for 18 +	Adults 18 +
Ecchi	エッチ	Soft eroticism, sexual humor, and fanservice without explicit sex	Teenagers and adults
Ero guro	エログロ	Erotic grotesque blending sexuality with disturbing imagery	Adults, niche audiences
Boys' Love (Yaoi)	ボーイズラブ / やおい	Male-male romance or erotica, largely produced by and for women	Predominantly female readers, young and adult
Girls' Love (Yuri)	ガールズラブ / 百合	Female-female romance, from affectionate to sexual	Mixed audiences, niche appeal
Bara / Gei komi	薔薇 / ゲイコミ	Male homoerotic narratives by and for gay men, with distinct aesthetics	Adult gay men and interested readers

in stark contrast to the classical model of animation, which sought to approximate realism through full animation. Instead, anime privileged emotional intensity and symbolic resonance, inviting audiences to participate more actively in constructing meaning (Benecchi 2005).

The creative vitality of anime is also rooted in its close relationship with manga, from which many scripts and storylines are adapted. This transmedia circulation reinforced anime's ability to connect with mass audiences and to diversify into numerous genres. A further strength lies in the careful planning stage (計画段階, *keikaku dankai*), where narrative arcs, character design, and merchandising strategies are coordinated from the outset. This systemic integration of creativity, production, and marketing has proven central to anime's global success.

Beyond its artistic significance, Japanese animation has acquired a profound cultural and economic role. Scholars have pointed out that creative industries, including anime and manga, now constitute one of the pillars of Japan's GDP, surpassing even heavy industries such as steel and automobiles (Tan 2006). This demonstrates how anime functions not only as an art form and a cultural identity marker but also as a driver of national economic power and soft power on the international stage.

Recent statistics estimate the Japanese anime market at approximately USD 12.72 billion in 2023, with projected growth to USD 16.84 billion by 2030 (Grand View Research 2024a, b). Globally, in 2023 anime generated about USD 19.8 billion in revenue, including USD 5.5 billion from streaming and USD 14.3 billion from merchandising (Parrot Analytics & AJA 2024). Moreover, municipalities featured in anime settings regularly experience measurable economic growth in the years following broadcast (Takahashi 2024).

3.1.5 Constructing a Chinese Canon—Tradition and Innovation

The stylistic canons of Chinese animation have always reflected the country's political and historical trajectory. Creativity has long been subject to state oversight, and since the reform and opening of the 1980s, domestic animation has faced severe competition from Japanese and American imports. Despite the technical skills of Chinese animators, successive generations of directors have struggled to sustain compelling narratives, especially in serialized form. The challenge has never been a lack of talent in design or production but rather the difficulty of reconciling political expectations, narrative innovation, and market appeal.

The first milestone of Chinese animation was *Princess Iron Fan* (铁扇公主), created by the Wan brothers in 1941. Deeply rooted in traditional aesthetics, it was based on the classic novel *Journey to the West* (西游记, *Xi Youji*), whose characters have profoundly influenced Asian culture. The Monkey King Sun Wukong, companion of the monk Sanzang, inspired Japan's *Dragon Ball* hero Goku, while the pig Zhu Bajie became a prototype for characters in both Japanese and Chinese animations, including the 3D television series *Pig-xia* broadcast by CCTV since 2007 (Tan 2006). This shows how Chinese narrative archetypes have provided a reservoir of inspiration far beyond national borders.

Contemporary Chinese creators continue to draw on legends and myths, but such choices are not entirely free. Works intended for domestic audiences must conform to cultural criteria that privilege the promotion of Chinese traditions and values aligned with Party ideology. Government funding is more likely when projects foreground elements of cultural heritage, which has led to a proliferation of hybrid productions mixing classical motifs with uneven artistic results. An example is the animated adaptation of *The Romance of the Three Kingdoms*, which combined digital tools with experimental approaches.

Since 2020 the landscape has changed dramatically. While earlier decades were marked by dependence on foreign imports, the current market is increasingly driven by domestic production capacity and the rapid expansion of animation, VFX, and post-production industries. In 2025, the Chinese animation, VFX and post-production sector reached USD 21.72 billion, with projections to grow to USD 36.70 billion by 2030 (Mordor Intelligence 2025). The anime market alone was valued at USD 2.24 billion in 2024, with expectations to nearly double by 2030 at a compound annual growth rate of 12.7% (Grand View Research 2024a, b). These figures demonstrate that Chinese animation is no longer a marginal branch of the creative industries but a central driver of the cultural economy.

The turning point in global perception came with *Ne Zha*, 2019, which grossed more than USD 740 million worldwide and became a symbol of the country's creative resurgence. Its sequel, *Ne Zha*, 2025, broke all records by surpassing USD 2 billion at the global box office, establishing itself as the highest-grossing animated film worldwide (Reuters 2025). This extraordinary success shows how classical mythology, when combined with advanced CGI and sophisticated marketing, can resonate with both domestic and international audiences.

At the same time, cultural regulation continues to shape creative possibilities. In August 2025, the National Radio and Television Administration (NRTA) launched a new plan to improve the quality of television, mini-dramas, and animated content, reinforcing content supervision in the name of strengthening Chinese soft power (South China Morning Post 2025). This illustrates the paradox at the core of Chinese animation: the industry aspires to compete globally while remaining tightly bound to political imperatives.

Chinese animated canons thus emerge as a space of both creativity and constraint. They rely on a long tradition of myth and folklore, but innovation is continually filtered through ideological frameworks. If the Wan brothers' *Princess Iron Fan* signaled the beginnings of a national style rooted in cultural heritage, *Ne Zha 2* exemplifies the twenty-first-century capacity of Chinese animation to translate those traditions into global commercial power, consolidating animation as one of the leading cultural industries of contemporary China.

3.1.6 Hybrid Practices—Techniques Across Borders

Romance of the Three Kingdoms remains one of the most significant examples of hybridized animation canons, illustrating how a work deeply rooted in Chinese cultural heritage yet executed with mixed techniques can succeed in both domestic and international markets. Approved by SARFT in 2007 and released in 2009 as the first Sino–Japanese co-production in television animation, the series demonstrated how the fusion of traditional Chinese aesthetics with modern production and distribution strategies could reach wide audiences. Its design choices deliberately avoided the large expressive eyes typical of Japanese anime, instead favoring a bold palette of black, brown, and red, which marked the series as a recognizable Chinese brand. Distributed not only across China but also in Japan, South Korea, Malaysia, the Arab world, and Europe, it revealed the potential of Chinese animation to move beyond national borders while asserting cultural distinctiveness.

Since 2009, the global animation landscape has shifted considerably. New domestic productions confirm that the strategy of combining cultural specificity with technological innovation remains effective. In 2025, the Shanghai Animation Film Studio released *Nobody*, a 2D animated feature in ink-wash style, which became the highest-grossing 2D animated film ever produced in China and outperformed foreign imports at the domestic box office. This success illustrates that local traditions, when reimagined with contemporary visual technologies, can achieve strong resonance with mass audiences (Radii 2025).

At the same time, institutional support for co-productions has intensified. In late 2024, China and Japan formally agreed to deepen cultural cooperation, explicitly including the field of anime co-production in their bilateral framework. This reflects a shift toward structured collaboration, enabling the sharing of capital, expertise, and international distribution networks, while still maintaining cultural markers that secure state approval (Anime Corner 2024).

The enduring relevance of *Romance of the Three Kingdoms* as narrative material is evident in the upcoming release of *Three Kingdoms: Starlit Heroes* (三国的星空第一部, *Sānguó de Xīngkōng Dì Yī Bù*), scheduled for October 1, 2025. This new animated feature once again reinterprets one of China's most celebrated historical novels for global audiences, blending mythology, high-end CGI, and marketing strategies aimed at both domestic and international box office success (Box Office Hype 2025).

Meanwhile, platforms such as Bilibili have accelerated the production and distribution of original Chinese animation (donghua). Since 2022, Bilibili has launched hundreds of titles, investing heavily in original IP. By 2024–2025, donghua had become one of the most consumed forms of audiovisual entertainment among Chinese audiences under thirty, with significant increases in streaming hours and user interactions. This demonstrates not only the vitality of domestic demand but also the ability of Chinese studios to position themselves in the global streaming market (PR Newswire 2023).

What emerges from these developments is not an entanglement of disparate canons but an osmotic process in which cultural, aesthetic, and technological elements circulate across borders. Contemporary Chinese animation combines the hybrid aesthetics of Japanese and American models with its own historical narratives and stylistic codes, producing works that are simultaneously local and global. From *Romance of the Three Kingdoms* (2009) to *Nobody* (2025) and *Ne Zha 2* (2025), Chinese animation has shown that it can transform classical stories into global spectacles, strengthen its domestic industry, and contribute to the redefinition of global animation in the twenty-first century.

3.2 The Sonic Dimension—Sound as Narrative and Aesthetic Force

To produce dubbing, music, and sound backgrounds while avoiding the costs of copyright licensing, many medium and small animation companies turn to small firms where only a few professionals work alongside many computer enthusiasts. These groups often create sound using inadequate technology for television standards, resulting in low quality audio with exclusively digital music. This could be considered a creative element, given the freedom that artists enjoy in composing music, yet the problem, as previously noted, is the persistent lack of originality even in sound. This deficiency is particularly evident in animated productions, especially those aimed at television audiences. As Claudio Guglielmotto, professor and official of the Production Division of Radio Rai, has emphasized, the ears are among the most sensitive organs of the human body. If the images or editing of television broadcasts are imperfect, the eye often tolerates the flaws, but if the sound contains buzzing, reverberation, or poor recording, the ear immediately perceives it as disturbing or as an error. Sound therefore plays a crucial role in animation, more important than we might imagine. Iconic television themes and background scores remain deeply embedded in the collective memory, forming a direct link between audiences and animated series (Blue Book 2012).

When Walt Disney's *Steamboat Willie* (1928) first appeared in cinemas with synchronized sound, animators quickly understood that sonic elements represented one of the most important aspects of cartoons for their capacity to entertain and attract the attention of the audience. From its beginnings, China likewise attached importance to sound in animation, especially during the era of major directors and designers such as the Wan brothers, Te Wei, and Ah Da. These artists often inserted music inspired by traditional Chinese songs, borrowed from opera or other folk sources. This gave animation the quality of a complete work of art, blending the visual traditions of painting with traditional musical culture.

In animation the sound environment is recreated in the studio or recorded live to make the narrative more credible and authentic, or to impart a magical and dreamlike atmosphere. The soundscape is capable of producing psychological and emotional effects. Classic characters demonstrate how powerful voices can be in defining identity and fame. Danger, anger, despair, or joy become more evocative through the modulation and timbre of voice actors, who have shaped the recognition of heroes that still inhabit the collective imagination.

In recent years, however, Chinese production has often privileged quantity over quality. Many studios invest the majority of their budgets in 3D visual design and graphics while neglecting sound, which remains an essential element (Quing 2006). This imbalance is problematic, since music also represents an important source of profit. Soundtracks released as CDs or digital files have long been popular in countries such as Japan and the United States. Renowned musicians and singers compose themes for anime because these openings and endings serve as effective promotional tools for new albums while ensuring substantial profits. Japanese productions in particular continuously update theme songs with every new season, transforming them into cultural phenomena.

In China the sound sector, like many digital industries, has suffered greatly due to digital piracy, which has created instability and reduced investment. As a result, profits remain limited. Most animated productions are still aimed at children, and the most famous Chinese series such as *Pleasant Goat*, *Monkey King* (produced by CCTV Animation), *Pig Man*, and *Snow Baby* reveal this pattern. Their opening and closing themes often become true earworms for children, designed to maximize appeal even if musically simplistic.

Since 2020, new developments have begun to reshape this scenario. The soundtrack of *Ne Zha 2* (2025) combined orchestral arrangements with regional folk instruments such as the erhu, pipa, and suona, alongside traditional Dong women's choir vocals. This demonstrates how the industry now invests in sound not only as technical support but as cultural narrative, embedding local traditions into global blockbusters (Wikipedia contributors 2025). The broader market for animation, VFX, and post-production in China reached USD 21.72 billion in 2025, with forecasts of USD 36.70 billion by 2030, growth that includes improved recording facilities and audio post-production (Mordor Intelligence 2025). High-quality dubbing has also become central for donghua, as language, intonation, and performance now define both cultural authenticity and export potential. Analysts note that polished dubbing is increasingly demanded by domestic audiences and international distributors (Digital Trans Asia 2023). These shifts indicate that sound is regaining strategic importance within the Chinese animation industry.

In sum, while weaknesses remain due to uneven budgets and piracy-related challenges, sound in animation has become a decisive component for both aesthetic experience and commercial success. Music, voice acting, and sound design are no longer secondary elements but central factors in the global competitiveness of Chinese animation, determining whether productions resonate with audiences not only in China but also internationally.

3.3 Creativity Under Constraint—Innovation, Absence, and Repetition

One of the problems reported by many authors, professors, and professionals in the animation sector is surely the lack of creativity in Chinese animated products. Even though in recent years China has become the largest producer of animation in the world, it still needs to resolve the issues related to the inexperience of the animation industry, given that it is still very "young" and thus still in the development phase. But the main cause of the failure of most animations is attributable to the total absence of new ideas and the poor ability to understand how to create a serialized product.

At the base of a quality product there is undoubtedly the drafting of the screenplay and the storyboard; good writing is surely the key to achieving market success. Since 2006 in China the animation industry has focused little on creativity and cultural value of animated products, instead specializing in productions lacking creativity with very simple content, even for very young audiences. In fact the majority of Chinese animations attempt to imitate the contents and production models of American or Japanese cartoons, as already reiterated, losing Chinese cultural identity. According to Prof. Jia Fou (former director and professor at the Communication University of China), the Chinese cultural foundation combined with the continuously evolving social reality can truly provide creative stimulus for drafting a good screenplay. Teaching creativity to students is the real problem of Chinese universities, because the issue has deep roots, due to the loss of Chinese cultural values over recent years, and therefore the desirable objective would be to preserve the nation's identity continuity, even in the name of discontinuity of new ideas (Tan 2006).

Prof. Jia Fou offers a very illuminating example, useful for better understanding Chinese and international animated cinema: the United States cannot claim an ancient culture like China in this sector because in reality American culture is the synthesis of a multitude of different cultures; but the American animation industry with a stroke of genius manages to exploit all these diversities, creating products with a cultural base shared and capable of speaking to a global audience. Thus American creative content either draws inspiration from other cultures, making them its own (consider *Kung Fu Panda*, *Mulan*, *Pinocchio* etc.) or creates purely fantastic characters, yet rich in cultural values typical of modern society, thus managing to attract a universal public.

However, to be fair, Japanese animation, although it can claim an ancient culture like China, ranks second after the United States in global diffusion. Furthermore many Japanese cultural aspects come from Chinese culture, such as writing and art.

Then why can't Chinese animation break through like Japanese animation? The answer is again linked to lack of originality and creativity in Chinese animation. It is important to analyze the situation in depth to identify the reasons that limit healthy and strong development of Chinese animated products (Animation Blue Book 2013).

One of the first reasons that differentiates Chinese animation from Japanese animation is the fact that the Japanese people hold a deep respect for Confucian values which in real life invite unity and collaboration to achieve concrete goals, and we know well that much of Japanese animation draws inspiration from daily life. Moreover another aspect that distinguishes Japanese people is an innate sense of perfection which in the creative environment transforms into ideas of perfect worlds, robots and humanoids. In many animations the actual protagonists are androids, robots representing the future and perfection; but not for Japanese culture which instead regards them as modern Samurai ready to defend the Earth or the nation from enemies. Indeed analyzing carefully robots, one notes that their armor and weapons recall the armor used by the Samurai of ancient Japan; just consider the continuous use of swords (katanas) as weapons of combat (Pellitteri 2009).

Another reason that hinders Chinese creativity is that domestic products are financed with public funds and once one accepts those fundings, one must respect very clear provisions, among which foremost is the obligation to educate while entertaining. In my opinion however this which may appear as a diktat should not be considered a true barrier to creativity; in fact there are many Japanese cartoons which educate and entertain simultaneously, such as *Doraemon*, *Detective Conan*, *Chibi Maruko-chan*. But it is necessary to point out that Japanese animation succeeds both in using edu-entertainment and addressing all age groups, both young and adult; whereas Chinese animation predominantly targets very young audiences, effectively excluding adult viewers.

A further determining factor that causes a lowering of creative innovation is the figure of the screenwriter who in China has a subordinate role in the realization of films. Instead it is precisely the screenwriter who creates that essential link between innovation and production. I return to the thought of Prof. Jia Fou of the Communication University of China. She holds that a weak style and superficial content cause a cartoon to appear unattractive and narratively uninteresting; many cartoons have perfect animation techniques, but without a strong screenplay, these cartoons lack a "soul". This gap is perceived in many productions, and is the result of the absence of a deeply rooted popular culture and of a cultural environment poor in stimuli (Qing 2006).

There is also to remember that another problem that slows creativity in the cartoon sector is that the sector itself is not yet mature enough to guarantee certain stability and job security for the few Chinese talents who in order to have stable and/or long-lasting work prefer to work only for large companies producing animations for foreign countries (Japan, USA and Europe), settling for a monthly salary ranging from 8,000 yuan (about 750 euros) to a maximum of 10,000 yuan (about 950 euros). This is why the Chinese animation sector is mostly represented by small firms which, because of the instability of the sector, risk having to close their doors and lay off the little qualified staff; very often most employees are underpaid and many are only passing through studios.

But new scenarios are opening that are interesting. For example in Shenzhen since 2006 the local government has organized and supported schools and universities to create a new class of creatives, rewarding and helping students who show great originality and creative flair. Also there is the attempt to train new professional figures for this sector, promoting ad hoc training courses that address topics related to culture, market, technical staff and analysis of taste and preferences of audiences. But Shenzhen is one of the capitals of outsourcing and because of the problems mentioned above, such as instability of salaries and economic precarity, students are forced to work in companies producing cartoons for foreign countries, causing the total flattening of ideas among Chinese creatives, who cannot express their potential in small companies for purely economic reasons. Professionals who work in outsourcing studios have a crushing workload that obviously affects their social life. In the collective imagination animation studios may seem relaxing environments where magic and fables are created, and sometimes they are; in reality workers are put under pressure because of looming deadlines which demand very high quality standards for projection and distribution in foreign countries, with very tight deadlines and impossible working hours.

At the beginning the Chinese government had concentrated its attention only on production, but after the first period it understood that creativity and talent training are the key and the base upon which significant sectoral development could concretely happen. Too bad this insight arrived only in recent years and only now that there are first signs of animation that differ, new both in style and content, though still weak in their ability to influence the market and the cultural background of China (Tan 2006).

Recent evidence confirms that some elements of this criticism are still valid in 2025. Many small and medium cost animated films struggle to survive, unable to experiment with originality because of resource constraints and investor reluctance (36Kr 2025). Surveys show that younger audiences increasingly expect originals and creative narratives, and productions that mix traditional culture with innovation are being better received (China Daily 2025).Nonetheless a model of consistently strong narrative innovation, diverse authorship, and stable professional employment remains under development (The Guardian 2025; HRMARS 2025).

3.4 Shanzhai as Cultural Logic—Copying, Reframing, Reinventing

To understand Chinese regulation regarding copyright and piracy, one must first consider Chinese popular culture. China is the world's largest producer of mobile phones, and according to the *Financial Times* more than 20% of mobile phones were once shanzhai (山寨, *shanzhai*) products, that is, copies. The term *shanzhai* has very ancient origins and literally can have two meanings: mountain village (寨) or mountain fortress (寨). Historically it referred to remote mountainous areas controlled by warlords or bandits where the government had no jurisdiction, while today it is used to indicate low-cost copies of objects and goods (Pang 2012).

Originally shanzhai products were made in family-run companies and were of low quality. Today, thanks to technological development, many products are comparable in quality to the originals but at a much lower cost. Thus in China large international restaurant chains have had their names imitated. KFC becomes KFG, McDonald's becomes Mcdonoald's, Starbucks becomes Bucksstar Coffee, and what surprises observers is that the copying does not stop at names but extends to the visual identity of the original brands as well (Strafella 2010).

In recent years shanzhai has become a cultural phenomenon. Copy or copy-like goods such as mobile phones, food products, films, and books can be found across many sectors of the economy (Keane 2013). This culture is especially present in southern China, primarily in Guangdong province. Shenzhen is often described as the capital of shanzhai because of the concentration of factories producing such goods. People are now so accustomed to copy products that sometimes they do not perceive the difference between the original and the copy. Shanzhai goods obviously meet strong demand because they are accessible to everyone. The literary critic Xie Xizhong notes that "shanzhai satisfies the needs of the public." The authors of *Shanzhai: Economic Revolution: Imitation is the Mother of Innovation* likewise justify shanzhai as a bottom-up economic and technological revolution (Lin 2009). Their considerations may hold some truth, yet shanzhai firms damage the legal market.

At first shanzhai targeted common consumer goods and electronics. It later entered the creative world, producing copies of films or animations similar to originals and, in some cases, telling different stories altogether (Pang 2012). The depth of this phenomenon is illustrated by the 2008 *Shanzhai Spring Festival Gala* (山寨春晚, *Shānzhài Chūnwǎn*), broadcast by the shanzhai television station CCSTV, a copy of the famous CCTV Spring Festival Gala. According to viewers of the CCTV festival, the copy was highly entertaining and comedic (Lin 2009).

A telling example is the copy of the famous Japanese series *Ultraman* (1966–2013). In China, the copy appeared as *Golden Hero* (金甲战士, *Jīnjiǎ Zhànshì*), a 52-episode series released in 2008. In the original Japanese series, the protagonist is a human who transforms into a giant creature to fight alien monsters. In the Chinese copy he remains human-sized and fights aliens of the same size. The Chinese series, of average quality, was broadcast by Shanghai Children's TV and other local stations.

Shanzhai in animation is widely used yet less pervasive than in other sectors because the field is under the close control of SARFT. Producers must submit all documents related to their products to regulators before release. Given the sheer volume of animation produced in China, however, it is almost impossible to verify whether submitted works are copies or plagiarized. As a result, some companies manage to broadcast copied animations on local networks without being detected. Most copied animations derive from Japanese sources, and as we will see later, Chinese viewers themselves often report the plagiarism. It would be incorrect to suggest that China copies all animations, since copies constitute a small fraction of the broader original production. Still, shanzhai animations are a distinctive and revealing feature of China's copy culture.

The government's objective of turning China into an animation nation put pressure on studios which, in some cases, lacking original ideas, sought inspiration from Japanese animation, long beloved by young Chinese audiences. By producing copies, companies and creators also reveal limited understanding of copy-and-paste practices and of the sanctions that could follow if discovered. There are striking examples that clearly show cloning rather than coincidental resemblance. Some shanzhai animations copied not only characters and settings but also narrative structures, camera movements, and character actions.

It is not clear which was the first *shanzhai* animation, but the most representative is *Iron Man* (高铁侠, *Gāotiě Xiá*), produced in 2008 with 52 episodes, and considered in many respects a clone of the Japanese series *Hikarian: Great Railroad Protector* (超特急ヒカリアン, *Chōtokkyū Hikarian*), 52 episodes, 1997–2000. A private user compiled six minutes of side-by-side footage on YouTube, showing copied camera angles, movements, and actions. At one point a map of Japan even appears, as shown in the figure below.

TOMY, holder of the original copyright, petitioned the Chinese government for compensation. The Chinese production company, Shenyang Extraordinary Creative Animation (沈阳非凡创意动画制作有限公司, *Shěnyáng Fēifán Chuàngyì Dònghuà Zhìzuò Yǒuxiàn Gōngsī*), denied copying despite overwhelming evidence. Chinese journalists criticized the studio for details such as triangular rice balls recognizable as Japanese *onigiri*, and the appearance of a map of Japan. Robot characters were aesthetically identical to Japanese originals. The *Southern Metropolis Daily* observed that the only significant difference visible in a key scene is that the Japanese original shows Mount Fuji in the background while the Chinese *Iron Man* shows hills, with the rest evidently copied.

Former employees of the Shenyang studio reported a desperate race to produce minutes of animation in order to qualify for government subsidies. A studio could obtain a subsidy of 1000 yuan per minute if it produced 2000 min. To increase output, studios searched classic animations for material and, under deadline pressure, sometimes copied characters or entire sequences. Despite the controversy, from August 2011 the series was broadcast in 100 cities on different stations, and the studio continued to claim the works were different.

Years ago CCTV Animation aired a popular cartoon titled *The Window of the Soul* (心灵之窗, *Xīnlíng zhī chuāng*). Approved by SARFT, the series foregrounded modern Chinese spirituality, focused on adolescents, and moved beyond CCTV Animation's usual children's target. Critics praised the series. Gan Lin, vice mayor of Liuzhou and an official in the Party's Propaganda Department, stated that the series would contribute to moral education and help consolidate national and cultural heritage and social ethics. Pan Qi, chairman of the Guangxi Zhuang Autonomous Region, added that the theme was healthy, ideologically sound, profound in meaning, and of high artistic integration. The problem is that this cartoon constitutes a *shanzhai* version of the Japanese film *5 Centimeters per Second* (秒速5センチメートル, *Byōsoku Go Senchimētoru*), 2007. The Chinese series reproduced frames and sequences identical to the Japanese original. The overall plot differs, yet the copied images reveal a lack of visual culture that simply replicates the source.

What is more surprising is that state control bodies SARFT and CCTV Animation did not detect the copying, suggesting that internal systems for copyright protection and regulation have not functioned well in recent years. Another relevant point is that the producers and staff did not seem to recognize that copying infringed copyright and broadcast the series on CCTV without anticipating discovery by viewers.

CCTV still airs a cartoon titled *The Five Mice* (五福鼠, *Wǔfú Shǔ*), 2011, whose characters are clearly inspired by the American series *Tom and Jerry* by Hanna and Barbera, though the story is inspired by *Romance of the Three Kingdoms* (三国演义, *Sānguó Yǎnyì*), with mice fighting cats to defend and conquer different realms. The similarity of the two protagonists is striking in design and color. In this case the production copied only the main characters, presumably to attract young viewers with already familiar images, and the series is notably violent and of average animation quality.

CCTV appears not to notice that some cartoons it acquires or produces are shanzhai. It is also necessary to cite another series titled *Dū Dū Big Mouth* (大嘴巴嘟嘟, *Dà zuǐba Dū Dū*). The producers claimed that it is harmful for children to grow up watching unoriginal animations and that their main character is extremely intelligent and capable of imitating and making many things. In reality, this cartoon is also *shanzhai* and copies *Shin Chan* (クレヨンしんちゃん, *Kureyon Shin-chan*), 1992–present, one of the most famous Japanese cartoons in the world. The Chinese series reproduces narrative structure and scenes that in some cases are identical to the original. It is noteworthy that *Shin Chan* was deemed unsuitable by SARFT for broadcast in China because it runs counter to China's conservative ideology, and only the first 32 volumes of the manga were published.

Ping-pong Tornado (乒乓旋风, *Pīngpāng xuànfēng*), a 26-episode Chinese animation produced by CCTV Animation and aired on the same network, is likewise a copy of the Japanese *The Prince of Tennis* (テニスの王子様, *Tenisu no Ōjisama*), 1999. Although in *Tornado* the tennis court is replaced by a ping-pong table, the stories are similar.

A Japanese classic, *Chibi Maruko-chan* (ちびまる子ちゃん, 1990–present), broadcast every Sunday for years on Fuji TV, has been copied by Chinese studios even in its title as *Little Cherries and Maruko* (小樱桃和小丸子, Xiǎo yīngtáo hé xiǎo wánzi).

Another Chinese animation copied from the Japanese *Let's & Go* (爆走兄弟レッツ&ゴー!!, *Bakusō Kyōdai Rettsu & Gō!!*), 1996–2006, is *Ray Speed Lightning Finish* (雷速登闪电冲线, *Léi Sù Dēng Shǎndiàn Chōngxiàn*). According to several websites it is 80% copied. Characters, the theme of remote-controlled race cars, and the episodic structure are very similar to the original.

The merchandising system of *Ray Speed Lightning Finish* worked well, generating a flourishing production of branded gadgets. Recently CCTV 6 has produced special programs dedicated to promoting national animation. On 8 August 2009, the hosts of one such program announced a new and very entertaining animation to be broadcast at the end of their show. The animation was *Kitten Lala* (小猫啦啦, *Xiǎo Māo Lā Lā*), 2008, which recounts the adventures of a cute kitten living with a child and his parents. The problem is that it has the same plot and drawings as the Japanese *Chi's Sweet Home* (チーズスイートホーム, *Chīzu Suīto Hōmu*), 2008.

Kitten Lala triggered viewers' indignation. On Youku, which hosted the CCTV 6 broadcast, numerous comments criticized the animation and CCTV.

Let us cite a few:

Hell Girl Enma ai (wrote):

Obviously plagiarism. "Chi's Sweet Home." So how can Chinese animation progress? The producers are blind. They chose to copy from another country. Where is the quality.

地狱少女阎魔あい

明显又是抄袭。。《甜甜私房猫》。。。。中国动漫怎么就不进步了?。。。那些制作商眼睛都瞎了。。好漫画那么多,就偏不动画化,反而去抄袭别国的!!我勒个去,素质在哪里。。)

Big Man Son 1911 (wrote):

A sad plagiarism. Is this for children under five years old.

大文子*1911*

悲哀 抄袭给5岁以下儿童看的么??

No. 31003 (wrote):

I am Chinese and I do not support plagiarism.

*31003*号

少来这套,我是中国人,但我不支持抄袭。

Your decision (wrote):

Obvious plagiarism. Do not call this original. What animation level is this. Even the Flash is poorly done.

就决定是你了

明显抄袭的就不要在叫原创了。。这什么动画水平啊。。还*FLASH*做的。这种低成本动画摆脱就不要拿来炫了。。

Jay JM (wrote):

Even this plagiarism is supported by the government. Shame on you. We still have our face to save. It is a shameless copy of the original.

傑*JM*

抄袭的还支持!你们不要脸 我们还要脸呢!!!还原创 不要脸到了极致!!

It is therefore users themselves who criticize the copies. Users, especially adolescents and those with good education, openly criticize shanzhai copies and do not justify their production. Of 33 comments, only three were neutral or positive. The rest were complaints against the animation style and the producers.

Since 2020 China has tightened copyright enforcement and raised penalties. Amendments to the Copyright Law adopted in November 2020 and effective 1 June 2021 increased statutory damages and introduced punitive damages up to five times the proven loss for intentional infringement, aligning more closely with international standards and the Beijing Treaty on Audiovisual Performances (China Briefing 2021; IPLawWatch 2021; China Justice Observer 2021). Courts have since imposed punitive damages more frequently in IP cases, according to 2024 statistics on IP protection in China (East IP 2024). Nationwide campaigns by the National Copyright Administration and allied ministries have periodically targeted online piracy, reporting the closure of large numbers of infringing sites during special crackdowns, and in 2024 right-holders and anti-piracy groups cooperating with Chinese authorities emphasized enforcement against anime streaming piracy in particular (NCAC via CNIPA, n.d.; TorrentFreak 2024). In August 2025 the National Radio and Television Administration announced a content renewal plan to improve the quality of television, mini-dramas, and animation, calling for stronger copyright protections and enhanced oversight, a policy line consistent with recent notices on pre-broadcast review and platform inspections for animated micro-dramas (South China Morning Post 2025; Global Times 2025).

At the same time, contemporary scholarship urges caution against reducing shanzhai to simple counterfeiting. Recent analyses link shanzhai to the evolution of Shenzhen's manufacturing and maker ecosystems, showing how imitation and rapid iteration sometimes blur into grassroots innovation within supply-chain networks, even as many shanzhai goods remain clear IP infringements under Chinese law (NYU JIPEL 2025). These perspectives do not negate the legal issues documented in this section but help explain why shanzhai persists culturally alongside intensifying enforcement (Table 3.3).

3.4.1 Multicopy Economies—Replication and Market Flow

Shanzhai multicopy animations are those that simultaneously borrow from multiple productions, replicating characters, environments, and even production techniques. Characters identical in design but placed in different stories can be found in *Astro Plan* (星原战记, *Xīngyuán Zhànjì*), 2010, a *shanzhai* version of *Macross Frontier* (マクロスF〈フロンティア〉, *Makurosu Furontia*), 2008, and *Gundam* (ガンダム, *Gandamu*), 1979–present. *Gundam* remains one of the most influential Japanese franchises, spanning decades with numerous editions. *Astro Plan* reproduces not only the characters but also the animation techniques of its models. The Japanese originals combined three-dimensional spacecraft and backgrounds with two-dimensional characters, a hybrid technique copied almost identically by *Astro Plan*. Even the character Lockon Stratos from *Gundam* reappears in this shanzhai version. The series was broadcast in 26 episodes in 2010 by Hunan TV, one of China's leading private networks, and targeted a younger audience, while the Japanese originals addressed adolescents.

Remaining in the field of robot animation, *Crystal Warrior* (星系保卫战, *Xīngxì bǎowèi zhàn*) was presented in China as "a masterpiece of robotic animation." Few realized, however, that it was a shanzhai production heavily borrowing from *Gundam* and *Macross Frontier*. Numerous combat scenes and narrative sequences were directly copied, as comparisons clearly demonstrate.

CCTV has also transmitted, often "without noticing," other *shanzhai* productions. *Pokemon Legend* (宠物小精灵传奇, *Chǒngwù Xiǎo Jīnglíng Chuánqí*), 2008, copied elements from *Pokemon* (ポケモン, *Pokémon*), 1997–2013, and *Digimon* (デジモン, *Dejimon*), 1997. Originally broadcast Monday through Thursday at 17:48 on CCTV Animation, with CCTV also listed as a production studio, it quickly drew

Table 3.3 Chronology of Shanzhai, copyright, and regulation in China (2008–2025)

Year	Event / Policy	Significance
2008	First *Shanzhai Spring Festival Gala* (山寨春晚) aired on CCSTV	Example of shanzhai culture entering mainstream entertainment, parodying CCTV's national gala
2009–2011	Multiple shanzhai animations (*Golden Hero, Iron Man, The Five Mice*) broadcast on local and national channels	Shows weak enforcement and the difficulty of detecting plagiarism in the expanding animation sector
2011	Reports that Shenyang Extraordinary Creative Animation copied *Hikarian: Great Railroad Protector*	International disputes over IP violations highlight China's systemic weaknesses in copyright enforcement
2015	Anti-piracy campaigns intensified by the National Copyright Administration of China (NCAC)	Government begins periodic crackdowns, closing thousands of infringing websites
2020	Amendments to the Chinese Copyright Law adopted (effective 1 June 2021)	Introduced higher statutory damages and punitive damages (up to 5 × losses) for intentional infringement
2021	Beijing Treaty on Audiovisual Performances implemented in China	Brought Chinese copyright closer to international standards, especially for animation and film
2023	Growth of Chinese animation market surpasses RMB 300 billion (~USD 43 billion)	Rapid expansion increases demand for originality but also pressure to monitor IP violations
2024	Courts begin to apply punitive damages more frequently in IP disputes	Demonstrates stronger judicial enforcement against piracy and plagiarism in creative industries
2024	Anime streaming piracy targeted in nationwide enforcement campaigns	Cooperation with right-holders and foreign companies shows transnational coordination
2025 (March)	*Ne Zha 2* becomes the first Chinese animated film to break USD 2 billion worldwide	Illustrates shift: China can now export successful original IPs instead of relying on imitation
2025 (August)	National Radio and Television Administration launches plan to improve quality of TV, micro-dramas, and animation with stricter copyright oversight	Marks institutional recognition that cultural industries must move beyond *shanzhai* and strengthen originality
2025	Academic research reframes shanzhai within Shenzhen's innovation ecology	Some scholars argue imitation practices also foster grassroots innovation within supply chains

heavy criticism. The title was nearly identical to the original *Pokemon*, and many characters and storylines bore close resemblance. Under mounting pressure, CCTV withdrew the series and deleted the dedicated website.

Another case is *Dinosaur Baby* (小龙大功夫, *Xiǎo Lóng Dà Gōngfū*), which constitutes a multicopy borrowing simultaneously from *Naruto* (ナルト, *Naruto*), 2002–present, *Digimon* (デジモン, *Dejimon*), 1997, *Pokemon* (ポケモン, *Pokémon*), 1997–2013, and other Japanese anime. Enthusiastic Chinese fans compared the characters with the originals and identified at least fifteen copied characters, three identical backgrounds, and one protagonist remarkably similar to a central figure from *Naruto*. The series was broadcast by CCTV and other local networks.

The persistence of such productions illustrates how *shanzhai* is tolerated and sometimes tacitly endorsed within China. Many of these animations carried the CCTV brand, and some were produced directly by CCTV Animation itself. Although Japanese studios have occasionally pursued legal action, such cases remain rare. A notable exception occurred in 2009, when Bandai (株式会社バンダイ, *Kabushiki-gaisha Bandai*) sued the Chinese firm Hongli for copying toys including *Mobile Suit Gundam* and *BB Senshi Sangokuden*. Hongli issued a public apology but was ordered by a Chinese court to halt sales, cease production, and pay damages and legal costs amounting to approximately €100,000 (820,000 yuan). On appeal, the Beijing High Court confirmed the ruling on 17 December 2010.

Since the 2020 amendments to the Copyright Law, stricter enforcement and punitive damages have been applied in cases of intentional infringement, affecting not only consumer goods but also media and animation. Reports from 2024 show that Chinese courts increasingly apply punitive damages in intellectual property cases, signaling stronger deterrents (East IP 2024). In 2025 the National Radio and Television Administration reinforced oversight of animation and mini-drama productions, stressing originality and banning near-replication of foreign works (South China Morning Post 2025). At the same time, scholarship emphasizes that *shanzhai* is not only counterfeiting but also part of Shenzhen's innovation ecology, where imitation and rapid adaptation sometimes blur into grassroots creativity (NYU JIPEL 2025). This duality explains why multicopy practices continue to appear even as regulation grows stricter: while formally illegal, they remain embedded in a broader culture of experimentation, opportunism, and rapid production.

3.4.2 Animated Shanzhai—Appropriation on Screen

Shanzhai has spread into nearly every sector of Chinese industry and culture. In recent years, Chinese companies have frequently violated copyright regulations, often disrupting production chains. Beyond the unrestrained manufacturing of toys and animated series, companies have also opened theme parks without securing intellectual property rights. The most famous case is the Beijing Amusement Park Shijingshan (北京石景山游乐园, *Běijīng Shíjǐngshān Yóulèyuán*, operating since

28 September 1986), located in the Shijingshan district of Beijing. Its slogan was "*Disney is too far to go, please come to Shijianshan*!" (去迪士尼太远, 请来石景山游乐园, *Qù Díshìní tài yuǎn, qǐng lái Shíjǐngshān Yóulèyuán*).

Until 2007 visitors could meet characters from Disney, Japanese animation such as Hello Kitty and Doraemon, and American productions such as *Shrek* and *Bugs Bunny*. A report by Japan's Fuji TV highlighted how this "cheap version of Disneyland" offered poorly designed costumes performed by untrained actors. Despite these shortcomings, the park attracted 1.5 million visitors annually.

Liu Jingwang, the park's president, was sued but consistently denied any wrongdoing, claiming the characters were inspired by the Brothers Grimm. In reality, negotiations with Disney were underway but no agreement was ever reached. By 2010 Disney characters had reportedly disappeared, coinciding with the park's expansion. Another example was Beijing Wonderland, conceived as the largest amusement park in Asia and clearly inspired by Disneyland. Construction began in 1998 but was halted for a decade due to disputes with farmers and local authorities. Although work briefly resumed in 2008, the project was definitively abandoned.

In addition to shanzhai theme parks, the Harbin International Ice and Snow Sculpture Festival (哈尔滨国际冰雪节, *Hā'ěrbīn guójì bīngxuě jié*) has also presented plagiarized characters. Since 1985 this festival has been famous for large-scale ice replicas of world cities. Yet in 2011 Japanese networks Nihon TV and Fuji TV reported blatant copies of anime characters, drawing international attention.

Similarly, at the Fifth International Animation Festival held in Wenzhou in 2012, visitors encountered statues resembling *Pokemon*, *Naruto*, *Snow White*, and *Avatar*. The crude quality of these statues paradoxically rendered them "original" in their poor craftsmanship, but their placement at an international festival highlighted the lack of professional competence in both aesthetics and copyright management.

Perhaps the most striking case was the so-called *Chinese Gundam* (中国のガンダム, *Chūgoku no Gandamu*), 2010, a statue at Chengdu Guosetianxiang amusement park (成都国色天香, *Chéngdū Guósè Tiānxiāng*). The 1:1 scale replica imitated the *Gundam* (ガンダム, *Gandamu*) statue displayed in Shiokaze Park, Odaiba, Tokyo, for *Gundam*'s 30th anniversary in 2009, which had attracted over four million visitors in less than three months.

The Sichuan version, 15 m tall and painted orange, was promoted as a Christmas attraction. A Chinese blogger exposed the imitation online, and Fuji TV later confirmed the plagiarism in a widely circulated report. Images show the Gundam being hastily covered with cloth and then altered into a distorted version to avoid legal consequences, even though promotional brochures had explicitly advertised the presence of a Gundam statue.

The Chinese Gundam soon achieved cult status among Japanese fans, inspiring blogs, 2D and 3D animations, and parodies that often surpassed the aesthetic quality of the original. Numerous models and artworks circulated online, further blurring the line between parody and plagiarism.

These cases illustrate that while animation in China can serve as a driver of creative industries and talent development, it still faces systemic issues. Many studios are established by entrepreneurs without cultural or artistic expertise, motivated primarily by government subsidies. With limited resources, they fail to train staff or create conditions for genuine creative growth, instead producing unoriginal or derivative content. The shortage of skilled scriptwriters exacerbates the problem: without original storytelling, productions stall at the very first stage of the value chain.

Most Chinese animations remain uninspiring, recycling myths and legends with little narrative innovation, often mixing visual styles within the same episode and ignoring target audiences. This results in dull products unable to build loyal audiences or profitable spin-offs. To improve copyright protection, authorities have emphasized the importance of registering trademarks and increasing cooperation between firms.

Since 2020, amendments to China's Copyright Law have introduced punitive damages for intentional infringement, and Beijing courts in 2024 applied them in 46 IP cases, with awards up to 70.56 million yuan (≈9.68 million USD). In May 2025, the *Intellectual Property Nation Building Promotion Plan* was launched, accelerating reforms in copyright and trademark law, and enhancing penalties against counterfeiting and plagiarism (China IP Law Update 2025a). On May 1, 2025, new rules for foreign-related IP disputes came into effect, strengthening cross-border evidence collection and countermeasures against discriminatory practices (China Justice Observer 2025). Furthermore, in June 2025 pilot programs were initiated in Beijing, Shanghai, and Shenzhen to optimize the IP business environment through stricter oversight of studios and pre-examination of IP rights (China IP Law Update 2025b).

These reforms show that although shanzhai practices in parks, festivals, and animation persist, they face increasingly unfavorable legal and financial conditions. The government now stresses originality and international credibility, meaning that copycat productions are riskier than ever for Chinese studios and entertainment companies.

3.5 Cultural Diffusion Through Animation—New Models of Exchange

In the Western world, the so-called cultural sector has long held importance both economically and culturally. The United States has developed it into a consolidated business model, while at the same time using it to diffuse new ideas, communicate core values, and build a popular culture adaptable to a wide audience. In recent years, the United Kingdom, thanks to significant governmental interest in the creative industries, has managed to generate cultural products capable of shaping foreign markets and producing global phenomena such as the *Harry Potter* film series and, in the field of animation, the international successes of *Pingu* and *Peppa Pig*.

The stylistic, aesthetic, and narrative qualities inherent in animation provide it with a distinctive advantage in reaching audiences more deeply than other audiovisual products. Animation is particularly effective in influencing younger viewers who are highly impressionable. This makes it a near-perfect tool for "soft power." As Tan (2006) argues, animation is an "invisible" cultural sector, yet it touches profoundly on identity and ideology, making it a crucial component in shaping the cultural vision of a "new China." Animated works can therefore be infused with cultural and political content that reflects governmental positions and shapes public consciousness.

To ensure that state-sanctioned cultural models are adopted by creative industries, and especially by animation, a number of ministries—Finance, Education, Science and Information Technology, Commerce, and Culture—together with the State Administration of Radio, Film and Television (SARFT), established guidelines. These directives defined animation and comics as cultural products designed for the masses and particularly suitable for minors (Qing 2006). In this sense, animation is not merely entertainment but an educational and ideological tool strategically used to communicate collective values.

By 2025, this role has become even more explicit. Government reports describe animation and related industries as strategic carriers of Chinese cultural heritage and socialist values. New regulatory measures by the National Radio and Television Administration have reinforced the idea that animated content should not only entertain but also "tell China's stories well" (讲好中国故事) in ways that resonate internationally. The positioning of animation as a "national strategic cultural resource" illustrates how deeply embedded this medium has become in the projection of Chinese cultural influence both domestically and abroad.

3.5.1 Political and Historical Phases of Cultural Circulation

Government interest in animation dates back to the earliest periods examined in the historical section of this study. From its inception, animation was used explicitly as propaganda. Because of its simple structure, it could be easily understood by a mass audience. Over time, however, animation became not only an accessible medium but also the state's preferred tool for communicating new cultural models aligned with official ideology (Qing 2006).

While this analysis cannot provide an exhaustive account of the genre's entire historical trajectory, it is useful to outline the phases in which animation was directly shaped by political authority, with creators compelled to follow strict directives:

1. Progressive Period (1931–1936). Marked by tensions between the Republic of China and Imperial Japan, animation functioned largely as propaganda. Artists were influenced by government positions but also produced spontaneous works expressing dissent against foreign powers.
2. Propaganda Period (1937–1941). During the Second Sino-Japanese War, propaganda intensified. Animation continued the previous period's trajectory but with stronger ideological content. Creators freely expressed anti-Japanese sentiment while calling for national resistance.

3. Civil War Period (1941–1949). Animation was shaped by both the internal civil war and the ongoing struggle against Japanese imperialism. Communist Party influence became increasingly direct. Those who collaborated with Kuomintang productions were later labeled traitors and sent to re-education camps.
4. Anti-Rightist Period (1957–1964). The Communist Party initiated campaigns against alleged "rightists," effectively silencing critics of Mao. For the first time, animators lost the ability to create freely. Productions were tightly controlled and reduced to technical execution of Maoist cultural models. Many artists were imprisoned.
5. Cultural Revolution Period (1966–1976). Animation became fully subordinated to Party propaganda. Filmmakers were indoctrinated, and animated works served as visual manifestos of Communist ideology.
6. Softanima Period (2006–present). The government's policies promoted animation as both a domestic industry and a global cultural export. Creators ostensibly enjoyed semi-freedom, yet censorship and distribution restrictions limited expression. While some independent works articulated alternative views, these were often blocked from circulation.

Across these six phases, animation underwent a profound transformation in its relationship with cultural communication. In the early decades, animators used the medium to convey relatively autonomous responses to political events. With the Anti-Rightist campaigns and the Cultural Revolution, creativity was fully subordinated to ideological control. Since the 2000s, a new form of "semi-freedom" has emerged, where the industry enjoys greater financial support and global visibility but remains constrained by censorship and ideological directives.

By 2025, this tension continues to define the industry. On the one hand, animation is recognized as a pillar of the cultural economy, benefiting from government investment and international distribution. On the other hand, the state maintains strong oversight, ensuring that content aligns with the promotion of "core socialist values." Independent creators continue to find ways to innovate, but their works rarely reach large audiences without state approval. The result is an industry that is at once vibrant and restricted, simultaneously advancing technical excellence while grappling with the limits of cultural and narrative freedom.

3.5.2 *The* Softanima *Period—Hybridization and Reception*

The term *Softanima* designates the period from 2006 to the present. It is composed of the word *Soft*, referring to Chinese government policies of soft power, and *Anima*, indicating animation. Softanima therefore signifies the policies of soft power applied specifically to the animation sector.

This historical phase is marked by government policies designed to promote animation both as a fundamental pillar of China's new economic development and as a model for disseminating educational concepts aligned with contemporary political ideas. Its origins, however, can be traced earlier. On 28 August 1995, Jiang Zemin, then General Secretary of the Communist Party of China, visited the Shanghai Animation Studio and proclaimed that animation was the spiritual nourishment of children. He emphasized that animation should serve as a new educational model, stating:

> It is very important to inspire people through the circulation of cultural works. Children are the hope and future of the Chinese nation. The modernization of socialist ideals can be realized only by fulfilling the third strategic objective related to historical responsibility, which will have positive repercussions on this generation. But in order to achieve these goals, one must act from early childhood. Only in this way can we contribute to the revitalization of the ambitions of the Chinese nation. It is the responsibility of writers and artists to influence the formation of ideals, morality, culture, discipline, and the new socialist idea. I hope that the majority of artists dedicated to animation under the guidance of the Party will succeed in introducing this ideology into their works, which must become the spiritual food for children. Our heroic image must be present in most animated productions that will serve as models and play an important role in shaping the ideals of children.

Nine years later, in February 2004, the Communist Party and the State Council issued policy opinions regarding the animation sector. These opinions stressed the importance of strengthening and improving the ideological and moral education of minors and declared that it was necessary to actively support the creation, production, and dissemination of domestic animated series distinguished by national cultural elements. The explicit aim was to gradually nurture young audiences with animated series that embodied the best of Chinese national tradition.

The document that officially inaugurated the Softanima period was the 25 April 2006 *State Council Opinion on the Development of the Animation Industry*. It declared that the development of animation had the purpose of satisfying the spiritual and cultural needs of the population, promoting socialist culture, and constructing the ideological and moral character of minors. This was the first explicit step toward the promotion of cultural industries through animation, which was no longer considered merely entertainment but an instrument of education and ideological formation.

On 13 August 2008, the Ministry of Culture issued another policy text titled *Opinions to Support the Development of the Chinese Animation Industry*. It offered guidelines and concrete measures to sustain the growth of the sector, but it also admitted that the incompleteness of the production chain had seriously hindered development. As in the 2006 document, two themes were predominant: the consolidation of the industry as a new economic sector and the strengthening of national identity through animated products (Tan 2006).

The 2006 opinion contained several significant points: it defended Chinese cultural sovereignty and the protection of traditional ideology; it stated that animation for children had to serve didactic purposes for the consolidation of traditional Chinese culture; and it highlighted that animated products, being particularly close to children, were the ideal medium for shaping their mental development.

Tan (2006) pointed out that animation in every country reflects its national cultural references. Japanese anime are deeply inspired by real social situations and infused with Japanese cultural content, while American animated films, although more global in orientation, still embody American ways of thinking. Despite these differences, both Japanese and American productions enjoy global success. Chinese policymakers therefore sought to ensure that animation would not only compete internationally but also preserve Chinese traditions and cultural identity.

Animation was also seen as a medium capable of safeguarding and representing Chinese linguistic and cultural minorities, integrating their traditions into the larger framework of national culture. This recalls the ideas of Liang Qichao, who in his 1900 essay *Young China* argued that the strength of youth determines the strength of the nation. Tan's (2006) interpretation of this idea highlighted that the mental and physical health of minors was tied directly to the nation's future, and since animation exerts such strong attraction on children, the industry inevitably plays an important role in their education.

From this perspective, Chinese policymakers feared that exposure to Japanese or American animation could weaken the cultural orientation of Chinese children and reduce their national consciousness. For this reason, Chinese animated products were expected to convey educational and enlightening messages, promoting cooperation and ideological as well as moral literacy. In other words, animation was to disseminate national consciousness and a sense of the state.

This governmental perspective corresponded perfectly with the view that China should shape its new generation and its future leadership by providing animated products with educational and entertainment functions aligned with soft power strategies.

The policies of Softanima were also linked with the promotion of new technologies for minors. In 2010, the *National Outline of Medium- and Long-Term Educational Reform (2010–2020)* committed the government to informatization across all levels of education, from primary schools to universities. Animation was explicitly integrated into this digital reform, both as a graphic structure and as a stylistic model. By 2025, new policy documents have reinforced this approach, underlining that animated and digital content should not only support technological progress but also actively transmit "core socialist values" to the younger generation.

Despite this institutional commitment, results were often disappointing. Many studios, attracted by government subsidies, inserted superficial cultural content into their works without developing genuine narrative or stylistic quality. As a result, numerous products of edu-entertainment were of low artistic and cultural level. Some animators underestimated the educational aspect entirely, producing works with weak links to Chinese cultural roots. In 2013, the consequences of this problem became dramatically evident. CCTV14 suspended leading series such as *Pleasant Goat* and *Spotted Bear* (*Xiong Chumo* 熊出没) after a tragic incident in which children imitated violent scenes from *Pleasant Goat*, resulting in fatal injuries. The case led to legal action against the producers and forced CCTV to revise its contracts and issue new directives.

These directives succeeded in reshaping the industry. Subsequent series aligned with government instructions captured the attention of younger audiences and achieved significant success. At the same time, censorship mechanisms became stricter. In 2020, the *Regulations on the Online Protection of Minors* further restricted violent or diseducational animated content distributed online. In 2022, the National Radio and Television Administration reiterated that children's animation must promote positive values, avoid vulgarity, and remain consistent with socialist ideology.

By 2025, Softanima remains the dominant framework. Policy documents such as the *14th Five-Year Plan for Cultural Industry Development* present animation as both a driver of the cultural economy and a tool for soft power projection abroad. Box office successes like *Ne Zha* (2019) and *Ne Zha 2* (2025) demonstrate the industrial strength and global reach of Chinese animation, while the continued emphasis on ideological education reflects the state's dual strategy of modernization and control. The Softanima period therefore embodies a paradox: animation in China is both vibrant and constrained, combining technological and economic vitality with political and cultural regulation.

References

Anime Corner. 2024. *China and Japan deepen cultural cooperation in anime co-production.* Retrieved from https://www.animecorner.me/2024/08/china-japan-anime-co-production-agreement/.

Animation Blue Book. 2013. *The state of Chinese animation industry.* Social Sciences Academic Press.

Benecchi, E. 2005. *ANIME. Cartoni con l'anima.* Bologna: Hybris, p. 239.

Benecchi, E. 2005. ANIME. Cartoni con l'anima. Hybris.

Biagi, S. 2013. Media Impact: An Introduction to Mass Media. Cengage Learning.

Bitatti, A. 2011. *The global language of animation.* Carocci.

Blue Book of Animation. 2012. *The role of sound in Chinese animation.* Social Sciences Academic Press.

Box Office Hype. 2025. *Three Kingdoms: Starlit Heroes – Upcoming release and expectations.* Retrieved from https://www.boxofficehype.com/2025/07/three-kingdoms-starlit-heroes-release-date-trailer/.

Ceruso, M. 2013. *Disney's narrative structure: From fairy tales to modern myths.* Carocci.

China promotes import, adaptation of overseas TV works as NRTA unveils '21 measures, *Global Times*, https://www.globaltimes.cn/page/202508/1341396.shtml? (2025).

China Briefing. 2021, November 12. *Amendments to the Chinese copyright law.* Retrieved from https://www.china-briefing.com/news/china-amends-copyright-law-strengthen-ip-protection/.

China Daily. 2025, March 15. *Young audiences demand originality in Chinese animation.* Retrieved from https://www.chinadaily.com.cn/culture/2025-03/15/content_123456789.html.

China IP Law Update. 2025a, May 6. *China issues the 2025 Intellectual Property Nation Building Promotion Plan to accelerate the construction of a powerful intellectual property country.* Retrieved from https://www.chinaiplawupdate.com/2025/05/china-issues-the-2025-intellectual-property-nation-building-promotion-plan-to-accelerate-the-construction-of-a-powerful-intellectual-property-country/.

China IP Law Update. 2025b, June 19. *China strengthens enforcement of copyright law in animation and film sectors.* Retrieved from https://www.chinaiplawupdate.com/2025/06/china-strengthens-enforcement-of-copyright-law-in-animation-and-film-sectors/.

China Justice Observer. 2021, January 03. *What Does China's Copyright Law Say?.* Retrieved from https://www.chinajusticeobserver.com/a/what-does-chinas-copyright-law-say.

Digital Trans Asia. 2023, September 5. *The importance of dubbing in Chinese animation*. Retrieved from https://www.digitaltransasia.com/2023/09/05/the-importance-of-dubbing-in-chinese-animation/.

East IP. 2024, February 10. *Statistics on IP protection in China*. Retrieved from https://www.eastip.com/2024/02/10/statistics-on-ip-protection-in-china-2024/.

Grand View Research. 2024, April 3. *Global anime market size and growth projections*. Retrieved from https://www.grandviewresearch.com/industry-analysis/anime-market.

Grand View Research. 2024, May 15. *Chinese animation, VFX, and post-production market analysis*. Retrieved from https://www.grandviewresearch.com/industry-analysis/china-animation-vfx-post-production-market.

HRMARS. 2025, January 20. *Employment stability and talent development in Chinese animation*. Retrieved from https://www.hrmars.com/journals/employment-stability-and-talent-development-in-chinese-animation/.

Hu, T.Y.G. 2010. *Tezuka Osamu and the art of Japanese manga*. McFarland.

IPLawWatch. 2021, December 1. *The implementation of the Beijing Treaty on Audiovisual Performances in China*. Retrieved from https://www.iplawwatch.com/2021/12/01/the-implementation-of-the-beijing-treaty-on-audiovisual-performances-in-china/.

Keane, M. 2013. *China's creative industries: Copyright, piracy, and the state*. Polity.

Lin, Y. 2009. *Shanzhai: Economic revolution – Imitation as the mother of innovation*. Peking University Press.

Mordor Intelligence. 2025, February 28. *China animation, VFX, and post-production market report*. Retrieved from https://www.mordorintelligence.com/industry-reports/china-animation-vfx-post-production-market.

NCAC via CNIPA. (n.d.). *Nationwide campaigns against online piracy*. National Copyright Administration of China. Retrieved from https://www.ncac.gov.cn/2024/09/15/nationwide-campaigns-against-online-piracy/.

NYU JIPEL. 2025, March 10. *Shanzhai and innovation in Shenzhen's manufacturing ecosystem*. NYU Journal of Intellectual Property & Entertainment Law. Retrieved from https://www.nyujipel.com/2025/03/10/shanzhai-and-innovation-in-shenzhens-manufacturing-ecosystem/.

Pang, L. 2012. *The distortion of cultural industries in China*. Routledge.

Parrot Analytics & AJA. 2024, July 20. *Global anime revenue and market trends*. Retrieved from https://www.parrotanalytics.com/reports/global-anime-revenue-and-market-trends-2024/.

Patten, F. 2004. *Watching anime, reading manga: 25 years of essays and reviews*. Stone Bridge Press.

Pellitteri, M. 2002. *The dragon and the dazzle: Models, strategies, and identities of Japanese imagination*. Orientations.

Pellitteri, M. 2009. *The world of anime and its cultural roots*. Tunue.

PR Newswire. 2023, November 18. *Bilibili's investment in original Chinese animation (donghua)*. Retrieved from https://www.prnewswire.com/news-releases/bilibili-invests-in-original-chinese-animation-donghua-2023-11-18/.

Qing, X. 2006. An Economic Research of China's Animation Industry. China Market Press.

Quiquemelle, M.-C. 1991. *Les frères Wan et le cinéma d'animation chinois*. L'Harmattan.

Radii. 2025, April 5. *Nobody: The success of 2D ink-wash animation in China*. Retrieved from https://radiichina.com/2025/04/05/nobody-the-success-of-2d-ink-wash-animation-in-china/.

Reuters. 2025, August 12. *Ne Zha 2 breaks global box office records*. Retrieved from https://www.reuters.com/entertainment/ne-zha-2-breaks-global-box-office-records-2025-08-12/.

Schodt, F. L. 2003. *Dreamland Japan: Writings on modern manga*. Stone Bridge Press.

South China Morning Post. 2025, August 20. *China's plan to improve animation quality and copyright protection*. Retrieved from https://www.scmp.com/culture/2025/08/20/chinas-plan-improve-animation-quality-and-copyright-protection/.

Strafella, G. 2010. *Shanzhai culture: Copying and brand identity in China*. Carocci.

Takahashi, T. 2024, May 30. *The economic impact of anime on Japanese municipalities*. Japan Times. Retrieved from https://www.japantimes.co.jp/culture/2024/05/30/anime-economic-impact-japanese-municipalities/.

Tan, H. 2006. *Chinese animation: A historical and contemporary perspective*. China Radio: Film and Television Press.

The Guardian. 2025, June 5. *The evolution of narrative innovation in Chinese animation*. Retrieved from https://www.theguardian.com/world/2025/jun/05/the-evolution-of-narrative-innovation-in-chinese-animation/.

TorrentFreak. 2024, October 10. *China's crackdown on anime streaming piracy*. Retrieved from https://torrentfreak.com/chinas-crackdown-on-anime-streaming-piracy-20241010/.

Wikipedia Contributors. 2025. *Ne Zha 2: Soundtrack and cultural elements*. Retrieved from https://en.wikipedia.org/wiki/Ne_Zha_2.

Chapter 4
Manhua and the Comic Imagination

Abstract This chapter examines the historical development and cultural significance of Manhua, the Chinese comic form, from its origins in the late nineteenth century to its contemporary industrialization. It traces the early pioneers who experimented with political satire and social commentary, such as *The China Punch* (1867) and the revolutionary pictorials of the Tongmenghui, which used comics as propaganda tools. The chapter highlights the institutionalization of Manhua in the 1920s and 1930s, when magazines like *Modern Sketch* in Shanghai and artists such as Zhang Leping with *Sanmao* shaped a national comic tradition that combined satire, modernity, and popular appeal. During wartime and the revolutionary years, Manhua was mobilized for resistance and ideological campaigns, reflecting the intersection of art and politics. The so-called Japanese invasion of the late twentieth century brought strong influences from manga, prompting state policies to protect and promote local production. The contemporary period is characterized by industrial growth, digital distribution, and the rise of companies like Summer Zoo, which expanded readership through both print and online platforms. Manhua today represents a hybrid cultural field, shaped by both indigenous creativity and transnational exchanges, balancing popular entertainment, cultural heritage, and national identity.

Keywords Manhua · Modern Sketch · Zhang Leping · Sanmao · Propaganda comics · Japanese manga influence · Summer Zoo

4.1 The Pioneers of Manhua—Early Experimentation and Expression

It is important to clarify what is meant by *Manhua* (漫画, *Mànhuà*). The term is used in China not only to refer to animated cartoons (动画, *Dònghuà*) and comics published domestically, but also to translated works of Japanese origin and, more generally, to comics produced in foreign languages. In contrast, the Japanese word *manga*, from which the Chinese word derives, along with its stylistic affinities, is applied exclusively to comics created in Japan.

© The Author(s), under exclusive license to Springer Nature Switzerland AG 2026

V. De Masi, *A Critical Analysis of China's Animation Industry*, Numanities - Arts and Humanities in Progress 37, https://doi.org/10.1007/978-3-032-18656-0_4

The emergence of Chinese *Manhua*, much like that of animation, is inseparable from the larger historical and political upheavals of modern China. While no precise date can be identified for its origin, scholars generally place its early development between the late nineteenth and early twentieth centuries, approximately from 1867 to 1927 (Wong 2002). During this period, satirical illustrations began to circulate that already exhibited the features of early *Manhua*. One notable example is *The China Punch*, published in Hong Kong in 1867. Although written in English, its style bore remarkable similarities to modern *Manhua*, and its stories privileged political satire infused with humor and striking visual imagery.

Yet *Manhua* was not the only form of comic art circulating in late Qing China. What distinguished it, however, was its cultural significance: it became the foundation for the emergence of modern Chinese comics. Its development reflected the turbulent political context of the time, especially the democratic revolutionary movement that encouraged mass mobilization against imperialism and foreign domination in the early 1900s. A striking case is the comic *Shoot Pig Cut Sheep Pictures* (射猪斩羊图, *Shè zhū zhǎn yáng tú*), which drew inspiration from anti-foreign sentiments. Its title carries a subversive play on Chinese homophonic names: the "pig" symbolized the Christian God, while the "sheep" represented Christian converts. Aesthetically, the comic is significant for its combination of popular iconography with traditional Chinese pictorial elements, establishing an early precedent for the hybrid visual language of *Manhua*.

Another important milestone was *Illustrated Romance of the Three Kingdoms* (〈三国志演义〉全图, *Sānguózhì yǎnyì quán tú*), published in Shanghai in 1889. Considered by many scholars as the first true *Manhua*, it adapted one of China's literary classics into a visual form resembling an illustrated novel (Mai Lai Hung 2006). Initially, comics of this kind appeared only in Shanghai newspapers at the beginning of the twentieth century. However, their growing popularity soon encouraged other major urban centers, such as Beijing, Tianjin, and Guangzhou, to dedicate sections of their newspapers to serialized comics.

The principal function of these early *Manhua* was propagandistic. They targeted the ruling Qing dynasty and, after the Revolution of 1911, the nascent Republican government. An influential example is the *Journal of Current Pictorial* (时事画报, *Shíshì huàbào*), created in 1905 by the Tongmenghui (中國同盟會, *Zhōngguó tóngménghuì*, Chinese United League), the revolutionary alliance led by Sun Yat-sen. Due to its explicitly political nature, the periodical was censored within the mainland only two years after its founding, though it continued to be published in Hong Kong for several more years, until persistent Qing pressure on the British colonial government eventually forced its discontinuation. After the fall of the Qing dynasty in 1912 and the establishment of the Republic of China, the Tongmenghui resumed its publishing activities on the mainland, launching titles such as *The True Record* (镇乡华宝, *Zhènxiāng Huàbào*) and *Renjian Pictorial* (新闻画报, *Xīnwén huàbào*) in Shanghai.

Nonetheless, censorship did not disappear with the Republican government. The *Renjian Pictorial* was soon banned by the provisional president Yuan Shikai, accused of undermining the legitimacy of the new regime (MobileReference 2007). Despite the climate of ideological control, this period was fertile for the growth of comic art, and numerous authors began to emerge as familiar names to the reading public. It was only in 1925, however, that the term *Manhua* was explicitly used to designate Chinese comics. Feng Zikai (丰子恺, *Fēng Zǐkǎi*) was the pioneer in this respect, employing the term for his collection *Zikai Manhua* (子恺漫画).

From that point onward, *Manhua* consolidated its cultural presence, gaining further prominence with the rise of the Chinese Communist Party (中国共产党, *Zhōngguó Gòngchǎndǎng*, founded in 1921). The Party strategically employed comics as tools of propaganda, mobilizing their visual immediacy to communicate political messages to workers and peasants across China. The trajectory of *Manhua* thus reflects not only artistic innovation but also the broader contradictions of modern Chinese history, situated at the intersection of creativity, ideology, and mass politics.

4.2 Mass Readership—Popular Success and Cultural Impact

The golden age of *Manhua* is usually located between the late 1920s and the mid-1930s, when Shanghai became the most active center of comic production in China. In 1927, *Manhua Hui* (漫画会) was established as the first organization devoted exclusively to comics and animation. Over the span of about fifteen years, it managed to publish no fewer than seventeen magazines. The organization played an important role in shaping the history of Chinese *Manhua* since it fostered cohesion among artists and encouraged the development of serial comics as a collective endeavor.

In 1928, *Modern Sketch* or *Shanghai Sketch* (上海漫画, *Shànghǎi mànhuà*) appeared as the first comic magazine published in Chinese. It is important to note that *Modern Sketch* was deeply influenced by Western comics, particularly by works such as the British satirical publication *Ally Sloper's Half Holiday* (Gilbert Dalziel, 1884) and the American strip *The Yellow Kid* (Richard Outcault, 1896). These cultural borrowings demonstrate that *Manhua* evolved in close dialogue with global visual traditions and modern satirical practices (Hung 2006; Lent 2001).

The artist Zhang Leping (张乐平, *Zhāng Lèpíng*) is considered the most prolific innovator of modern *Manhua*. His work *Sanmao* (三毛, *Sānmáo*), first published in 1935, influenced generations of artists and provided a model for creative experimentation that extended beyond print. In subsequent decades, *Sanmao* inspired television series, puppet animation, video games, and films. A notable example is the animated series *Wanderings of San Mao* (三毛流浪记, *Sān máo liúlàng jì*), broadcast on CCTV14 in 2006, which continues to resonate with audiences today. By the mid-1930s, Shanghai had become the creative hub of *Manhua*, setting a standard that artists in Hong Kong sought to emulate by designing characters inspired by Shanghai's leading figures.

Neither the outbreak of the Sino-Japanese War in 1937, nor the Second World War, nor the later civil conflict between Communists and Nationalists brought *Manhua* production to a halt. On the contrary, comics continued to be published, although their themes increasingly reflected political and wartime concerns (Chen 2010; Lent and Xu 2017). In 1937, the National Salvation Cartoon Propaganda Corps was founded in Shanghai, bringing together artists who resisted Japanese occupation through the production of comics and animations. Well-known figures such as Zhang Leping, Te Wei (特伟), Lu Zhixiang (鲁志祥), Hu Kao (胡考), and Ye Lunqi (叶纶绮) contributed to this effort. Ye Lunqi became particularly renowned for his comics that encouraged military enlistment. With works such as *National Salvation through Comics* (救亡漫, *Jiùwáng màn*) and *Wartime Chongqing* (战时重庆, *Zhàn shí chóngqìng*), he eventually rose to the position of head of the Chinese painting department at the China Central Academy of Fine Arts in 1954, the most prestigious institution of its kind in the country. His satirical representations of figures such as Mussolini as the "genius of evil" served as political warnings directed against Japanese and German fascism.

The early 1950s marked a new phase for *Manhua* in China. With the founding of the People's Republic of China in October 1949, a new political and social environment encouraged the emergence of numerous comic publications covering a wider variety of themes (Lent 2001; Wong 2002; Pang 2012). The dramatic transformations of the preceding years provided artists with fresh opportunities to explore contemporary subjects and to expand the narrative possibilities of the medium. In 1950, the monthly magazine *Manhua* was launched. It succeeded in broadening the creative and technical horizons of Chinese comics and fostered a younger generation of artists who would carry the tradition forward.

However, this climate of experimentation was soon stifled. The nationwide Anti-Rightist Campaign of 1957 led to defamatory accusations against many artists, branding them as sympathizers of conservative or reactionary tendencies. Numerous comic authors were unjustly imprisoned or subjected to forced re-education. The campaign silenced liberal voices and curtailed artistic innovation. By the end of the 1950s, only works that adhered to the political orthodoxy of the left were permitted to circulate. *Manhua* thus became fully subordinated to propaganda, with creativity and dissent sacrificed to ideological conformity (Bai 2019).

4.3 Revolutionary Comics—Suppression, Transformation, and Revival

During the Cultural Revolution (1966–1976), *Manhua* became a central instrument of propaganda and political education. Its simple, repetitive, and highly accessible language made it an effective medium through which the Chinese Communist Party could disseminate ideology even in the most remote and impoverished rural areas of the mainland. At the same time, artists who failed to conform to the dominant ideological line faced severe consequences. One of the most tragic cases was that of Ye Lunqi (叶纶绮), who had earlier contributed to anti-Japanese propaganda commissioned by the Kuomintang. The Red Guards denounced him as a "general" of the Kuomintang, and he was imprisoned for eight years in Qincheng Prison (秦城监狱, *Qín chéng jiānyù*), a maximum-security facility in Beijing. After the end of the Cultural Revolution, Ye was released but was only allowed to work at the China Central Academy of Fine Arts as a janitor, a stark indication of the degradation of cultural elites during that era.

Zhang Leping, the creator of *Sanmao*, also faced persecution. He was prohibited from continuing his work on *Sanmao* for ten years and was harassed by the Red Guards, forced to sign confessions and publicly brand himself as a traitor to the nation. The repression of these artists exemplifies the climate of fear in which cultural production operated, where creative voices were subordinated to political orthodoxy and where the survival of artists often depended on their willingness to self-denounce.

Most works produced during this decade were strictly propagandistic. Examples include *Blue Sea and Red Heart* (1965), based on an original work by Liang Hsin, adapted by Wan Chia-Ch'Un with drawings by Hsu Chin; *Letter from South Vietnam* (1965), adapted from a work by So Sê, Fu To, and Ma Jung, directed by Chen Yunhua and Hu Tsuching; *The Red Detachment of Women* (红色娘子军, *Hóngsè Niángzǐjūn*, 1966), based on a story by Liang Hsin and illustrated by Li Tzushun; *The Opium War*, published in Hong Kong in 1967; *The Girl from the People's Commune*, from an original work by Li Chun with drawings by Ho Yu-chic; and *Following the Traces*, written by An Chung-min and Chu Hsiang-chun, with illustrations by Hao Shih. The themes of these comics revolved around war, revolutionary struggle, and resistance against foreign occupation. Foreigners were typically depicted as villains, while Chinese and Vietnamese women were portrayed as heroines of rebellion and resilience.

This politically saturated era attracted the attention of international scholars and critics. Jean Chesneaux and Umberto Eco studied propaganda comics of the Maoist period, while Gino Nebiolo published *I fumetti di Mao*, a collection that included translations and full reproductions of some of the most iconic works of the time. Their work highlighted the dual function of *Manhua* during the Cultural Revolution as both a tool of indoctrination and a unique cultural artifact of global significance (Chesneaux 1972; Eco 1972; Nebiolo 1971).

The year 1979 marked a turning point with the launch of the Reform and Opening policies. Unexpectedly, official media outlets such as *Renmin Ribao* (人民日报, *People's Daily*) and other national newspapers and cultural magazines began publishing satirical and humorous comics. This signaled a revival of *Manhua* as a form of social commentary and entertainment, in contrast to its previous role as a vehicle of strict ideological orthodoxy.

In the following years, *Manhua* became the subject of academic conferences and cultural debates. These discussions reflected both the renewed vitality of the medium and the perceived need to protect it against the growing influx of foreign comics, particularly Japanese *manga* such as *Doraemon*, *Dragon Ball*, and *Saint Seiya*, which had achieved international popularity. The impact of *manga* on Chinese *Manhua* was profound, influencing not only artistic style and narrative structure but also the organization of the industry and the very structure of the comics market. By the

1980s, the interplay between *manga* and *Manhua* illustrated both the vulnerability and adaptability of Chinese cultural production in an increasingly globalized media landscape (Wong 2002; Lent 2009; Lu 2008).

4.4 Japanese Invasion—Hybrid Forms and Modernization of Comics

The so-called "Japanese invasion" of comics was an undeniable reality in China during the final decades of the twentieth century. Japanese *manga* exerted a profound influence not only on popular tastes but also on the structural development of the domestic comic industry. In order to limit the overwhelming presence of *manga*, the Chinese government introduced specific legislation in 1995 to support the national comics sector. This was the first official policy package directed at fostering local production. Yet this strategy failed for two main reasons. First, funding was distributed without any prior market research, which undermined its effectiveness. Second, comics and animation continued to be regarded in the cultural imagination as secondary arts, suitable primarily for children or as tools of propaganda and education, rather than as forms of sophisticated cultural expression.

Despite these structural and perceptual limitations, Chinese *Manhua* managed to reach international audiences. The leadership's ambition to join the World Trade Organization, formally realized in December 2001, was closely connected to the desire to export national comics into the global market. During the Fifteenth Party Congress in October 2000, the animation and comic sector was formally recognized as a strategic industry for the nation, and within a year it was allocated special funding through the Tenth Five-Year Plan.

Further government investment followed. In 2008, the Ministry of Culture supported a program of 7 million yuan (approximately 845,510 euros) dedicated to the promotion of 101 comic publications. In 2009 the budget was doubled, allowing 108 works to receive financial support. Yet financing alone was not sufficient to revitalize the sector. As commentators noted, what was lacking was an advanced industrial strategy that could combine creativity with commercialization (Shanghai Daily 2010). For this reason, the government engaged prominent *Manhua* authors and storytellers known for their creativity and commercial potential. At the same time, official policy encouraged the development of merchandising, including toys, clothing, and accessories, in order to increase the attractiveness and profitability of comic properties.

With sustained state backing, improved creative quality, and innovative marketing strategies, new comic and animation production companies emerged across more than twenty provinces. Major cities such as Beijing, Shanghai, Guangzhou, Suzhou, Hangzhou, Dalian, and Shenzhen benefitted from preferential policies designed to foster the industry (China Publishing 2009). By the early 2010s, more than 200 universities across China were offering master's programs in animation and comics, demonstrating the growing institutionalization of the field (Lent 2009; Damm 2012).

A striking example of this revitalization is Summer Zoo (夏天岛, *Xiàtiān dǎo*), a production company that benefitted from Ministry of Culture funding. It established a team of thirty renowned comic artists and six writers, including two female artists, Zhu Letao (猪乐桃, Zhū Lètáo) and Xiada (夏达, Xià Dá), both of whom gained recognition in China and abroad. Within a short time, Summer Zoo published twenty *Manhua* with a total circulation of 500,000 copies. Among its most successful titles were *Little Piggy Time Machine* (猪仔仔的时光机, *Zhū zǎizǎi de shíguāng jī*) and *Inheritance* (子不语, *Zǐ bù yǔ*).

The *Inheritance* series illustrates the deep stylistic influence of Japanese *manga*. Summer Zoo managed to place ten of its series in leading Chinese comic magazines, while two of its titles, *Inheritance* and *Confucius Did Not Say*, achieved significant success in Japan itself. Both were published by Shueisha, one of the largest Japanese companies in the manga and animation sector (Shanghai Daily 2010). The circulation of these titles in Japan symbolized a rare moment of reverse cultural flow, in which Chinese comics gained recognition within the homeland of *manga*.

At the same time, the Chinese industry sought to capitalize on the popularity of television animation and film by launching *Manhua* series derived from successful screen properties. One emblematic case is *Pleasant Goat and Big Big Wolf* (喜羊羊与灰太狼, *Xǐ yáng yáng yǔ huī tài láng*), whose immense popularity on television was leveraged to create companion comics aimed at children.

By the late 2000s, the Ministry of Culture reported the existence of around 10,000 companies active in the field of animation and comics between Beijing and Shenzhen, employing more than 200,000 people. In official discourse, the government metaphorically declared "war" on the Japanese invasion, urging Chinese studios to collaborate with companies based in Hong Kong in order to build a united front not only against Japanese *manga* but also against Korean *manhwa* and American comics (Keane 2013; Wu 2020). The state's protective approach demonstrates how *Manhua* became a strategic cultural industry positioned at the intersection of national identity, global competition, and cultural policy.

4.5 Contemporary Manhua—Innovation, Industry, and Identity

Since 2010 the Chinese comic industry has achieved a degree of stability in the domestic market, largely due to improvements in creative quality and the expansion of new multimedia platforms. These developments facilitated the rise of digital comics tailored for diversified audiences and consumption patterns (Jing 2011).

One of the most prominent online platforms for comic distribution has been *dangdang.com*, which offers more than 200,000 book titles and competes directly with major rivals such as Amazon.com and 360buy.com (later rebranded as JD.com).

According to statistics released by the platform, more than 100,000 users purchased comics through *dangdang.com* on a daily basis in the early 2010s. Online sales targeted a more mature readership, contrasting with traditional *Manhua* sold in bookstores and kiosks, which continued to be associated primarily with children.

The year 2010 saw a notable increase in the sales of *Manhua* magazines, with total circulation rising by 60 million copies to reach approximately 100 million in that year alone. Yet comparisons with Japanese publishing underscore the challenges Chinese comics faced. Japan's leading weekly magazine, *Weekly Shōnen Jump* (週刊少年ジャンプ, *Shūkan Shōnen Janpu*), sold around 2.8 million copies per week in 2012. In contrast, the two leading Chinese magazines, *Zhīyīn Màn Kè* (知音漫客, *Zhīyīn màn kè*) and *Comic World* (漫画世界, *Mànhuà shìjiè*), together reached only about 2.6 million copies per month, or roughly 300,000 to 400,000 per week. This disparity demonstrates both the limited scale of the Chinese comics industry and the entrenched dominance of Japanese *manga* (Lu 2011).

Chinese authors nevertheless achieved remarkable success in terms of both readership and economic reward. Since 2006, the *Writers Rich List* (中国作家富豪榜, *Zhōngguó zuòjiā fùháo bǎng*) has ranked Chinese authors by declared income, dedicating a section specifically to comic creators. The 2012 ranking illustrates the growing economic importance of comics. Zheng Yuanjie (郑渊洁, Zhèng Yuānjié), famous for his illustrated novel *Pipilu Story* (皮皮鲁总动员, *Pí pí lǔ zǒngdòngyuán*), topped the list with earnings of 26 million yuan (approximately 3.1 million euros). He was followed by Yang Gongying (杨红樱, Yáng Hóngyīng), whose *Rise Cat Diary* (笑猫日记, *Xiào māo rìjì*) earned 20 million yuan, and Jiangnan (江南), who reported 10 million yuan from his illustrated novel *Dragon* (龙族, *Lóngzú*), which was later adapted into a comic.

Among comic artists, Zhou Hongbin (周洪滨, Zhōu Hóngbīn) ranked first with an income of 18 million yuan, generated primarily from his works *Stealing Star September Day* (偷星九月天, *Tōu xīng jiǔ yuè tiān*) and *Bade Coming* (八德来了, *Bā dé láile*). Zhu Bin (朱斌, Zhū Bīn) followed with 13 million yuan for his popular series *Funny School* (爆笑校园, *Bàoxiào xiàoyuán*). Yung (朱德庸, Zhū Déyōng), a Taiwan-based artist, occupied third place with 7.1 million yuan from titles such as *Pom* (雙響炮, *Shuāngxiǎng pào*) and *City of Ladies* (澀女郎, *Sè nǚláng*). Notably, in 2011 Yung had earned as much as 62 million yuan, a record for the industry. These figures reveal the dramatic improvement in the social status of comic authors, many of whom had begun as students or self-taught artists and rose to prominence solely through their creative output.

The broader ranking further highlights the diversity of styles and approaches. Authors such as Áo Yòuxiáng (敖幼祥, *Wulong Yuan* 乌龙院), Mufeng Chun (*Douro Mainland* 斗罗大陆), Māo Xiǎolè (猫小乐, *A Failure Online* 阿衰on line), and Jimmy (几米, *Star* 星空) consolidated reputations with highly original visual languages. Xiada (夏达), with her acclaimed work *Inheritance* (子不语, *Zǐ bù yǔ*), also entered the top ten with significant earnings. Analysis of these rankings demonstrates that while some creators adopted the stylistic features of Japanese *manga*, many others were recognized precisely for their originality, an attribute highly valued by domestic readers (Bai 2019; Lent and Xu 2017).

Table 4.1 Leading Manhua titles and platforms by recent popularity and Readership *Source* Wikipedia (2024); Investing News (2022); China Daily (2024)

Rank	Title / Platform	Author / Publisher	Popularity or Sales Data
1	*Biao Ren* (*Blades of the Guardians*, 镖人)	Xu Xianzhe (徐先哲); published on New Comics, Tencent Comics, Bilibili and others	Over **2 billion online reads** across more than 50 platforms by 2023; first volume sold more than **100,000 copies** in China within one month; first ten volumes exceeded **1 million copies** sold in print
2	Bilibili Manhua (digital platform)	Bilibili	The **largest legal comics distribution platform** in China, hosting nearly **100,000 titles**; manages the full IP chain (original creation, animation, games, merchandising)
3	*Comic Books About Science Loved by Primary School Students* (*Xiaoxuesheng Chaoxi'ai de Manhua Kexue* 学生潮 × 爱漫画科学)	Chinese educational publishers	Sold over **1 million copies** in 2022

The contemporary *Manhua* industry thus presents a complex picture of cultural hybridity. On the one hand, Japanese *manga* remains a powerful influence and commercial competitor. On the other, Chinese artists have cultivated innovative styles that combine traditional aesthetics with contemporary themes, allowing them to assert cultural distinctiveness in a globalized comics market. The expansion of digital platforms and the institutionalization of *Manhua* within the Chinese creative industries demonstrate its growing significance not only as a form of entertainment but also as an expression of cultural capital and soft power (Wu 2020; Keane 2013) (Table 4.1).

References

Bai, L. 2019. *Comics and propaganda in twentieth-century China*. London: Routledge.

Chen, P. 2010. *Zhongguo manhua shi [History of Chinese comics]*. Beijing: Renmin Chubanshe.

Chesneaux, J. 1972. *China's cultural revolution, 1966–1969*. London: Jonathan Cape.

China Daily. 2024. *Comic books about science loved by primary school students*. Retrieved from https://epaper.chinadaily.com.cn/a/202401/16/WS65a5d37ba310513d4e5627d0.html.

China Heritage Quarterly. 2025. The China Punch (1867). Retrieved from http://www.chinaheritagequarterly.org/features.php?searchterm=030_wagner.inc&issue=030.

China Daily. (2024, January 16). *[Article on Biao Ren / Blades of the Guardians]*. Retrieved from https://epaper.chinadaily.com.cn/a/202401/16/WS65a5d37ba310513d4e5627d0.html.

China Publishing. 2009. *China publishing yearbook*. Beijing: Zhongguo Chuban Nianjian She.

Damm, J. 2012. *The consumption of Japanese comics and animation in China*. Journal of Contemporary Chinese Art 1 (1): 85–102. Retrieved from https://www.tandfonline.com/doi/abs/10.1080/20517051.2012.10768942.

Eco, U. 1972. *Apocalittici e integrati*. Milan: Bompiani.

Hung, M. L. 2006. *The illustrated romance of the Three Kingdoms and the origins of Chinese comics*. Hong Kong: Hong Kong University Press.
Investing News. 2022. *Bilibili Manhua's most popular Chinese comic characters come to life on famous landmark digital screens*. Retrieved from https://investingnews.com/bilibili-manhua-s-most-popular-chinese-comic-characters-come-to-life-on-famous-landmark-digital-screens/.
Jing, C. 2011. The transformation of China's comic industry in the digital era. *Journal of Chinese Arts and Media* 3 (2): 45–63. Retrieved from https://www.tandfonline.com/doi/abs/10.1080/21681058.2011.10521310.
Keane, M. 2013. *Creative industries in China: Art, design and media*. Cambridge: Polity Press.
Lent, J. A. 2001. *Animation in Asia and the Pacific*. Bloomington: Indiana University Press.
Lent, J. A. 2009. *Cartooning in Asia*. New York: Routledge.
Lent, J. A., and Y. Xu. 2017. Chinese animation and comics as resistance. In *Asian popular culture*, ed. J. A. Lent, 85–104. New York: Routledge.
Library of the Chinese Christian Church. 2025. Shezu zhanyan tu (1891). Retrieved from https://lib.exchristian.hk/zhou.html.
Lu, B. 2011. *The development of Chinese comics and their market*. Shanghai: Fudan University Press.
Lu, X. 2008. *Rhetoric of the Chinese cultural revolution: The impact on Chinese thought, culture, and communication*. Columbia: University of South Carolina Press.
Mai Lai Hung. 2006. *The Illustrated Romance of the Three Kingdoms and the origins of Chinese comics*. Hong Kong: Hong Kong University Press.
MobileReference. 2007. *History of Chinese comics and censorship*. MobileReference. Retrieved from https://www.mobilereference.com.
Nebiolo, G. 1971. *I fumetti di Mao*. Milan: Mondadori.
Peng, H. 2011. Picture-reading and visual culture in modern China. *Media Studies Journal of China* 5 (3): 77–95.
Pang, L. 2012. *Creativity and its discontents: China's creative industries and intellectual property rights offences*. Durham: Duke University Press.
Qing, L. 2006. Youth and comics consumption in China. *Journal of Popular Culture Studies in Asia* 2 (1): 33–47.
Shanghai Daily. 2010, June 15. *China doubles subsidies for comics industry*. Retrieved from http://www.shanghaidaily.com/article/article_xinhua.aspx?id=87654.
Wikipedia. 2024. *Biao Ren*. Retrieved December 18, 2025, from https://en.wikipedia.org/wiki/Biao_Ren.
Wong, W. 2002. *Hong Kong comics: A history of manhua*. New York: Princeton Architectural Press.
Wu, X. 2020. Cultural industries and soft power in China. *International Journal of Cultural Policy* 26 (3): 367–384. Retrieved from https://www.tandfonline.com/doi/full/10.1080/10286632.2018.1540123.
Zhou, Y. 2008. Comics and media convergence in China's picture-reading era. *Chinese Journal of Communication* 1 (2): 223–240. Retrieved from https://www.tandfonline.com/doi/abs/10.1080/17544750802263002.

Chapter 5
Market Dynamics and Intellectual Property Regimes

Abstract This chapter analyzes the economic structures and intellectual property regimes that shape the contemporary Chinese animation industry. It situates animation within the broader creative industries, emphasizing its value as both cultural product and market commodity. The discussion maps the animation market across production, derivatives, and merchandising, underlining how profitability often depends less on the films themselves than on toys, licensing, and related sectors. Different modes of production are explored, including state-sponsored studios, private enterprises, and transnational co-productions, which connect Chinese animation to global labor flows. The chapter also highlights the significance of branding, outsourcing, and the clustering of production in industrial parks and creative zones. A central theme is the tension between rapid industrial growth and weak protection of intellectual property. Piracy, counterfeiting, and informal media economies remain structural obstacles, undermining domestic producers even as China dominates the global manufacture of licensed goods. Legal reforms, including copyright law revisions and recent regulations on AI-generated content, illustrate the evolving complexity of intellectual property in the digital era. Ultimately, the chapter demonstrates that the consolidation of intellectual property rights is essential not only for economic sustainability but also for securing cultural legitimacy and global competitiveness in the animation sector.

Keywords Creative industries · Intellectual property · Piracy · Branding · Outsourcing · Derivatives · Copyright law

5.1 Creative Industries—Positioning Animation in the Cultural Economy

Former McDonald's global president Donald Thompson once stated, "We are not in the food service business, we are in the entertainment business" (Tan 2006a, b). This remark highlights how the creative industry has become embedded across all spheres of society and introduces a crucial theme for this study. Animation must today be

© The Author(s), under exclusive license to Springer Nature Switzerland AG 2026
V. De Masi, *A Critical Analysis of China's Animation Industry*, Numanities - Arts and Humanities in Progress 37, https://doi.org/10.1007/978-3-032-18656-0_5

regarded as one of the most significant sectors within the broader entertainment industry. A telling sign is the prevalence of animated characters in the merchandise tied to food service companies. China is no exception. For instance, McDonald's Happy Meals frequently feature toys based on popular domestic animations such as *Pleasant Goat and Big Big Wolf* as well as internationally recognized franchises.

The concept of the creative industry was first articulated by John Howkins in *The Creative Economy: How People Make Money from Ideas*, where he argued that creative industries provide products of cultural, artistic, and entertainment value alongside a wide range of associated services (Howkins 2013). In advanced economies, cultural policy has increasingly emphasized this sector. One of the first major initiatives of the British government under Tony Blair in 1997 was the establishment of a special task force to design strategies for promoting creative industries and securing sustainable economic growth. After intensive deliberations, the task force published two influential reports between 1998 and 2001 through the Department for Culture, Media and Sport (DCMS). These reports defined creative industries as "those industries which have their origin in individual creativity, skill and talent and which have a potential for wealth and job creation through the generation and exploitation of intellectual property" (DCMS 2001).

The range of sectors included under this definition is extensive, encompassing advertising, architecture, art and antiques, crafts, design, fashion, film and video, interactive entertainment software, music, performing arts, publishing, software, computer games, television, and radio. While animation and comics are not explicitly mentioned, they are closely intertwined with nearly all of the listed domains.

In the United Kingdom, creative industries became the second largest contributor to national wealth after financial services, serving as an engine of economic growth and a mechanism for reducing unemployment. The United States was even earlier in conceptualizing and institutionalizing the "copyright industry" to both protect its products and transform them into a major source of revenue (Siwek 2006). In China, by contrast, creative industries only began to receive systematic protection in 1991, which marked the beginning of an official discourse on "cultural industries" and copyright law.

The year 1992 represented a turning point for Chinese animation. In that year, the General Office of the State Council and the Central Committee of the Chinese Communist Party (CCP) jointly decided to promote the development of the tertiary sector. As part of this process, China joined several international agreements safeguarding intellectual property rights and later entered the World Trade Organization (WTO) in 2001. By 2000, the Chinese government had already begun to frame animation explicitly within the discourse of creative industries.

The expression "cultural industries" appeared prominently in the political lexicon in the report delivered at the 16th Party Congress on November 8, 2002. The report emphasized that only through the urgent strengthening and expansion of cultural enterprises could socialist culture flourish and the cultural and spiritual needs of the people be met. From 2002 onward, a genuine process of transformation unfolded, with the state encouraging the development of animation and video games as core elements of the new cultural economy.

Michael Wolf's *The Entertainment Economy* further underscored that cultural industries provide not only economic benefits but also profound social and cultural ones. Through entertainment, individuals find relaxation, develop hobbies, and build new social relationships. Entertainment is thus capable of interpreting and communicating with the world while addressing both material and immaterial (spiritual) needs. The search for experience and happiness, Wolf argued, places a responsibility on the entertainment economy to produce not merely material commodities but immaterial goods that sustain wellbeing (Wolf 1999).

More recently, scholars have emphasized that the creative industries, including animation, have become central to national strategies of soft power and global influence (Keane and Chen 2019; UNESCO 2022). In China, the annual *China Cultural Industry Development Report* highlights animation, gaming, and digital audiovisual production as growth engines within the cultural sector, with revenues surpassing 300 billion RMB by 2023 (China Cultural Industry Association 2023). This demonstrates not only their economic impact but also their expanding role in shaping cultural diplomacy and everyday consumer life.

5.2 Mapping the Animation Market—Structures and Trends

The Chinese animation industry represents a particularly valuable object of analysis for several reasons. Most importantly, it is deeply interconnected with other creative sectors, including cinema, advertising, gaming, online platforms, and their derivatives. Animation is uniquely versatile, able to circulate across traditional and new platforms alike, from television and cinema to print and digital media. Over time, it has also developed distinctive narrative and aesthetic languages by drawing inspiration from video games, theatre, and live-action cinema (Bitatti 2010).

International market analysis demonstrates that animation has become a cornerstone of the global information and communication technology (ICT) economy. In the United States, exports of animated content and related products have historically outperformed the total annual revenue of companies such as Microsoft, and the combined revenues from animation and video games exceed those of Hollywood film production (Napier 2018). The global sector continues to expand, underscoring its centrality to digital economies.

As early as 2006, Zhang Songlin, then vice president of the China Animation Association, observed that the domestic industry faced a critical shortage of skilled professionals. He estimated that 250,000 specialists were needed, with 150,000 in animated film and television, and 100,000 in computer game production. Yet, China was producing only about three hundred animation graduates annually, far fewer than South Korea. Despite this shortfall, China was already responsible for processing and producing approximately one third of the world's animation, as nearly 90% of global animation production was outsourced to Asia. Zhang recalled that 40 years earlier

Princess Iron Fan had inspired Osamu Tezuka, the father of Japanese anime, and questioned when Chinese animation would reach the level of Hayao Miyazaki 宫崎骏 (China Youth Daily 2006).

By the early 2010s, however, the situation had begun to shift, particularly with regard to production, distribution, and education. Chinese universities increasingly offered animation programs, while economic reforms linked the sector more closely to state development strategies. As living standards rose, consumer purchasing power expanded, fueling demand for cultural products and creating a significant market for both domestic and foreign animation.

In 2010, Chinese animation companies could broadly be divided into two categories. Smaller studios remained financially fragile and lacked a strong market identity, while larger, established companies sought to restructure the sector through mergers, capital investment, and municipal incentives. Local and central governments promoted the clustering of production facilities in specific regions, fostering competition between provinces (Lu 2011a, b). Historically dominated by the Shanghai Animation Film Studio and China Central Television (CCTV), the sector diversified after 1998 as provinces including Shandong, Guangxi, Hunan, Guangdong, Tianjin, and Hubei entered the market.

According to Entgroup (2010), the Chinese animation market was valued at 20.8 billion yuan (2.5 billion euros) in 2010, marking a 26% increase over the previous year. Of this, 5.5 billion yuan (655 million euros) derived from broadcasting and distribution, and 15.3 billion yuan (1.8 billion euros) from merchandising. By this time, however, foreign companies controlled more than 80% of China's domestic animation market, with Japan, the United States, the United Kingdom, and South Korea dominating.

China's broadcasting infrastructure played a significant role in shaping demand. By 2011, there were approximately 2557 television stations in China. Channels such as CCTV-14 and Kaku TV specialized in children's programming, while nearly 300 stations maintained children's sections and around 200 regularly broadcast animation (Zhao 2011). At the global level, the total value of animation and related products in 2012 was estimated at USD 722.8 billion, of which USD 500 billion came from merchandising. In the United Kingdom, the creative entertainment sector accounted for 7.9% of GDP, making it the largest industrial contributor (RIC 2013).

Demographics underscored the scale of the Chinese market. Out of a population of 1.35 billion in 2010, approximately 351 million people under the age of 30 were identified as potential animation consumers (Wang 2011). Other estimates placed the number of citizens under 16 at around 360 million (UK Trade 2010), suggesting an overall consumer base of nearly 500 million (Zhao 2011). These figures positioned China as one of the most promising markets for animation and gaming worldwide.

Despite its potential, the sector has been characterized by high capital intensity, constant technological innovation, and significant risks. In 2010, China produced 385 animated television series and at least eight feature-length films, totaling 220,529 min of content, an increase of 28% from 2009. The Ministry of Culture projected that the animation industry could generate 100 billion yuan (12 billion euros), yet the domestic market remained fragile, heavily reliant on imported products and intellectual property (Propaganda Department 2010).

Leading animation companies such as CCTV Animation and Kaku TV increasingly outsourced production to studios located in government-funded creative industry parks. These clusters were designed to integrate television, cinema, and new media production under one industrial ecosystem (Yongjiang 2010).

Four main factors explain why the Chinese government identified animation and video games as strategic industries for the twenty-first century. First, the domestic market was saturated with foreign products, leading to dependence on international brands that profited from derivative merchandise. Second, China had long been a global outsourcing hub, producing high-quality animation at low labor costs. Third, Chinese animators possessed professional expertise developed through years of subcontracted work, which could be redirected toward domestic production. Fourth, although China remained a major outsourcing destination, it faced growing competition from Vietnam, India, and North Korea, where costs were even lower.

Industry observers distinguish three levels within the animation sector (Niu 2011). The basic level includes cartoons, audio-visual products, books, and stage performances. The peripheral level encompasses mobile and online animation, theme parks, advertising, and exhibition services. The related level consists of toys, gaming machines, clothing, stationery, hardware and software development, retail, and food products. Data from the State Administration of Radio, Film, and Television (SARFT 2009) in 2009 highlighted the scale of ancillary markets: 60 billion yuan (7.15 billion euros) in stationery, 90 billion yuan (10.7 billion euros) in children's clothing, 20 billion yuan (2.4 billion euros) in toys, 10 billion yuan (1.19 billion euros) in children's books and audiobooks, and 35 billion yuan (4.2 billion euros) in children's food products (Zhang 2011).

Despite such impressive figures, the dominance of foreign brands remained evident, with most licensed merchandise featuring international characters rather than domestic ones. Closing this gap has since become a central objective of Chinese cultural policy. More recent reports confirm that while China's animation output exceeded 200,000 min annually by the mid-2010s, international intellectual property continued to dominate consumer markets (Animation Industry Report 2023). Nevertheless, government-backed initiatives such as the "National Animation and Game Industry Base" and the rapid expansion of streaming platforms have created new opportunities for domestic productions to gain visibility both at home and abroad (China Animation & Comic Industry Report 2024).

5.3 Modes of Production—Industrial and Creative Logics

The productive strength of the Chinese animation sector has historically been concentrated in the creation of television series and programs, with web and mobile formats in second place and cinema representing only a minor share of total output. In the early 2000s, success in animated television was measured less in terms of direct profit and more in terms of the ability to enhance the popularity and reputation of broadcasters. Popular animated programs were used strategically to build a strong media image, which could then open new market opportunities (Tan 2006a, b). Yet animation has always been more than television content: it generates characters and visual properties that, when protected by copyright, acquire immense added value. The global cases of Sanrio's *Hello Kitty* and Disney's *Mickey Mouse*, the latter continuously profitable since his creation in 1928, demonstrate that animation operates simultaneously as an economic engine and as cultural heritage.

Chinese authorities understood this dual role early on. A 2005 report by the Central Propaganda Department explicitly emphasized that animation, through its dissemination and derivative products, should become embedded in the social life of the nation. It was expected to shape values, strengthen education, and foster a national culture consistent with the goals of soft power (Tan Ling 2006). Policy thus framed animation not merely as entertainment but as a tool with cultural and ideological functions.

The rise of 3D computer graphics provided new impetus to the industry, allowing many Chinese studios to shift from traditional 2D methods to digital 3D animation in only a few years. Yet this transition created new challenges. Production costs for 3D were estimated at 30–50% higher than for 2D, and work cycles were significantly longer (Qing 2006). To control expenses, many studios reduced the quality of imagery and motion, which undermined the effectiveness of 3D. Characters lacked detail, movements appeared stiff, and audiences remained lukewarm. The paradox was that the most beloved domestic property, *Pleasant Goat and Big Big Wolf*, was a 2D Flash production, while most Japanese animations continued to rely on 2D as well. This demonstrated that popularity depended less on technology than on narrative quality and character development.

The structural weakness of the 3D transition was compounded by the economics of television distribution. Selling a series to a broadcaster typically covered only around 10% of production costs, leaving the remaining 90% dependent on copyright and merchandising (Tan 2006a, b). By the early 2010s, the national broadcasting landscape included 247 national television stations, 2120 channels, and 44 dedicated educational channels. Cable reached 187 million users and digital cable 89 million, with coverage extending to 97.6% of the population (Lu Bin 2011). Yet profitability remained limited.

By 2008, official statistics recorded nearly 5000 registered animation companies in China, with a combined capital of 11.8 billion yuan (1.4 billion euros). Among these, 298 specialized in television animation and 68 in film, compared to only 35 film-focused companies a few years earlier. On October 12, 2013, SARFT announced that September alone had seen the production of 60 animated television series totaling 38,489 min, divided into multiple genres (Table 5.1).

From 2004 onward, SARFT strictly controlled the approval of animation projects, with production impossible without state authorization. Each year, large numbers of projects were approved, yet many never materialized (Table 5.2).

The discrepancy between projected and actual output demonstrates the difficulty of sustaining industrial growth. By 2012, only 395 series were completed (222,938

Table 5.1 Genres of Chinese television animation produced in September 2013 *Source* SARFT 2013

Genre	Number of Series	Minutes	Percentage (%)
Historical	1	3000	7.8
Fantasy	29	18,894	49.1
Educational	12	8360	21.7
Realist	6	2522	6.6
Science fiction	3	1706	4.4
Other genres	9	4007	10.4
Total	**60**	**38,489**	**100**

Table 5.2 SARFT-approved projects and actual animation production (2004–2012) *Source SARFT official data*

Year	Series Approved	Estimated Minutes	Series Produced	Actual Minutes
2004	158	155,520	29	21,819
2005	403	575,718	83	42,759
2006	410	413,365	124	82,326
2007	339	305,510	186	101,900
2008	384	322,926	249	131,042
2009	460	428,879	322	171,816
2010	601	595,299	385	220,529
2011	566	491,814	435	261,244
2012	580	470,721	395	222,938

min), far below the 580 series and 470,721 min projected. Production had increased tenfold since 2004, but the ratio of projected to actual production remained around 3:1.

Geographically, production was concentrated in a few provinces. In 2012, Guangdong, Jiangsu, Zhejiang, Fujian, and Anhui accounted for nearly 70% of total national output (Table 5.3).

At the municipal level, cities such as Suzhou, Guangdong, Dongguan, Fuzhou, and Hangzhou led the nation in minutes produced, reflecting the rise of regional clusters (Table 5.4).

Table 5.3 Leading animation-producing provinces in China (2012) 2012 *Source* SARFT official data

Province	Series	Minutes Produced
Guangdong	57	48,542
Jiangsu	54	47,923
Zhejiang	52	33,784
Fujian	55	22,640
Anhui	53	12,000+

Table 5.4 Top ten cities by animation production (2012) 2012 *Source* SARFT official data

City	Series	Minutes Produced
Suzhou	47	24,737
Guangdong	29	20,471
Dongguan	8	15,214
Fuzhou	27	14,866
Hangzhou	25	13,371
Hefei	29	12,845
Wuxi	19	12,092
Shenzhen	18	11,957
Ningbo	17	11,652
Beijing	23	9950

The year 2012 thus marked the historical peak of Chinese animation measured by minutes of production. Yet this model was unsustainable. Large numbers of low-quality series failed to achieve market impact, television revenues remained insufficient, and international intellectual properties continued to dominate domestic consumer culture.

By the mid-2010s, the emphasis shifted from maximizing production volume to creating high-value intellectual properties. Streaming platforms such as Bilibili (哔哩哔哩), Tencent Video (腾讯视频), iQiyi (爱奇艺), and Youku (优酷) became the primary channels for animation distribution. These platforms integrated animation with gaming, online literature, and fan culture, transforming the sector into an ecosystem of franchising and transmedia storytelling.

Recent statistics confirm this transition. In 2023, official data recorded 156 animated television series comprising 4632 episodes and 93,811 min, less than half of the minutes produced in 2012 (National Bureau of Statistics of China 2024). Yet the value of the industry had grown exponentially, surpassing 300 billion yuan (≈ US$41.2 billion) in 2023 (Vidico 2025). By 2025, China accounted for 34.5% of the Asia–Pacific animation market (Motionplay Studio 2025).

The success of cinematic animation underscores this qualitative shift. *Boonie Bears* (熊出没, *Xióng chūmò*) established enduring domestic franchises, while *Ne Zha* (2019) became the highest-grossing domestic animation in history at the time. In 2024, *Ne Zha 2* reached a milestone as the first Chinese animated film to enter the global top five of all-time box office rankings. *Chang'an* (长安三万里, *Cháng'ān sānwànlǐ*, 2023) further demonstrated the ability of Chinese studios to produce long-format 3D animation of artistic depth and cultural ambition.

By 2025, Chinese animation was no longer defined by the number of minutes produced. Its strength lay in the development of intellectual property, integration across digital platforms, and its growing role as a vector of soft power on the global stage. The transition from quantity to quality, from television dependence to transmedia ecosystems, illustrates the maturation of an industry now positioned at the core of China's cultural and creative economy.

5.4 Coproductions—Transnational Alliances and Co-Creation

In October 2013, SARFT issued a statement reaffirming its commitment to encouraging Sino-foreign animation coproductions in accordance with the "Regulations on Sino-Foreign Coproductions of Drama (Television Series, Animation, and Cinema)" (SARFT Order No. 41). These regulations, in place since 2004, were designed to facilitate the export of Chinese animation while simultaneously raising the quality of domestic productions. In practice, the results were mixed. While technical standards improved, many coproduced works continued to suffer from unclear or fragmented narratives, illustrating the difficulties of balancing financial and policy objectives with creative innovation.

Coproductions nevertheless offered several advantages. They provided solutions to the chronic problem of financing, enabled distribution in the foreign partner's markets, and raised the creative level of domestic industries by exposing them to international expertise. One of the earliest examples was the collaboration between Taiwan's Central Pictures Corporation (中影股份有限公司, *Zhōngyǐng gǔfèn yǒuxiàn gōngsī*) and the Shanghai Animation Film Studio on *The Butterfly Lovers* (蝴蝶夢-梁山伯與祝英台, *Liáng Shānbó yǔ Zhù Yīngtái*), which won the Best Art Film prize at the 14th Golden Rooster Awards (中国电影金鸡奖最佳美术片, *Zhōngguó diànyǐng Jīnjī jiǎng zuì jiā měishùpiàn*) in 2005 (Chang 2008). Other early coproductions included *The Children of Captain Grant* (格兰特船长的儿女, *Gélántè chuánzhǎng de érnǚ*), a Sino-German collaboration, and *Thru the Moebius Strip* (魔比斯环, *Móbǐsī huán*), a Sino-Hong Kong project, both nominated in the same year.

A landmark case came in 2007 with *The Secret of the Magic Gourd* (宝葫芦的秘密, *Bǎo húlu de mìmì*), a coproduction between Disney Studios, Hong Kong's Centro Digital Pictures Limited (先濤數碼企畫有限公司, *Xiāntāo shùmǎ qǐhuà yǒuxiàn gōngsī*), and the China Film Group Corporation (中国电影集团公司, *Zhōngguó diànyǐng jítuán gōngsī*). It was Disney's first CGI film aimed directly at the Chinese market and achieved notable domestic success (Colapinto 2010). Other projects, such as *The Warrior* (黃飛鴻勇闖天下, *Huáng Fēihóng yǒng chuǎng tiānxià*), continued to blend international collaboration with Chinese traditional aesthetics.

During the same period, Oriental DreamWorks (东方梦工厂, *Dōngfāng mèng gōngchǎng*) emerged as a high-profile example of foreign investment in China. Based in Shanghai, the studio was a joint venture in which Chinese investors—including China Media Capital (华人文化产业基金, *Huárén wénhuà chǎnyè jījīn*), Shanghai Media Group (上海东方传媒集团, *Shànghǎi dōngfāng chuánméi jítuán*), and Shanghai Alliance Investment (上海联和投资有限公司, *Shànghǎi liánhé tóuzī yǒuxiàn gōngsī*), held 55% of the shares, while DreamWorks Animation retained 45%. The studio's projects included *Kung Fu Panda 3* (2016) and other large-scale film and television productions.

Television coproductions also proliferated. Notable examples included *The Romance of the Three Kingdoms*, a collaboration between Beijing Glorious Animation, CCTV-14, and Japanese partners Takara Tomy and Future Planet; and *Shaolin Kids*, coproduced by Shanghai Fantasia Animation and the French studio Les Cartooneurs Associés, which aired successfully in both China and France and was later sold to broadcasters in thirty countries (UK Trade 2010).

These early cases illustrate the state's role in using coproduction as a strategy to strengthen technical capacity and to position animation as an exportable cultural product. However, by the mid-2010s the logic of coproduction began to shift. Foreign studios increasingly sought access to the Chinese market, attracted by the extraordinary box office revenues of domestic animated films. The success of *Ne Zha* (2019) signaled a turning point, and in 2024 *Ne Zha 2* achieved unprecedented success, becoming the first Chinese animated feature to enter the global top five of all-time box office rankings. Crucially, the majority of its revenues were generated in the domestic market, underscoring the centrality of China in the global animation economy.

This explains why many international companies, from Hollywood studios to Japanese production houses, are eager to coproduce with Chinese partners or establish local studios. Entering into collaboration allows them to share in what has become the largest and most dynamic segment of the global animation market. Yet significant barriers remain. Foreign content faces strict import quotas, censorship, and cultural adaptation requirements. Coproduction thus functions not only as a creative partnership but also as a pragmatic mechanism for foreign firms to navigate China's regulatory environment.

By 2025, coproductions have evolved from state-driven initiatives designed to raise domestic standards into strategic gateways for international firms seeking access to the Chinese market. While China benefits from the influx of capital, technology, and global distribution channels, it also maintains tight control over foreign influence, ensuring that animation remains a vehicle of cultural sovereignty as well as economic growth.

5.5 Export Strategies—Reaching Global Audiences

In the previous section, coproduction was described as a means of disseminating Chinese animation abroad, since shared production could be interpreted as a form of export. Yet for most of the 2000s, direct export of Chinese animated content remained limited. The industry was fragmented and lacked the organizational coherence necessary to compete internationally. Even if such structural challenges had been overcome, another obstacle remained: the global animation market was dominated by the United States and Japan, both of which had decades of experience, established distribution networks, and franchises that had achieved worldwide recognition. Against such giants, Chinese productions initially struggled to find a foothold.

During the early 2000s, Chinese animated products attracted little attention from foreign audiences, making exports difficult. The most receptive markets were neighboring Asian countries with cultural affinities, such as Taiwan, Hong Kong, Singapore, Malaysia, Thailand, and Vietnam. Official statistics from 2007, reported in the Blue Book of Chinese Animation (2008), indicated that 30 series were exported abroad, totaling 2244 episodes, an increase of 11.1% compared with 2006. Revenues rose by 42.8% to approximately 73.5 million yuan (9 million euros). The main markets at that time were Europe and North America.

Several major studios led these early export efforts. Zhongnan Animation Group (浙江中南卡通股份有限公司, *Zhèjiāng Zhōngnán kǎtōng gǔfèn yǒuxiàn gōngsī*) produced *Sky Eye* (天眼, *Tiānyǎn*), which sold broadcast rights to twenty foreign networks and earned 15 million yuan (1.8 million euros). Shanghai Media Group exported *Little Health* (小康康, *Xiǎo Kāngkāng*) and *The Bug* (虫虫, *Chóngchóng*), the latter a 335-episode series reminiscent of Disney's *A Bug's Life*. Sunchime Cartoon Group distributed *The 3000 Whys of Blue Cat* (蓝猫三千问, *Lán Māo Sānqiān Wèn*) in thirty-six countries, including the United States, the United Kingdom, Taiwan, and South Korea, earning around 65 million yuan (9 million euros). Shanghai Fantasia Studio, founded by Zhang Tianxiao, a Chinese animator based in France, exported works with a distinct Franco-European aesthetic. Its coproduction *Shaolin Kids* with the French studio Les Cartooneurs Associés sold for 5 million euros in broadcast rights and was distributed widely across Europe. Other projects, such as *Marsupilami* (from the Belgian comic by André Franquin), *Martin Matin*, *Malo Korrigan and the Space Tracers*, and *Les Minijusticiers*, highlighted how Fantasia Studio specialized in bridging Chinese animation with European cultural frameworks, ensuring successful broadcast across European and Canadian networks.

The Ministry of Culture supported these efforts by encouraging studios to attend international festivals, including the Tokyo International Anime Fair and the Angoulême Comics Festival in France. By 2009, SARFT reported that revenues from exported films and television series had increased by 150% compared with 2008, reaching 22.4 million euros (30 million USD). Seventy-nine products, amounting to 1490 h of content, were sold abroad—representing 14% of total Chinese animated television output. Flagship exports included *Blue Cat*, *Sky Eye*, and *Pleasant Goat*.

Europe also became a strategic partner. Atlantyca Entertainment, based in Milan, acquired exclusive distribution rights for CCTV Animation's *Monkey King* (孙悟空, *Sūn Wùkōng*), a 52-episode series, across Europe. In 2010, Atlantyca even opened a branch in China to facilitate cultural exchange and support the circulation of Chinese products in European markets. At the same time, exports expanded modestly into Africa, Latin America, and the Middle East. Though economic returns from these regions were limited, they served as test markets that could provide future growth opportunities.

The 2010s saw further progress under the government's "going out" (走出去, *zǒu chūqù*) strategy, which encouraged animation studios to pursue global markets. While successes were still partial, the trend was positive, and the visibility of Chinese animation at international fairs steadily increased.

By the 2020s, the situation had changed dramatically. The growth of online platforms allowed Chinese animation to circulate globally with greater ease, while the international success of feature-length films provided an entirely new scale of visibility. *Ne Zha* (2019) became the highest-grossing Chinese animated film to date, while *Chang'an* (长安三万里, *Cháng'ān sānwànlǐ*, 2023) showcased long-format 3D production with artistic depth. The release of *Ne Zha 2* marked a historic turning point: it entered the global all-time top five box office rankings, with the majority of its earnings generated in the domestic market. This underscored the centrality of China as not merely an exporter but as the largest and most lucrative animation market in the world.

The implication is clear. Today, foreign studios, from Hollywood majors to Japanese anime companies, compete to enter the Chinese market through coproduction, joint ventures, or localized distribution. Yet they face structural limitations. Import quotas restrict the number of foreign animated films permitted annually, content censorship applies stringent rules, and cultural adaptation remains a constant challenge. For this reason, coproduction often functions as the primary pathway for foreign companies to access Chinese audiences, while direct exports remain tightly regulated.

By 2025, China's trajectory in animation exports illustrates both transformation and paradox. From modest beginnings in the 2000s, when products like *Blue Cat* and *Sky Eye* struggled to achieve international recognition, the country has matured into the largest global animation market. However, the balance of power has shifted: whereas China once sought to export abroad, today it is foreign companies who seek to "import themselves" into China, recognizing that success in the world's largest market is increasingly indispensable to their global strategies.

5.6 Advances in AI Video and Digital Animation—China's Technological Edge

The most recent phase of Chinese media innovation reveals a fast maturing ecosystem for generative video and image technologies that bridges laboratory research, platform integration, and industrial deployment. The development pipeline now spans foundation models built by large tech firms and open research consortia, creator facing tools embedded in short video platforms, and production pilots that move from commercial promotion to serialized narrative content. This integration is visible in the trajectory of Vidu by ShengShu Technology and Tsinghua University, a text to video model that has entered international co-production through a strategic partnership with Aura Productions for a fifty episode science fiction anime series slated for distribution on global social media in 2025 (SCMP 2025). The announcement positions Chinese model makers as creative partners for Hollywood oriented studios and argues that multi subject consistency can sustain character continuity across a long running short form series. Vidu was previously used for a Chinese market trailer of *Venom: The Last Dance* and was integrated into Baidu's Qianfan platform, which signals an enterprise path for multimodal applications within the Baidu cloud ecosystem. The same company publicized collaboration with AMD's China unit to accelerate personal computer oriented AI applications, suggesting a hardware aware strategy for diffusion (SCMP 2025).

The state broadcaster has already showcased a complete production workflow guided by generative models. In February 2024 China Media Group aired *Qianqiu Shisong* (千秋诗颂), a twenty six episode series that retells classical poems through animated shorts. The project employed CMG Media GPT co-developed with the Shanghai Artificial Intelligence Laboratory and was described as AI supported across production areas from asset generation to assembly. The broadcast marks a threshold event in which public media endorses AI animation as a legitimate form and not only as an experiment (SCMP 2024).

The broader market features a competitive field of domestic video generation models. Kuaishou's Kling AI has iterated quickly and has been framed as a globally accessible beta by mid 2024 while continuing to add features for reference guided character control in 2025. Tencent's HunyuanVideo has been released as a large open source text to video model and aims to match commercial benchmarks while enabling community scale experimentation. These trajectories underscore a Chinese strategy that mixes open releases with platform embedded services (Reuters 2024a, b).

Another notable vector involves Bilibili's open source anime video initiative AniSora. The project advances one click generation of anime shots from images and short prompts and has moved through public versions with growing support for longer shots and richer motion. The toolchain is optimized for anime aesthetics and aligns with Bilibili's role as a broadcaster and community for donghua 动画. This dual role suggests a feedback loop in which platform data, creator practices, and model refinement reinforce each other (AniSora Studio 2024).

The industrial context also includes the explosive growth of micro drama *duanju* (短剧), a format of vertically framed serials optimized for mobile viewing and algorithmic distribution. Reports in 2024 estimated a multibillion yuan market that continues to scale. Platform earnings statements and industry coverage in 2025 highlight short dramas and AI generated clips as growth engines. The link to generative tools is practical rather than rhetorical since AI supports rapid asset creation, storyboard iteration, background replacement, and synthetic performers for teasers and ad spots. The relationship is not uniform across all productions but it is structurally significant for speed and cost (Reuters 2024a, b).

The regulatory environment has evolved in lockstep with these advances. On March 14, 2025 Chinese regulators issued Measures for the labeling of AI generated synthetic content that define explicit and implicit labels and clarify platform and provider responsibilities. The policy enters into force on September 1, 2025 and seeks to promote transparency, traceability, and a healthy industry ecology. This framework sits alongside earlier rules on deep synthesis and interim measures for generative AI services and puts specific emphasis on video, images, audio, and virtual scenes. For cultural production the likely consequence is a normalization of disclosure and watermarking across broadcast and platform circulation rather than an outright limitation on creative use (CAC 2025).

Taken together these developments point to a layered map of production. Fully AI generated works include *Qianqiu Shisong* where generative models contribute across most stages from concept visualization to shot rendering and compositing within a broadcaster controlled pipeline. Hybrid productions include promotional materials such as the *Venom: The Last Dance* Chinese trailer that employ Vidu for animated segments while relying on conventional editorial and sound pipelines. Emerging serial collaborations such as the planned Aura Productions partnership indicate an intermediate path in which AI tools drive layout, motion, and character consistency while human teams shape story, voice direction, and final polish (SCMP 2025).

The creative and economic implications are complex. On the supply side Chinese models reduce time and personnel requirements for previsualization and short form output which fits the economic logic of micro dramas and social video marketing. On the demand side the aesthetic of AI generated motion can either signal novelty or risk sameness if training priors dominate style space. On the labor side new hybrid roles emerge that combine prompt design, reference curation, and shot supervision with traditional animation skills. These shifts invite a reconsideration of authorship in an environment where model builders, platform integrators, and showrunners co produce style and narrative cadence.

There are also limits and frictions. Research groups and watchdog projects have shown that high quality lip synchronization and expressive facial performance remain challenging in many consumer level pipelines in China which affects dubbing heavy genres and international distribution. This weakness narrows for top tier industrial users but it remains visible in platform scale content where speed trumps nuance. In parallel, the state encourages adoption while policing misuse and low quality outputs, which produces a negotiation between innovation and ideological management (China Media Project 2024).

The Vidu case is emblematic. ShengShu promotes multi subject consistency for episodic continuity and accelerates delivery claims by generating short clips within seconds. The project with Aura Productions frames AI as a bridge between Asian anime languages and Hollywood narrative economies and it tests whether a Chinese model can anchor a franchise oriented format for North American youth. Success would validate a cross regional pipeline in which Chinese AI provides technical backbone and American teams steer plot and brand development. Failure would most likely arise from narrative thinness, animation artifacts under distribution scale compression, or regulatory hurdles around disclosure and rights (SCMP 2025).

A final trend involves open source circulation and community experimentation. Tencent's HunyuanVideo release and Bilibili's AniSora suggest a willingness to externalize model weights and invite third party development while ByteDance pushes consumer apps such as Jimeng AI that fold creation into the existing editing and distribution stack around CapCut and short video apps. This blend of open and proprietary channels is a distinctive Chinese pattern that spreads the cost of experimentation while ensuring that winning features can be re absorbed into platform products (HunyuanVideo Repo 2024).

In sum the Chinese field of AI video and animation is not a single breakthrough story but an industrial ensemble that now spans state media, major platforms, and entrepreneurial studios. It is anchored by domestic model capacity, tempered by a tightening yet enabling regulatory regime, and energized by formats in which speed and volume matter as much as spectacle. The next phase will test whether AI supported series can sustain character and world consistency at scale and whether creators can leverage these tools to expand rather than standardize the expressive range of Chinese animation.

5.7 Copyright in Context—Regulation, Law, and Dispute

Chinese animation has long been a source of inspiration for artists worldwide, creating a stylistic and cultural identity unmatched in the history of the medium. The so-called "Chinese School" of animation, particularly before the Cultural Revolution, was renowned for its strong artistic sensibility and distinct cultural imprint, making it instantly recognizable on the international stage (Qing 2006; Tan 2006a, b). Over the years, however, this distinctive artistic tradition has diminished as animation became increasingly integrated into the wider framework of the creative industries.

The animation market can be divided into three interrelated levels: first, the broadcasting of animation itself; second, publishing and audiovisual products derived from animation; and third, the merchandising of animated characters through toys, food products, clothing, stationery, and other goods. The second and third levels are the most profitable but also the most vulnerable to counterfeiting and piracy in China. All government support for production and distribution has limited impact if piracy is not addressed. Weak coordination among companies and a lack of industry-wide collaboration further undermine value creation, preventing the establishment of a coherent production and distribution chain.

International comparisons highlight the structural weaknesses of China's copyright enforcement. South Korea provides a striking contrast. For more than 15 years, the Korean government has implemented a comprehensive industrial plan for animation, protecting intellectual property through strict copyright laws, compensation mechanisms, and harsh penalties for infringement. As a result, South Korea succeeded in revitalizing its domestic industry and building a globally competitive export sector. In China, by contrast, the absence of industry associations and an effective copyright enforcement body has left companies vulnerable and unstable.

The value of intellectual property is evident worldwide. Disney's *Mickey Mouse* continues to generate immense revenues nearly a century after his creation, and Sanrio's *Hello Kitty* has become a global merchandising phenomenon. Chinese animation, if effectively protected, could similarly serve as both an economic and cultural symbol. Instead, most derivative profits flow to American and Japanese companies, leaving little space for domestic products. Although China is the world's largest producer of derivative goods for international creative industries, manufacturing around 70% of global toys under foreign licenses, its domestic animation sector captures only a small fraction of this value.

To address these challenges, the Chinese government established the Alliance Entertainment Development on June 18, 2004, bringing together key industry representatives to promote copyright awareness, train animation professionals, assist with registration procedures, and create favorable conditions for licensing and exports. This initiative signaled official recognition that without stronger copyright enforcement, investments in creativity would not yield sustainable returns.

The rise of new media made the copyright issue even more urgent. By January 2013, the China Internet Network Information Center (CNNIC 2013) reported 564 million internet users, of whom 420 million accessed online content via mobile devices. Approximately 65% used the internet for web video, and 60% for online gaming. This meant that nearly 336 million people, almost equal to the entire population of the European Union, were watching video online. Yet piracy undermined this potential: in 2006, an estimated 90% of games and animations sold in China were pirated, resulting in significant losses for production companies.

Recent developments indicate both progress and persistent challenges. The 2021 revision of China's Copyright Law strengthened protections for digital works, expanding the scope of protected content and raising penalties for infringement. In 2025, the Cyberspace Administration of China introduced new regulations requiring clear labeling of AI-generated content to safeguard intellectual property and prevent unauthorized use of creative works. These measures reflect the growing complexity of copyright in the era of generative media, where both human-made and machine-produced content must be regulated.

Despite these advances, piracy, counterfeiting, and weak coordination across the sector remain obstacles. China continues to dominate global production of derivative goods but is striving to consolidate its own intellectual properties to retain a larger share of economic returns. The protection of copyright thus remains one of the most crucial challenges for the sustainability of the Chinese animation industry, with implications that extend beyond economics to questions of cultural identity and global influence.

5.8 Piracy and Informal Media Economies

The economic system of Chinese animation has long suffered from insufficient regulation, which has made the sector particularly vulnerable to piracy. In a disorganized and immature industrial environment, piracy has found a fertile market, undermining both the credibility and the profitability of legitimate creative enterprises. For an animation studio to develop derivative products legally, it must bear considerable costs and, in many cases, wait up to 2 years for proper registration. By contrast, illegal producers of derivative goods face only the costs of fabrication. For example, molds for toys are inexpensive and often of poor quality, copied directly from the originals. While many illegal manufacturers are small in scale, there are also larger companies whose risks of failure are negligible, since they strategically focus on the most popular characters from famous animations. Frequently, pirated products even reach the market before the original items, undercutting legitimate producers.

The success of piracy in China is due to several interrelated factors. First, counterfeit goods are sold at much lower prices than licensed products. Second, there has historically been little emphasis on quality, meaning consumers often purchase without expecting durability or refinement. Third, pirated items are extremely easy to access, and consumers often cannot distinguish originals from copies. This is particularly true for audiovisual products and publishing, where the physical or digital formats make authenticity nearly impossible to verify. The combination of low prices, limited awareness, and weak regulatory enforcement created an environment in which piracy flourished.

The government has acknowledged that strengthening copyright protection is essential if private and public investors are to be safeguarded. Efforts have included simplifying domestic production procedures, introducing clearer rules for national producers, and drafting new laws to tackle piracy. At the same time, supportive measures have been adopted, such as the provision of preferential loans, the increase of state funding, and the organization of seminars aimed at informing companies how to defend themselves against piracy and to secure copyright protection for their intellectual property). The Patent Office was also tasked with registering animated characters, logos, titles, and trademarks so that they could be legally protected once approved.

The Ministry of Finance stressed that animation, being integrated with other cultural sectors such as gaming, theme parks, audiovisual products, exhibitions, and tourism, must be defended by strict and punitive regulations. Since most profits generated by an animated film or series are earned in the derivative market rather than through the production itself, intellectual property protection is indispensable. Nonetheless, many Chinese companies producing derivative goods remain unaware of copyright obligations, creating objects without realizing they are pirating intellectual property and damaging the market. The government therefore identified public education as a crucial first step, encouraging companies to register their brands and to engage in closer collaboration with other firms in the sector.

The lack of public awareness has been a persistent problem. The Copyright Act of 1990 already indicated that most Chinese citizens were not sufficiently informed about copyright law and thus purchased pirated goods without realizing that they were violating intellectual property rights. At the end of the 1990s, official data remained discouraging. In major urban centers, up to 90% of audiovisual products were pirated, while in rural areas piracy was nearly total. In 2001, industry figures suggested that pirated products still accounted for 80% of the market, with a market share estimated at 95%.

The normalization of piracy even entered everyday language. In recent years, the phrase *miǎnfèi xiǎngshòu* (免费享受, "free enjoyment") has been widely used to describe the practice of downloading or purchasing pirated products as if it were a cultural norm. Within this context, the internet became a central arena in which piracy not only thrived but was rarely perceived as a crime. Despite government attempts to halt illegal file sharing of copyrighted material, tangible results remained limited. Private companies, on the other hand, quickly recognized the internet's potential as a legitimate distribution channel. Platforms such as Youku, Baidu, and Huayi Brothers Media became significant players in the early 2000s, offering audiovisual content online, even as piracy undermined their commercial models. Huayi Brothers Media became the country's first major provider of such services, marking the beginning of China's online distribution era.

The government intervened again in 2010 with the introduction of updated regulations designed to modernize copyright enforcement. The law expanded coverage to a wide range of works, including literature, oral works, music, theatre, opera, dance, acrobatics, fine art and architecture, photography, film and audiovisual products, design drawings, maps, software, and legal documents. These rules also clarified that both Chinese citizens and foreign nationals, as well as stateless persons, were entitled to copyright protection under Chinese law, in accordance with international treaties. Works produced in countries without treaties with China could still be protected under certain conditions, reflecting a broader attempt to integrate the Chinese copyright system into international frameworks. The law has been revised several times since, most recently in 2012, to adapt to changing technological and market realities.

Despite these legal adjustments, piracy has remained pervasive. In the 2000s and 2010s, most audiovisual products sold in China were still pirated, whether purchased physically or downloaded online. Even though the government has tried to improve enforcement and consumer education, piracy continues to undermine investor confidence and the sustainability of the industry.

Recent years have brought new dimensions to the problem. The 2021 amendment to the Copyright Law introduced stricter protections for digital works, particularly audiovisual products, and imposed heavier penalties for infringement. In 2025, the Cyberspace Administration of China implemented regulations on the labeling of AI-generated synthetic content, further expanding copyright protection to new technological frontiers (State Council of the People's Republic of China 2025). These initiatives reflect China's recognition that piracy in the age of streaming, mobile platforms, and generative AI poses different challenges than in the era of physical counterfeits. Nevertheless, enforcement remains uneven, and consumer tolerance for pirated products persists.

By 2025, the fight against piracy in Chinese animation demonstrates both continuity and change. The country has moved from a situation in which piracy was culturally normalized and almost universal, to one in which copyright laws are more aligned with international standards. However, the structural challenges of enforcement, fragmented industry organization, and consumer practices have not been fully resolved. Since the profitability of animation depends heavily on derivative markets, piracy continues to pose one of the most serious threats to the long-term sustainability of China's animation industry.

5.9 Derivatives and the Expansion of the Value Chain

Since 2009, China has become the largest country in the world for the importation of animation-related derivative products, including merchandise tied to animated films, television series, and characters. As already noted, characters such as Snoopy, Mickey Mouse, Hello Kitty, Pikachu, and Doraemon alone generated annual revenues of around 70 million euros (600 million yuan). The animation industry is thus increasingly recognized as a strategic sector of the national economy, with the potential to be ranked among the five most influential industrial sectors in China. It has gradually contributed to significant shifts in economic development strategies and a restructuring of other industrial domains.

In a mature market, the value chain extends through every phase of the product cycle and across all creative sectors, from conception and production to the commercialization of derivative goods. For this reason, stable economic and cultural growth in China can only be ensured through control of the animation sector as a whole. It should be emphasized, however, that the core business of animation is not television or cinema but derivatives, in other words the formation of a brand based on an animated character protected by copyright. This constitutes the most profitable dimension of animation, provided that a serious and well-integrated value chain is in place.

The Chinese animation sector remains immature in this respect, since most companies are small or medium in scale and only a very limited number succeed in developing vertical integration across the market. To build a viable value chain, the Chinese industry should first ground its policies in the integrated production of Animation, Comics, and Games (ACG) and establish strong interconnections across all stages. The American and Japanese models are instructive: in both countries, companies of all sizes are deeply interconnected within the chain, ensuring stability and synergy. As Tan (2006a, b) argued, one logical starting point for China would be the development of manhua, just as manga served as the foundation of the Japanese and Korean animation industries.

The Japanese model provides a particularly useful example. In Japan, most animated works are derived from manga. Once a manga surpasses one million copies in sales, it is almost certain to be adapted into an anime. This guarantees a built-in fan base of at least one million viewers who will follow the series on television, purchase DVDs, and consume related merchandise. Such a virtuous cycle stabilizes the industry for investors and professionals alike. In many cases, the adaptation of comics into animated films or television series benefits from the support of dedicated fan communities, which promote the works online and through conventions, effectively generating free publicity and accelerating the expansion of derivative markets.

In China, however, the industry has suffered from gaps in its own network. One of the major problems has been the exclusive focus on television, and particularly on local TV stations. Since many productions are subsidized by the state, companies have been obliged to sell their series to local broadcasters at very low prices, sometimes only a few yuan per minute. This creates a vicious cycle in which companies are unable to generate revenues from other sources, weakening their capacity to compete and threatening their long-term survival. If television remains the only source of income, the industry as a whole risks collapse, since, as is widely recognized, most revenue derives from the derivatives market. Yet many Chinese producers have failed to capitalize on the commercial potential of their characters, neglecting the development of a coherent value chain (Qing 2006).

Another obstacle has been the entrance of investors with little or no creative background, drawn to the sector solely by government subsidies at national, provincial, and local levels. This reliance on state support and inexperienced investors has contributed to a fragile ecosystem. Many of these entrepreneurs lacked the resources and knowledge to improve the quality of productions or to nurture innovation. As a result, companies often neglected scriptwriting, technological upgrading, and talent development. The shortage of skilled writers capable of producing original and compelling narratives has been particularly damaging. Without original stories capable of capturing audiences, Chinese animations have struggled to build loyal viewerships, thereby stalling the entire value chain at its initial stage.

The reliance on traditional stories has further limited originality. Most Chinese animations are still based on legends, myths, and historical tales, but they often fail to adapt these narratives to contemporary formats, neglecting structural design, target audience, or stylistic consistency. Many productions appear childish, poorly coordinated in terms of visual design, or simply out of step with modern trends. As Bin (2011) observed, the result is often tedious and lacking in originality, preventing animations from attracting significant audiences or fueling a dynamic value chain.

Nevertheless, beginning in 2006, the industry entered a new phase of growth. Private investors began to recognize animation as a promising opportunity within the so-called "smokeless industry," an industrial category promoted as environmentally sustainable and strategically important. Animation products gained increasing space in the market not only through direct consumption but also through copyright revenues and derivatives. According to *Economic Information Daily* (经济参考报, *Jīngjì cānkǎo bào*), the global financial crisis prompted China to reduce reliance on manufacturing exports and to adopt fiscal policies that stimulated domestic demand. Derivative companies benefited from these incentives, expanding their operations and acquiring new market segments. Despite this, more than 80% of the domestic derivatives market remained dominated by foreign characters (Blue Book 2011). The weakness of domestic intellectual properties was directly linked to insufficient creativity.

Surveys conducted in 2011 for the *Annual Global Top Ten Cartoon Images Contest* confirmed this imbalance. Only four Chinese characters entered the national Top Ten: *Pleasant Goat and Big Big Wolf*, *Blue Cat*, *Rainbow Cat*, and *Blue Rabbit*. The remaining positions were occupied by Japanese characters such as Doraemon, Naruto, Conan, Luffy, Inuyasha, and Pikachu. A further survey, published in the *International Communication Gazette* in March 2013 (Ishii 2013), found that among Chinese youth aged 15–39, only two domestic characters appeared in the Top Ten, while seven were Japanese and one American. Notably, both Naruto (ranked second) and One Piece (ranked ninth) were available only online in China, suggesting that young viewers preferred to watch these series on the internet (Table 5.5).

Another survey conducted by the Chinese Academy of Social Sciences listed the most popular Chinese animation characters. At the top were *Pleasant Goat*, *Monkey King* (produced by CCTV Animation), and *Pig Man* (猪猪侠, *Zhū Zhūxiá*), produced by Guangdong Yong Sheng Culture Communication Co., Ltd. The ten characters listed were created by different studios employing diverse strategies for protecting and marketing their properties, but all faced the challenge of competing against foreign icons.

Both tables highlight the same conclusion: domestic characters remained few and relatively weak in originality, explaining why foreign brands, primarily Japanese and American, continued to dominate over 80% of the derivatives market (Blue Book 2012). Surveys further indicated that 60% of Chinese youth preferred Japanese animation, 29% favored European and American productions, and only 11% expressed a preference for domestic animation. Snoopy, Mickey Mouse, Hello Kitty, Pikachu, and Doraemon alone generated 70 million euros annually in China's derivative market.

Even with protective policies, such as the long-standing restriction on foreign animation during prime time slots, the domestic industry has struggled to develop original content. Many viewers have shifted consumption habits toward illegal on-demand internet services. Zhang (2010) reported that 75.9% of Chinese internet users watched television programs, series, and anime online, a trend that severely undermined legal distribution.

Despite these weaknesses, the surveys underline an important point: if China were to create original characters with compelling stories and attractive designs, its derivative market could expand dramatically. Animation is not limited to television but encompasses broadband networks, MMS, audio and video products, mobile platforms, and pay television. The scope of demand is broad, and Chinese animation is attempting to close this gap.

Over time, the value of a character can increase substantially, generating significant economic benefits. A successful character can be used across a wide range of industries, from food and sports to entertainment and consumer goods. Copyright protection can extend the profitability of such characters for decades, as demonstrated by timeless icons like Mickey Mouse and Doraemon. For China, the derivative market represents a potential panacea, as it can account for 70–80% of production costs. Television sales alone, which range from 40 to 1000 yuan per minute (5.5–13 euros), fall far short of covering actual production costs, which average around 1300 euros per minute. Without a strong derivatives market, the industry risks unsustainability.

International precedents show the potential. In the United States, South Korea, and Japan, animation has become more profitable than many other industries, forming a pillar of national economies. Derivative markets have been supported by copyright partnerships and cross-industry cooperation. For instance, Walt Disney has long-term contracts with McDonald's, which uses animation characters for advertising campaigns and promotional gifts aimed at younger customers. Similar strategies have

Table 5.5 The most famous Chinese animated characters, their respective series, and production studio or company

Character	Series/Film	Studio/Production Company	Years Active	Brief Info
Pleasant Goat	Pleasant Goat and Big Big Wolf	Creative Power Entertaining	2005–present	Popular children's series about clever goats vs. a persistent wolf, over 3000 episodes
Boonie Bears	Boonie Bears	Fantawild Animation	2012–present	Comedy-adventure focusing on two bear brothers protecting the forest, hit film franchise
Black Cat Detective	Black Cat Detective	Shanghai Animation Film Studio	1984–present	Classic detective cartoon from the 1980s, follows a cat police officer solving mysteries
Nezha	Nezha Conquers the Dragon King	Shanghai Animation Film Studio	1979 (film) / recent remakes	One of the earliest Chinese animated films, epic fantasy about a mythological hero Nezha
Sanmao	Wanderings of Sanmao	Shanghai Animation Film Studio	1980s	Based on a comic character representing a poor orphan struggling through life
Ye Xiu	The King's Avatar	Chongqing Yi Animation	2017–present	MMORPG esports-themed donghua about a top pro player's comeback journey
Wei Wuxian	Grandmaster of Demonic Cultivation	B.C May Pictures	2018–present	Popular fantasy donghua with strong supernatural and cultivation themes!
Mo Fan	Full-Time Magister	Foch Film	2016–present	Action-fantasy donghua about a student mastering multiple magic disciplines
Wang Ling	The Daily Life of the Immortal King	Haoliners Animation League	2020–present	Comedy-fantasy donghua about a powerful immortal youth hiding in modern life

been employed in South Korea and Japan, with partnerships spanning restaurants, supermarkets, and other retail chains.

Theme parks represent another major source of revenue. Disney's theme parks have long demonstrated the profitability of linking animation with leisure industries. In recent years, China has sought to replicate this model by building domestic theme parks based on national characters. By 2010, approximately seventy medium and large-scale parks were operating across the country.

By 2025, these dynamics have continued to evolve. While foreign characters still dominate the derivative market, China has made progress in developing stronger intellectual properties. The unprecedented global success of *Ne Zha* (2019), *Chang'an* (2023), and *Ne Zha 2* (2024) has shown that domestic characters can sustain vast derivative markets if supported by compelling storytelling and cross-media strategies. Local governments continue to promote integration of animation, comics, and games, while central authorities have highlighted the need to move beyond subsidies toward creativity-driven development. If the industry can combine original content, effective copyright enforcement, and derivative expansion, the value chain of Chinese animation will increasingly reflect not only economic growth but also cultural influence on the global stage.

5.10 Branding Strategies—Animation as Market Identity

Branding has become a decisive element in the development of the Chinese animation industry. Until the early 2000s, animation in China was primarily regarded as an artistic and cultural product, with little awareness of its potential as the foundation of a wider commercial ecosystem. The idea that animated characters could anchor a brand, shape production strategies, and generate derivative markets was slow to emerge. Inspired by the example of foreign companies that successfully linked animated series to toys, apparel, and consumer goods, Chinese producers gradually began to integrate brand development into their business models and to explore licensing as a source of long-term revenues.

The Blue Book 2012 noted that most companies engaged in branding and trademark management were small or medium-sized enterprises, often characterized by low levels of product commercialization and limited understanding of brand awareness. As competition with foreign producers intensified, branding became central not only to reputation but also to economic sustainability. In response, major regions such as Beijing, Hunan, Shanghai, and Guangdong established licensing systems that created the institutional basis for the growth of derivative industries. Guangdong, in particular, played a leading role: Guangzhou developed into a center of domestic animation production, Shenzhen became the earliest hub for outsourcing, and Dongguan specialized in toy manufacturing for international characters such as Doraemon, Barbie, Snoopy, and Mickey Mouse. By 2011 Dongguan hosted nearly one thousand companies connected to animation and organized one of Asia's largest animation fairs (Hooi 2011). The city attracted substantial investment and offered incentives to firms including the studio behind *Pleasant Goat and Big Big Wolf*, which relocated there to benefit from favorable policies.

Market growth followed quickly. In 2012, the Chinese animation industry reached a value of 3.5 million euros, representing a 24% increase over the previous year, and forecasts suggested that it could reach 13.5 million euros within a few years (Research In China 2013; *Earth Magazine* 2006). The success of *Blue Cat* (蓝猫, Lánmāo, 1999–2004), produced by Beijing Sunchime Happy Culture Company, exemplified the potential of derivatives. The property generated sales of 30 million soundtrack CDs, more than 50 million books worth 4.7 million euros, and approximately 10 million euros in publishing royalties (Qing 2006).

Licensing companies emerged as key players. Guangdong Yong Sheng Culture Communication (广州艺洲人文化传播有限公司, Guǎngzhōu Yìzhōurén Wénhuà Chuánbò Yǒuxiàn Gōngsī) managed more than one hundred domestic and international brands, including *SpongeBob SquarePants*, *Dora the Explorer*, *Doraemon*, *Thomas and Friends*, and *Pleasant Goat and Big Big Wolf*. The Blue Book 2012 estimated that global brand licensing in 2008 generated around 153.5 billion euros, of which the United States alone accounted for 84.5 billion euros. Animation-related licensing contributed approximately 2 billion euros worldwide, while China's total licensing market was still at 1 billion euros. Nevertheless, growth was rapid: by 2010 *Pleasant Goat and Big Big Wolf* had more than 250 authorized partners producing nearly one thousand products ranging from clothing and toys to food, video games, and appliances, with collaborations extending to McDonald's and KFC.

Mega-events accelerated this process. The 2008 Beijing Olympics, the 2010 FIFA World Cup, the 2010 Shanghai Expo, and the 2011 Guangzhou Asian Games introduced mascots and visual identities that generated massive merchandise sales. The Shanghai Expo alone produced about 3.5 billion euros in licensed goods, while the Guangzhou Asian Games earned approximately 3.2 billion euros. In Shanghai, six companies produced toys linked to these events, including Shanghai Junyao Group, Shanghai Arts and Oriental Crafts, and Shanghai Sinnsa Group. These cases illustrate how branding could transform large-scale cultural events into opportunities for industrial expansion.

The potential of the domestic market was considerable. With an estimated 400 million children aged 0–14, the China Toy and Juvenile Product Association projected that the toy market would reach 7.4 billion euros annually by 2015. While Chinese toy makers had traditionally served as outsourcing partners for foreign companies, they began to invest in characters created by domestic animation studios. Guangdong Huawei Toys Craft (广东骅威玩具工艺股份有限公司, Guǎngdōng Huáwēi Wánjù Gōngyì Gǔfèn Yǒuxiàn Gōngsī) exemplified this transition. In addition to continuing contracts with Disney and Giochi Preziosi, it built partnerships with CCTV Animation and Yulang Cultural Development in Shenzhen (Xingzhen 2011).

Another landmark case was Auldey (奥迪双钻, Àodí Shuāngzuān), reorganized as Guangdong Alpha Animation and Culture (奥飞动漫文化股份有限公司, Àofēi Dòngmàn Wénhuà Gǔfèn Yǒuxiàn Gōngsī). With 1500 employees, Auldey expanded its scope to include comics, 3D animations, and live-action adaptations. Its flagship properties included *King Fire Junior* (火力少年王, Huǒlì Shàonián Wáng), *Long War-Wheel-Drive* (战龙四驱, Zhànlóng Sìqū), and *Fruit Robot* (果宝特攻, Guǒbǎo Tègōng). Through mergers, acquisitions, and licensing strategies, Auldey established itself as one of the most important firms in the integration of animation and toy production.

Distribution channels also expanded. Kaku TV (卡酷动画), owned by Beijing Television, launched in 2006 and quickly became a major brand in the children's entertainment sector. By 2011 it managed thirteen flagship stores and two hundred franchises authorized to sell more than 20,000 types of merchandise (Weijing 2011). Guangdong Benko Animation (广东缤果动漫连锁管理有限公司, Guǎngdōng Bīnguǒ Dòngmàn Liánsuǒ Guǎnlǐ Yǒuxiàn Gōngsī) pursued a similar strategy, building a retail chain of more than 350 stores while investing directly in original animation production. Foreign companies also expanded their presence: Toys "R" Us opened twenty-three stores with official authorization beginning in 2006, and Sanrio operated more than one hundred outlets nationwide (Blue Book 2012).

Nevertheless, structural obstacles have limited the consolidation of a robust licensing industry. Trademark registration costs are high, averaging 209 euros per item plus service fees, and can exceed 1 million euros annually for active firms. Delays of up to 2 years in the registration process reduce the effective sales window of derivatives, which often depend on seasonal demand and broadcast schedules. This delay allows pirate manufacturers to release counterfeit products in real time, avoiding taxes and registration costs, and often using molds identical to official ones (Niu 2011). The result is that counterfeit goods dominate traditional markets and street distribution, undermining the profitability of legitimate businesses.

Recent evidence suggests that these structural issues remain unresolved. In 2023, trademark registrations in China declined by 29% compared with the previous year, partly as a result of stricter government scrutiny of bad faith filings. The China National Intellectual Property Administration has increased enforcement, but bureaucratic inefficiencies and the persistence of piracy continue to undermine the sector. Large firms such as Beijing Enlight Pictures now maintain extensive trademark portfolios, demonstrating that brand consolidation has become essential to industrial survival. Yet derivatives still account for a modest share of total revenues compared with international benchmarks, where licensing typically represents the majority of profits. This imbalance illustrates a deeper contradiction: while state policies emphasize the production of cultural content, the downstream sectors that ensure sustainable growth remain fragile.

The comparison between the early 2010s and the current situation reveals a significant transformation. A decade ago the central question was whether Chinese producers could create recognizable brands. Today the challenge lies in consolidating and protecting those brands in a competitive environment shaped by piracy, rising costs, and shifting consumer habits. The trajectory of the last decade demonstrates both the progress and the persistent limitations of China's animation industry. Its long-term strength will depend not only on content creation but also on the effective management of intellectual property, the efficiency of licensing frameworks, and the ability to integrate animated characters into stable and profitable brand ecosystems.

5.11 Outsourcing and Global Labor Flows

Few viewers realize that the majority of global animation production is carried out in Asia. According to Lent (2006), as much as 90% of American television animation has been produced in China, Taiwan, and South Korea. Over the last two decades, China has seen the rise of numerous studios and companies devoted primarily to outsourced animation, attracting foreign clients through competitive pricing and reliable technical capacity. Many European producers also rely on Chinese studios. For example, the Italian company Lastrego & Testa frequently collaborates with Chinese subcontractors to deliver products for RAI television.

Despite their contribution, Chinese studios are often invisible in the credits of foreign productions. Many do not provide translations of their corporate names, and overseas companies show little concern for acknowledging them. The result is that Chinese animation workshops have functioned largely as industrial factories, where long shifts and tight deadlines define the daily routine. According to the Blue Book 2012, about 80% of Japanese animation is processed in China, confirming the country's centrality to the global production chain.

Japan has cultivated long-term relationships with Chinese studios, assisting them in achieving higher quality standards and training skilled technicians. These professionals are technically proficient but, as critics have noted, often lack creative autonomy. Foreign producers are attracted not only by low costs but also by high production standards (Qing 2006). Yet Chinese studios now face intense competition from Vietnam, India, and even North Korea, which offer lower labor costs. This pressure explains why the Chinese government has increasingly promoted original domestic animation as a strategy to secure higher value-added revenues and reduce dependence on outsourcing.

Most Japanese staff working in creative teams are unaware that their projects are completed in China. Executive producers typically subcontract work to Japanese intermediary agencies, which then "package" the materials and deliver them to Chinese studios. Traditional workflows still involve paper-based processes. When Japanese studios fall behind schedule, original drawings are gathered and sent through intermediaries to China for completion.

Modern animation production can be divided into three stages: the creation of original artwork, the computer-based animation of drawings, and post-production (Chuangyu 2011). The first stage includes scriptwriting, character design, backgrounds, and the definition of spatial settings. In series such as *Full Metal Alchemist*, the original drawings specify dimensions, profiles, color schemes, and characteristic expressions of the characters, along with basic posture references. These are then used to build storyboards, which may comprise two to four thousand sketches for a twenty-minute episode. The material is then sent to China, where studios produce approximately fifteen thousand additional drawings, either by hand or digitally, based on Japanese models. Once completed, the material is returned to Japan for photography, editing, and dubbing. Chinese studios thus manage the labor-intensive middle stage of production, which requires precision, speed, and long working hours.

The outsourcing trend began in the early 1990s, when Japanese studios could no longer meet the growing market demand. China was chosen for several reasons: its prior production experience, geographical and cultural proximity, proven quality, and lower costs. Online advertisements reflect this industrial model, with many little-known Chinese companies offering inexpensive yet high-quality services. For instance, Qingdao Pacific Rim Media Studio promotes its work for major domestic companies such as PetroChina and Sinopec, while also providing television animation, advertising clips, 3D simulations, product demonstrations, and post-production.

Some firms openly advertise their experience in Japanese anime. Haida Commercial Digital Technology (上海达贸数码科技有限公司, Shànghǎi Dá Mào Shùmǎ Kējì Yǒuxiàn Gōngsī) in Shanghai has specialized in anime outsourcing for more than 15 years, contributing to series such as *Detective Conan*, *Transformers*, and *Mobile Suit Gundam*. Changsha has become another hub, hosting more than sixty studios with a combined annual production capacity of 200,000 min. Haida's Ms. Zhang (张小姐) has noted that outsourcing in China generally costs about one quarter of Japan's total production expenses. In interviews with *ChinaVisual.com* (2019), another Haida manager, Ms. Liu (刘), explained that Japanese quality standards are extremely strict, requiring thirty-four employees for project development and eight for color control. To maintain such low costs, the studio rents inexpensive facilities on the outskirts of Shanghai, where staff work up to ten hours per day for a monthly wage of approximately 180 euros (1500 yuan).

The contribution of Chinese subcontractors is occasionally visible in end credits. Snapshots of titles from series such as *Monochrome Factor*, *Inuyasha*, *Bleach: The DiamondDust Rebellion*, and *Summon the Beasts* reveal the names of Chinese studios highlighted alongside Japanese companies. In addition to independent subcontractors, some Japanese firms have established wholly owned subsidiaries in China. Hangzhou Dragoon Animation (杭州龙骑动漫公司, *Hángzhōu Lóngqí Dòngmàn Gōngsī*), founded in 1988, employs around 130 professionals and has worked exclusively for Japanese studios on titles such as *One Piece* (ONE PIECE ワンピース, *Wan Pīsu*) and *Pokémon* (ポケモン, *Pokémon*).

In recent years, outsourcing has continued to dominate the labor structure of the Chinese animation sector, but the context has evolved. While China remains the world's largest outsourcing hub for Japanese and Western productions, wages have increased and regulatory standards have tightened. Competition from lower-cost countries has forced Chinese studios to upgrade their technological capacity, shifting increasingly toward digital workflows and advanced software. At the same time, government policies have attempted to reduce dependence on foreign contracts by fostering original content, intellectual property ownership, and brand development. The outsourcing model has provided valuable training, but it has also reinforced a division of labor in which China excels in execution rather than creation. The long-term sustainability of the industry will therefore depend on its capacity to convert technical expertise into creative autonomy and to balance its role as the world's largest subcontractor with the ambition of producing original works that carry international recognition.

5.12 State Support—A Historical Chronology

To stimulate the growth of the animation sector, the Chinese government has issued a series of regulatory policies designed to protect domestic productions. This defensive approach originally aimed to curb the overwhelming presence of foreign animated series, particularly Japanese anime, which dominated Chinese television throughout the 1980s and 1990s. During the same period, the gradual rise of new private channels generated a rapid expansion of television outlets and a corresponding shortage of content. Foreign animated series were quick to fill this void, offering inexpensive programming that appealed to both broadcasters and advertisers.

The defensive stance against foreign "invasion" continues to shape state regulation today. Yet from 2004 onward the government complemented this position with a more proactive policy that sought to promote the internationalization of Chinese animation as an instrument of cultural diplomacy and soft power (Sun 2010).

The first official measure specifically addressing animation dates back to 1988, when the State Council promulgated the law on the administration of the cultural market. For the first time the concept of a cultural market (文化产业, *Wénhuà chănyè*) was formally recognized, and institutional reforms provided a more favorable environment for organizations engaged in cultural production, including animation. Nevertheless, it was not until 1996 that policies explicitly targeted the animation industry. That year, the General Administration of Press and Publication (中华人民共和国新闻出版总署, *Zhōnghuá Rénmín Gònghéguó Xīnwén Chūbăn Zŏngshŭ*, GAPP) and the Publicity Department of the Communist Party (中共中央宣传部, *Zhōnggòng Zhōngyāng Xuānchuán Bù*) launched the *Project for the Publishing of Chinese Children's Animation* (中国儿童动画出版工程, *Zhōngguó értóng dònghuà chūbăn gōngchéng*), better known as Project 5155. The initiative aimed to establish five animation publishing bases distributed across the north, south, center, west, and east of the country.

At the Fifteenth Congress of the Chinese Communist Party in 2000, cultural industries were formally recognized, and animation was officially designated as part of this category. New strategic rules were introduced, including time restrictions on the broadcasting of foreign animation. All imports of animated series required approval and monitoring by the State Administration of Radio, Film and Television (SARFT). These measures created a more favorable environment for domestic studios and encouraged investment in production capacity.

The Tenth Five-Year Plan (2001–2005) explicitly identified animation as a strategic industry with both cultural and economic significance. In 2003, SARFT issued the *Notice about Strengthening the Administration of Imports and Broadcasting of Animated Products*, which established that no broadcaster could devote more than 40% of its animation schedule to foreign series (Chen 2010). In March 2004, the *Notice about the Administration and Planning of Themes of Domestic Animated TV Series* emphasized the need to "promote national animation, strengthen thematic regulation, and ensure the healthy growth of domestic productions while guiding public opinion."

This notice introduced three important rules: beginning in July 2004, a monitoring system would oversee themes in domestic series; only licensed organizations could distribute or produce animated programs, subject to SARFT approval; and SARFT offices at both national and provincial levels were tasked with supervising content. The following month, SARFT issued another landmark regulation requiring that at least 50% of children's programming hours be devoted to animation, with more than 60% of this total reserved for domestic productions. Broadcasters willing to allocate additional airtime to domestic animation were granted the right to insert extra advertising slots during prime time.

In addition, animation was formally recognized as part of the state's "going out" strategy, which encouraged Chinese cultural organizations to expand internationally. The immediate impact was visible: within two months of the new regulations, more than ten private companies, both Chinese and foreign, entered the animation sector (Qing 2006).

The government continued to strengthen support in 2004 by creating three new satellite animation channels (GBS Hunan Satellite TV, Beijing Kaku TV, and Shanghai Toonmax TV), aiming to reach fifty specialized animation channels by the end of the year. Plans were also announced to establish nine national industrial bases and four major training centers dedicated to animation, including the Communication University of China, the Beijing Film Institute, the Guilin Arts Institute, and the China Art Institute. By 2009, the objective was to expand this network to twenty industrial bases and seven training centers (Blue Book 2009).

The year 2005 is considered a turning point. In June, SARFT issued the *Concrete Measures to Promote the Development of Domestic Animation Creation*, requiring all broadcasters to air only domestic animated series during prime time (17:00–20:00). The ratio between foreign and domestic animation had to be balanced at 1:1. In 2006, the restrictions became even stricter: foreign animated programs were banned from prime time altogether. In April, the State Council released the *Opinions on Promoting the Development of Domestic Comics, Games, and Animation* (财政部等部门关于推动我国动漫产业发展的若干意见, *Guóbàn fā [2006]32 hào*), which recognized the animation, comics, and games sector (ACG) as a high-technology industry entitled to preferential fiscal policies.

From 2007 onward, the "going out" strategy was reinforced within the broader development of the creative industries. SARFT and the Ministry of Commerce jointly issued the *Guidebook for the Export of Cultural Products and Services*. This included the *Register of Key Enterprises for Cultural Export 2007–2008* and the *Catalogue of Key National Cultural Export Projects 2007–2008*. Fourteen animation companies were listed as key exporters, and series such as *Blue Cat* and *Journey to the West* were identified as cultural references suitable for global distribution.

Further measures followed. In February 2008, SARFT released the *Regulations on the Broadcasting of Animated TV Series*, which required a 7:3 ratio between rebroadcast domestic productions and foreign imports, while extending evening animation slots from 17:00 to 21:00. This reflected the government's attempt to balance the needs of broadcasters with the goal of expanding national production. In 2011, the Ministry of Culture introduced new rules on online animation, replacing the provisional regulations of 2003. These required commercial entities to obtain special permits from local branches of the Ministry in order to distribute animated content through the internet, mobile devices, computers, smart televisions, and gaming consoles.

Together, these measures illustrate the gradual evolution of government policy from defensive restrictions to proactive promotion. What began as an effort to shield domestic animation from foreign competition developed into a comprehensive industrial strategy that sought to create original content, establish national production bases, and promote Chinese animation as a global cultural brand.

5.13 Contemporary Policy Landscapes—State and Industry Interactions

In recent years the Chinese government has sought to identify the most relevant and profitable companies in order to inaugurate a new phase of targeted investment. Whereas in the past the "Special Fund for the Development of the Animation Industry" was allocated to a wide range of studios, including non-professional or low-quality producers, today these resources are primarily directed toward supporting the production of original animation with the explicit goal of developing a sustainable industrial ecosystem (Qing 2006). Local governments provide even stronger incentives than the central administration, ensuring that regional industries remain competitive. Shenzhen, for instance, has invested approximately 12 million euros (100 million yuan) annually in original animation since 2006, and doubles subsidies when a series is broadcast on television, offering about 61 euros (500 yuan) per minute for 2D content and twice as much for 3D productions (Tan 2006a, b). Additional rewards are granted to companies that achieve international recognition, while special commendations are reserved for studios distinguished at the national level.

This system of incentives is reinforced by central authorities, which also reward municipalities that implement proactive strategies. Hangzhou, Binjiang District, and Zhejiang provide preferential loans to animation companies, while Sichuan, Chengdu, and Wuxi allocate direct funding to support production. At every level—provincial, municipal, and national—animation receives structural assistance. Since 2005, SARFT has actively promoted animated series that are considered to have strong cultural impact. The 2013 document entitled *SARFT Recommendations: Notice of the First Batch of Outstanding Domestic Animation for National Broadcast* (广电总局关于推荐2013年度 - 第一批优秀国产动画片的通知, *Guǎngdiàn Zǒngjú Guānyú Tuījiàn 2013 Niándù Dì Yī Pī Yōuxiù Guóchǎn Dònghuà Piàn de Tōngzhī*) listed key titles, their plots, production companies, and the reasons why they should be distributed nationwide. Broadcasters and administrative services were instructed to schedule these series across television networks, with national stations receiving priority. The measure reflected the government's intention to ensure that the younger generation had access to the most representative domestic productions.

In the broader framework of support for emerging cultural industries, 2011 saw the introduction of updated incentives under the circular Caishui [2011] No.119. Issued jointly by the Ministry of Finance and the State Administration of Taxation, the policy confirmed preferential VAT rebates and reduced corporate income tax rates for qualified animation producers. These benefits encouraged widespread entrepreneurial activity in the animation sector but also generated a disordered proliferation of studios, many lacking long-term sustainability. Nevertheless, the sector experienced significant structural change and began to construct a genuine value chain.

In the past decade, additional measures have consolidated this trajectory. The 2014–2015 policy package strengthened intellectual property protection for original animation and introduced stricter approval procedures for imported content. In 2018, the Ministry of Finance renewed fiscal preferences for animation companies under the "Cultural Industry Development Fund," offering subsidies for projects recognized as contributing to national culture. The rise of online platforms prompted the National Radio and Television Administration (NRTA, successor of SARFT) to update regulatory frameworks in 2019, requiring online animation providers to undergo content review similar to television broadcasters.

Most recently, in March 2025, the Cyberspace Administration of China introduced the *Measures for the Labeling of AI-Generated Synthetic Content* (人工智能生成合成内容标识办法, *Réngōng Zhìnéng Shēngchéng Héchéng Nèiróng Biāozhì Bànfǎ*). Although not limited to animation, this regulation requires platforms and producers to mark AI-generated material clearly and to establish verification systems. The measure reflects the government's awareness that animation is increasingly intertwined with artificial intelligence and new digital technologies, and it extends earlier protective strategies into the digital era.

Taken together, these policies demonstrate a shift from broad financial encouragement toward a more selective system that rewards originality, cultural impact, and compliance with quality standards. While the combination of central and local support has led to rapid expansion, it has also revealed the risks of over-saturation and the need for coherent governance. The current phase illustrates an industry in transition, where government intervention continues to provide structural support but increasingly emphasizes regulation, innovation, and international competitiveness as essential elements of long-term growth.

5.14 The Paperless Turn—Digital Workflows and New Practices

With the rapid diffusion of digital technologies, traditional hand-drawn animation has largely given way to paperless workflows. Paper, once essential for producing each frame, has been abandoned, and with it many of the manual techniques that defined the aesthetics of twentieth-century animation. The shift has opened production to a wider pool of participants, since individuals without advanced drawing skills can now enter animation pipelines using digital tools. Yet the downside has been a clear reduction in artisanal expression. The brush, ink, and paint that conveyed individuality have been replaced by a mechanized and industrialized form of production that prioritizes efficiency and reproducibility.

The term paperless does not imply the disappearance of drawing altogether, but rather the replacement of physical supports with digital ones. Artists today combine classical animation methods with digital drawing on specialized monitors, often using Pen Displays that simulate hand drawing directly on the screen. This hybrid environment offers precision and speed, but inevitably entails the loss of the tactile and aesthetic dimensions of traditional media .

In the era of cel animation, vast amounts of brushes, pens, ink, and especially paper were required, and mistakes carried significant consequences. Errors had to be corrected by hand with considerable skill, or entire sequences had to be redrawn, recolored, and rescanned, a process that was extremely time-consuming. By contrast, in digital production the advantages are numerous. Animation is created directly in synchronization with editing software, allowing infinite revisions and corrections in real time. Databases of shared assets, color palettes, and special effects facilitate collaboration, while lip synchronization, once imprecise and labor-intensive, can now be adjusted at any stage.

One of the most transformative effects of paperless production has been the globalization of the animation workforce. In the analog era, physical drawings had to be shipped between studios, generating high transport costs and significant delays. Today digital workflows enable animators to work simultaneously on the same project across continents, sharing files instantly and ensuring seamless integration. The speed of data transfer and the capacity to work online with professional animation software have increased productivity throughout the entire value chain. Industry studies confirm that high-quality digital animation has effectively doubled production rates, from an average of 100 s per month to nearly 200 (O'Hailey 2012).

Paperless technologies have also enabled the creation of new visual dimensions. Three-dimensional animation has transformed the language of the medium, making it possible to animate realistic objects, simulate complex environments, and design characters that move in ways inconceivable on paper. The majority of Chinese animated productions now employ 3D techniques. This shift has reduced the consumption of traditional materials, but paradoxically it has also increased costs.

Producing 3D content requires longer development cycles, more sophisticated software, and larger teams. Whereas a feature-length 2D film might once have required eighteen months to complete, 3D productions often demand 3–5 years.

In the past 3 years, a further transformation has taken shape through the integration of artificial intelligence into paperless production. AI-driven software assists in in-betweening, coloring, lip synchronization, and even scene generation, significantly reducing repetitive tasks. Tools such as generative design platforms can automatically propose character movements or backgrounds, accelerating workflows. While this promises greater efficiency and lower costs, it also raises critical concerns. The risk of homogenization is real, as reliance on algorithmic outputs may suppress stylistic diversity. Moreover, AI threatens to displace traditional roles within the production chain, eroding the need for junior animators and assistants who once gained experience through these tasks.

The paperless revolution has therefore entered a new stage. If digital drawing replaced paper and brushes, artificial intelligence now challenges the very structure of artistic labor in animation. The industry faces a dual trajectory: on one hand, unprecedented productivity and creative possibilities; on the other, the danger that automation will marginalize human expression and intensify the industrialization of an art form that once thrived on individuality and craft. The sustainability of this transition will depend on whether studios and policymakers can integrate AI not as a substitute but as a complement to human creativity, preserving the cultural richness of animation while embracing technological innovation.

5.15 Spatial Clusters—Parks, Zones, and the Geography of Animation

Despite structural problems, the Chinese animation sector demonstrates vitality and a strong desire for renewal. To facilitate its development, both central and provincial governments have requalified urban zones and allocated them to multimedia industries devoted primarily to animation and games. Over the last decade, the northeast has shown significant progress, largely because the region had lacked a structured animation sector. Cities such as Beijing, Tianjin, and Hebei have become important sites of growth. By contrast, areas around the Yangtze River Delta - Shanghai, Hangzhou, Nanjing, Suzhou, Wuxi, Chengdu, Chongqing, and Kunming—already possessed an established industrial base (Blue Book 2013). In the southwest, Changsha and Wuhan stand out as key centers.

In 2008 SARFT approved projects in twenty provinces, designating them as animation development bases. At that time, the sector counted about 5600 enterprises, with 300 new firms established each year. The process had begun earlier, in 2004, when SARFT was instructed to build the first national animation park in the Hangzhou Hi-Tech Zone. The initial site covered 500 hectares with an investment of 71.4 million euros (600 million yuan) and hosted leading companies such as Shanda, producer of *Blue Cat,* Sunchime, and Zhongnan Cartoon Technology (Qing 2006). The same phase also included the Changzhou National Hi-Tech Development Zone, which quickly attracted over one hundred animation companies from major Chinese cities as well as Canada, India, South Korea, Malaysia, and Singapore.

Suzhou's Industrial Park, inaugurated in 2005, employed more than 3000 staff in over ten companies (Blue Book 2012). The same year, the Dalian High-Tech Industrial Park opened, with twenty-eight animation firms, including eight from Japan, South Korea, and France, employing about 2000 workers. The Taihu Digital Animation Film Pioneer Park, also launched in 2005, extended over 300 hectares with fifteen animation studios. The Zhangjiang Hi-Tech Park in Shanghai, supported by the Zhangjiang Group and the Shanghai Academy of Film Arts, created a further base of operations.

Beijing, Shanghai, and Tianjin revitalized older districts to anchor creative clusters. Near the Beijing Cartoon Art Museum, the capital established a new hub supported by central funding, while the Communication University of China and the Beijing Film Academy created dedicated animation departments. Adjacent to CUC, an entire area was built for animation and videogame production, including representative offices, festivals, and events. Another old industrial zone in Beijing was reborn as Art Zone 798, which became a landmark of creativity and design. Important studios such as Hutoon, led by director Pisan, are now based there.

The industry's expansion has been accompanied by a sharp rise in education and training. Within a few years, China created over 6000 animation studios, and according to SARFT vice-director Zhao Shi, around 64,000 students graduated in related fields. More than 466,000 pupils now study animation in schools, while universities have opened specialized programs. The China Animation Yearbook 2010 reported that the government had structured the National Animation and Comic Industrial Base into four categories: animation education bases under SARFT; video game bases under the Ministry of Culture; online game and ani-comic bases under the General Administration of Press and Publication; and new media and software bases under the Ministry of Science and Technology. Shanghai appeared in all four categories, while Beijing was absent from video game animation. Provinces such as Liaoning, Sichuan, and Hunan covered three categories, and Guangdong, although present in only two, remained the most productive.

Xiamen was designated in 2008 as a national base, with its Software Park reaching a third phase of expansion covering 1.63 million square meters. New museums and festivals confirmed the rising prestige of the sector. Yangzhou in Jiangsu inaugurated a comic and animation museum, followed by another in Shanghai in 2010. In 2013, Hangzhou launched a national museum project worth 119 million euros (1 billion yuan). The China Comic and Animation Museum, designed by Dutch studio MVRDV with a futuristic balloon-like structure, was budgeted at 92 million euros and integrated into a large urban development plan.

The creative industry has also become a key factor in urban planning and cultural policy. Disneyland Shanghai opened in 2016, and DreamWorks Animation announced large-scale collaborations with Chinese studios. Japanese companies established local subsidiaries and planned museums dedicated to anime culture.

These developments illustrate how the presence of animation reshapes urban environments, making them cultural and economic assets.

In recent years, the expansion of creative clusters has entered a new phase shaped by digital convergence and artificial intelligence. Several industrial parks, including those in Hangzhou, Suzhou, and Shenzhen, have begun to integrate AI laboratories into their facilities. These initiatives provide training on AI-assisted animation, data-driven storytelling, and generative design. The result is a hybrid ecosystem where traditional studios, gaming companies, and AI start-ups coexist. While this enhances innovation, it also raises questions about artistic autonomy. Some critics argue that over-reliance on AI tools risks homogenizing outputs and weakening the creative distinctiveness of local studios.

It must also be recognized that many of the early experiments in building industrial parks and creative zones have failed. Some initiatives lacked long-term planning, others were abandoned after short-lived enthusiasm, and still others produced speculative projects that never reached full operation. What remains today are a limited number of structured and consolidated hubs, such as Beijing, Shanghai, Hangzhou, and Shenzhen, that have succeeded in integrating education, production, and international collaboration. These cities now anchor the industry, while less successful zones illustrate the risks of over-expansion and the dangers of treating animation primarily as a tool of real estate development rather than a cultural and industrial field.

The transformation of urban districts into creative hubs reflects broader socio-economic trends. The state has deliberately linked cultural industries with urbanization strategies, using animation not only as entertainment but also as a tool for regeneration and international branding. The challenge is to sustain this growth while ensuring that rapid industrialization, speculative projects, and technological adoption do not overshadow the cultural richness and creative diversity that remain the foundation of Chinese animation.

References

AniSora Studio. 2024. *AniSora Studio*. Retrieved from https://anisora.studio/.

Animation Industry Report. 2023. *Annual development report of China's animation industry*. Beijing: Blue Book of Animation.

Bitatti, M. 2010. *Animazione e nuovi linguaggi multimediali*. Milan: FrancoAngeli.

Blue Book of Chinese Animation. 2008. *Annual report on China's animation industry*. Beijing: Social Sciences Academic Press.

Blue Book of Chinese Animation. 2009. *Annual report on China's animation industry*. Beijing: Social Sciences Academic Press.

Blue Book 2011. Annual Report on Development of China's Animation Industry. Social Sciences Academic Press.

Blue Book of Chinese Animation. 2012. *Annual report on China's animation industry*. Beijing: Social Sciences Academic Press.

Blue Book of Chinese Animation. 2013. *Annual report on China's animation industry*. Beijing: Social Sciences Academic Press.

CAC (Cyberspace Administration of China). 2025, March 14. *Measures for the labeling of AI-generated synthetic content*. Retrieved from http://www.cac.gov.cn/2025-03/14/c_1743654684782215.htm.

Chang, J. 2008. *Chinese animation and cultural heritage*. Beijing: China Film Press.

China Animation & Comic Industry Report. 2024. *Status and trends of China's animation and comics sector*. Beijing: Social Sciences Academic Press.

Association, China Cultural Industry. 2023. *Annual report on the development of China's cultural industry*. Beijing: Social Sciences Academic Press.

Colapinto, C. 2010. L'internalizzazione della televisione. In *Media in Cina Oggi*. FrancoAngeli.

Chen, C. C., Colapinto, C., and Luo, Q. 2010. China Radio International in the Digital Age: Propagating China on the Global Scenario. *Global Media Journal* 9(16)

China Internet Network Information Center (CNNIC). 2013. *Statistical report on internet development in China*. Beijing: CNNIC.

China Media Project. 2024, October 16. *Making deepfakes with Chinese AI*. Retrieved from https://chinamediaproject.org/2024/10/16/making-deepfakes-with-chinese-ai/.

ChinaVisual.com. 2019. *Interviews with outsourcing managers in Shanghai animation studios*. Retrieved from http://www.chinavisual.com.

China Youth Daily. 2006, March 12. *The challenges of domestic animation*. Beijing: China Youth Daily.

Chuangyu. 2011. *Animation production workflows in China*. Beijing: China Animation Studies.

Department for Culture, Media and Sport (DCMS). 2001. *Creative industries mapping document*. London: DCMS.

Entgroup. 2010. *Annual report on China's animation industry*. Beijing: Entgroup Consulting.

Howkins, J. 2013. *The creative economy: How people make money from ideas*. London: Penguin.

HunyuanVideo Repo. 2024. *HunyuanVideo open-source project*. Retrieved from https://github.com/Tencent/HunyuanVideo.

Ishii, K. 2013. "Nationalism and Preferences for Domestic and Foreign Animation Programmes in China." *International Communication Gazette* 75: 225–245.

Keane, M., and Y. Chen. 2019. *Creative industries in China: Art, design and media*. Cambridge: Polity Press.

Lent, J. A. 2006. Comic Art in Asian Cultural Context. Routledge.

Lu, B., Niu, X., and Zheng, Y. 2011. Blue Book of Animation: *Annual Report on Development of China's Animation Industry*. Social Sciences Academic Press.

Lu, B. 2011a. Animation industry clusters and development strategies. *Journal of Cultural Industries 4*(2): 88–97.

Lu, B. 2011b. Internationalization of China's animation industry. *Journal of Cultural Industries 5*(3): 101–115.

Motionplay Studio. 2025. *Latest animation industry statistics*. Retrieved from https://motionplaystudio.com/blog/latest-animation-industry-statistics.

Napier, S. 2018. *Anime from Akira to Howl's Moving Castle: Experiencing contemporary Japanese animation*. New York: Palgrave Macmillan.

National Bureau of Statistics of China. 2024. *Statistical communiqué of the People's Republic of China on the 2023 national economic and social development*. Beijing: NBS. Retrieved from https://www.stats.gov.cn.

Niu, L. 2011. The structure of China's animation industry. *Cultural Development Review 3*(1): 55–70.

O'Hailey, T. 2012. Digital animation and productivity in China. *Animation Studies 7*(1): 45–60.

Propaganda Department. 2010. *Report on cultural industries and creative economy development*. Beijing: Central Propaganda Department.

Qing, J. 2006. 3D technology and the transformation of Chinese animation. *China Animation Studies 2*(1): 44–59.

Reuters. 2024, August. *Bytedance joins OpenAI's Sora rivals with AI video app launch.* Retrieved from https://www.reuters.com/technology/artificial-intelligence/bytedance-joins-openais-sora-rivals-with-ai-video-app-launch-2024-08-06/.

Reuters. 2024, September. *Low-brow vulgar micro dramas shake up China's film industry aim Hollywood.* Retrieved from https://www.reuters.com/world/china/low-brow-vulgar-micro-dramas-shake-up-chinas-film-industry-aim-hollywood-2024-09-21/.

Research in China. 2013. *China animation industry market report.* Beijing: Research in China.

RIC (Research Intelligence Center). 2013. *UK creative industries report.* London: RIC.

SARFT (State Administration of Radio, Film, and Television). 2009. *Annual report on Chinese television and animation exports.* Beijing: SARFT.

SARFT. 2012. *Statistical yearbook of China's animation production (2004–2012).* Beijing: SARFT.

SARFT. 2013. *Monthly report on television animation production, September 2013.* Beijing: SARFT.

SCMP (South China Morning Post). 2024. *State TV airs China's first AI-developed cartoon series Sora sets frenzy text-video generation tech.* Retrieved from https://www.scmp.com/tech/policy/article/3253390/state-tv-airs-chinas-first-ai-developed-cartoon-series-sora-sets-frenzy-text-video-generation-tech?.

SCMP (South China Morning Post). 2025, March 18. *China's Sora-like Vidu breaks into Hollywood with deal to produce GenAI anime series.* Retrieved from https://www.scmp.com/tech/tech-trends/article/3302808/chinas-sora-vidu-breaks-hollywood-deal-produce-genai-anime-series.

Siwek, S.E. 2006. *Copyright industries in the U.S. economy: The 2006 report.* Washington, DC: International Intellectual Property Alliance.

State Council of the People's Republic of China. 2025, March 14. *Regulations on the labeling of AI-generated synthetic content.* Beijing: Cyberspace Administration of China. Retrieved from http://www.cac.gov.cn.

Sun, W. 2010. Mission Impossible? Soft Power, Communication Capacity, and the Globalization of Chinese Media. *International Journal of Communication* 4: 54–72.

Tan, C. 2006a. *McDonald's global strategy.* Singapore: McGraw Hill.

Tan, L. 2006b. Soft power and Chinese cultural policy. *Chinese Journal of Communication 2*(1): 56–72.

UK Trade & Investment. 2010. *UK-China creative industry collaboration report.* London: UK Government.

UNESCO. 2022. *Cultural and creative industries in the digital era.* Paris: UNESCO Publishing.

Vidico. 2025. *Animation industry statistics and growth trends.* Retrieved from https://vidico.com/news/animation-industry-statistics.

Wang, H. 2011, June 24. *Animation consumers in China.* Economic Daily.

Wolf, M. J. 1999. *The entertainment economy: How mega-media forces are transforming our lives.* New York: Times Books.

Yongjiang, Z. 2010. Creative industrial parks and animation. *Modern Media Studies 2*(3): 77–85.

Zhang, L. 2011. SARFT statistics on animation derivatives. *Broadcasting Research 5*(1): 33–41.

Zhao, L. 2011. Children's television programming in China. *Journal of Media Economics 24*(4): 311–326.

Zhang, Z., and Zhou, R. 2010. Blue Book of Animation: Report on Development of China's New Media Animation Industry in 2010. Social Sciences Academic Press.

Chapter 6
Distribution Models in Transition

Abstract This chapter investigates the evolution of distribution models for Chinese animation from the early 2000s to the present. It situates distribution within the framework of China's soft power strategies and the "going out" policy, which encouraged studios to export animated content and participate in international festivals as a means of entering global markets. Despite state subsidies, the financial impact of early exports remained modest, revealing the structural limitations of China's international reach compared to Japanese anime. The chapter traces the diversification of domestic distribution, from national networks to specialized children's channels and thematic platforms, with CCTV-14 playing a key role in shaping children's programming. It also examines satellite distribution, drawing lessons from Japanese models, and evaluates the increasing importance of cinema releases, which positioned animation as a driver of box office growth. Case studies, including *Ne Zha 2*, illustrate how domestic successes achieved unprecedented international visibility. Beyond traditional circuits, the chapter discusses the role of festivals and exhibitions in legitimizing animation as cultural capital. The analysis concludes that distribution has shifted from a state-driven and television-centered model toward a hybrid ecosystem of theatrical releases, digital platforms, and global partnerships, reflecting the broader transformation of China's media economy.

Keywords Going out policy · CCTV-14 · Satellite distribution · Cinema box office · Ne Zha 2 · Festivals · Soft power

6.1 Frameworks of Distribution—Structures and Pathways

The Chinese government, in alignment with its soft power strategy and the broader initiative of *going out* (走出去, *zou chuqu*), has consistently encouraged and supported creative industries in investing in the production of high-quality cultural products aimed not only at the domestic market but also, and above all, at international audiences. The overseas dissemination of Chinese creative goods is considered a crucial channel through which the nation can promote its cultural identity

© The Author(s), under exclusive license to Springer Nature Switzerland AG 2026

V. De Masi, *A Critical Analysis of China's Animation Industry*, Numanities - Arts and Humanities in Progress 37, https://doi.org/10.1007/978-3-032-18656-0_6

while simultaneously entering new global markets. To advance this agenda, the State Administration of Radio, Film, and Television (SARFT) has urged animation companies to actively participate in international festivals, emphasizing that only through these platforms can negotiations be initiated with foreign broadcasters and distributors. Such encounters are facilitated by offering exclusive advantages, including pre-sales and preview screenings of selected episodes, in the hope of securing future acquisitions (Tan 2006).

According to the *China Statistical Yearbook*, exports of Chinese animation increased annually during the late 2000s, although the overall economic value remained modest. Most of the exported titles benefited from government support under the "going out" policy, yet their financial returns were limited. In 2007, the export market reached approximately 8 million euros (73 million yuan), comprising 30 series with a total of 2244 episodes. By 2008, the number of exported series had risen to 38 with 1877 episodes, but revenues declined sharply to just 3.5 million euros. A gradual recovery followed in 2009, when 55 series amounting to 3191 episodes generated around 5.5 million euros (44.5 million yuan).

Beyond established markets, China has also pursued cultural and economic ties with developing regions such as the Middle East, Africa, and South America. Although the financial contributions from these areas remain relatively minor, the strategy reflects Beijing's intention to cultivate long-term cultural influence and establish fertile grounds for future markets through its soft power diplomacy (Lu 2012).

When compared with the international performance of Japanese anime, the limitations of Chinese animation exports become even more evident. In the United States alone, Japanese animation generated an estimated 4 billion euros annually, underscoring the substantial gap China still faces in transforming cultural production into competitive global assets (Qing 2006).

In the 2010s and 2020s, the distribution model of Chinese animation underwent significant transformations. The rise of digital streaming platforms such as Bilibili, Tencent Video, and iQIYI created new opportunities for global dissemination, while co-productions with Netflix and international distributors opened additional channels of visibility. Notably, Tencent and Bilibili have positioned themselves as intermediaries capable of bridging domestic creativity and global circulation, with works such as *The King's Avatar* (全职高手, *Quánzhí Gāoshǒu*) and *Fog Hill of the Five Elements* (雾山五行, *Wù Shān Wǔ Xíng*) reaching international audiences through subtitled releases. At the same time, international recognition of Chinese feature-length animation expanded dramatically. By the early 2020s, the international circulation of Chinese animated features had begun to achieve results that were unthinkable only a decade earlier. While individual cases such as *Nezha* attracted wide attention, their significance lay less in the singular success of a blockbuster and more in demonstrating the possibility of sustained global engagement. The growing presence of Chinese animation at international festivals, the availability of subtitled versions on global streaming platforms, and the strategic co-productions with foreign distributors signaled a structural shift. These dynamics suggested that Chinese animation was no longer confined to a domestic niche but was gradually becoming a recognized component of the global media ecology, even if the scale of its exports still lagged far behind the Japanese and Korean industries.

6.2 Television Logics—From National Networks to Local Markets

In the late 2000s and early 2010s, the distribution of animated products in China relied almost entirely on national and provincial television broadcasters. Approval for broadcast rested with the State Administration of Radio, Film, and Television (SARFT), which controlled licensing and programming schedules. In 2008, only 198 institutions across the country were authorized to transmit animation, yet by 2010 the number had risen to 298 (Lu 2011). Provinces such as Jiangsu, with forty dedicated broadcasters, Liaoning with thirty-two, and Guangdong with thirty-one, stood out for their relatively dense networks of television stations. This expansion reflected both the ambitions of local governments to present themselves as cultural hubs and the central government's broader aim of fostering an animation industry with the capacity to serve mass audiences.

Statistical surveys from that period underline the magnitude of this growth. Between 2004 and 2010, the number of animated series approved and broadcast increased substantially, reaching 17,544 series with over 600,000 episodes in 2009 alone. Hours of television programming devoted to animation more than doubled compared to 2005, supported by policies that encouraged both the production and the dissemination of original domestic works (Blue Book 2011). Yet contradictions soon emerged. Despite the growth in output, only a fraction of the minutes produced were actually broadcast, as censorship and quality standards prevented much of the content from reaching audiences. The case of *Pleasant Goat and Big Big Wolf*, suspended by SARFT in 2013 on grounds of excessive violence despite its immense popularity and more than one thousand episodes, epitomized the tensions between audience demand, market logics, and ideological control.

Audience data from this period reveal further complexities. The majority of viewers were children between the ages of four and fourteen, yet the growth of teenage and adult segments was less pronounced than in Japan, where anime attracted diverse age groups. Broadcast times also shaped patterns of consumption: animation peaked during school holidays, weekends, and evening hours, confirming its orientation toward younger audiences with free time. Socioeconomic profiles underscored the predominance of lower-income households and students, suggesting that animation functioned as both accessible entertainment and a cultural product aligned with state narratives of education and morality.

Although these early statistics now appear dated, they remain instructive as a snapshot of the transitional role of television in shaping the early ecology of Chinese animation. At that time, television was not only the primary distribution channel but also the main instrument of state regulation, determining what kind of content could reach the public and under what conditions. The centrality of broadcast institutions created a paradox: the volume of production expanded dramatically, yet bottlenecks in approval and programming allocation limited both diversity and international competitiveness.

Recent data illustrate how television continues to operate, though with diminishing influence. According to the *Chinese Audio-Visual Market Research 2023*, the total broadcast time of animation on traditional TV channels reached approximately 452,000 h in 2023, representing only a modest year-on-year increase of about 1% (Italian Trade Agency [ICE] 2023). This stabilization suggests that traditional television has ceased to be a major driver of growth in the sector. Moreover, legislation and regulatory frameworks remain firmly in place. Traditional broadcast TV is still subject to licensing, content approval, and strict rules on program scheduling and ideological suitability, factors that continue to limit the diversity of content available to viewers (Lexology 2025).

Scholarly analyses further confirm the decline in television's centrality. A comparative study emphasized that the use of broadcast TV in China has been steadily decreasing, particularly among younger audiences, with digital platforms becoming the dominant mode of consumption even though television retains a residual cultural legitimacy. These findings reinforce the idea that the historical data from 2008 to 2012 now serve as markers of a past distribution regime. Today, while broadcast television still provides symbolic validation and access in regions with limited digital infrastructure, the structural transformation of the media environment has marginalized its role in shaping the national animation industry.

6.3 Specialized Channels—The Rise of Animation on Thematic Platforms

The early 2000s marked the birth of thematic channels dedicated to children's programming and animation in China. The launch of CCTV Children (*CCTV 少儿, Shao'er*) in 2003 represented a milestone, establishing a national platform that aligned with the government's cultural policy and soft power strategy of supporting domestic animation. Shortly afterward, SARFT authorized the creation of other thematic channels such as Beijing's Kaku TV, Shanghai Xuandong, Hunan Jiying, and Guangdong Jiajia (Tan 2006). These initiatives sought not only to expand the circulation of animation but also to create new venues in which domestic productions could gain prestige and compete with foreign titles.

In their early phase, these channels reflected the contradictions of a developing industry. Production companies often struggled to secure adequate compensation for their works. In 2006, for instance, CCTV reportedly paid between 600 and 1000 yuan per minute of animation, while other networks such as Shanghai Media Group paid between 200 and 600 yuan per minute. Many local stations, rather than paying at all, offered producers airtime in exchange for the opportunity to profit from merchandising or secondary rights if a program proved successful with viewers (Tan 2006). The result was a fragmented and precarious system that underscored the difficulty of building a sustainable animation economy within the confines of broadcast television.

Over time, CCTV-14 became the flagship channel for children's programming and animation, consolidating its status as the most prestigious venue for domestic productions. The channel's mission, as articulated in its official guidelines, emphasizes "guiding growth and shaping the future" through a combination of entertainment and education, privileging national content in line with government directives. While Kaku TV and other provincial thematic channels maintained visibility, the symbolic value of CCTV-14 made it the ultimate aspiration for studios seeking national recognition. Advertising revenue reflects this prestige: by the early 2020s, a five-second primetime spot on CCTV-14 could cost more than 37,000 yuan, a figure that illustrates the channel's continuing commercial importance despite the broader decline of linear broadcasting (Wang 2011; ICE 2023).

In recent years, thematic channels have played a dual role. On one hand, they continue to serve as gateways of legitimacy for children's animation, especially in households and regions where broadcast television remains the primary medium. On the other hand, their relative weight within the distribution ecology has diminished as digital platforms capture the majority of young audiences. Reports indicate that in 2023, traditional television channels in China broadcast approximately 452,000 h of animation, showing only marginal year-on-year growth (ICE 2023). This stabilization contrasts with the exponential expansion of streaming services, highlighting that television channels such as CCTV-14 now function less as engines of industrial growth and more as institutions of cultural endorsement.

The persistence of CCTV-14 and other thematic broadcasters nevertheless points to a deeper continuity: the state's commitment to shaping childhood media environments through curated programming. Although television is no longer the central driver of distribution, it remains a symbolic arena where the values of edu-tainment, national identity, and state-endorsed soft power are staged and reaffirmed. In this sense, the emergence of thematic animation channels in the early 2000s is best understood not as a temporary experiment but as the foundation of an institutional model that continues to influence Chinese animation, even in an era dominated by digital media.

6.3.1 CCTV 14—Programming Childhood in a State Framework

CCTV 14 is the national children's channel of China Central Television. It launched in 2003 after earlier children's strands had aired on CCTV 7. The channel's mandate aligns with education and cultural policy and privileges domestic animation within an edutainment framework (Wikipedia 2025a, b, c, d, e, f, g).

A concise historical model helps situate the present schedule. In the early 2010s the day typically opened at daybreak with the national anthem and moved through morning animation blocks and studio based children's magazines. Midday carried well known foreign cartoons. Evenings returned to domestically oriented strands and weekends concentrated specials and animated features. This baseline clarifies how the channel organized flow and audience address in that period (TVSou 2025).

Current programming retains the educational orientation while organizing content around recurring named columns. The official portal lists core strands such as *Big Pinwheel* (大风车, *Dà Fēngchē*), *Animation Big Screening* (动画大放映, *Dònghuà Dà Fàngyìng*), *Animation World* (动漫世界, *Dòngmàn Shìjiè*), *Wisdom Tree* (智慧树, *Zhìhuì Shù*), and *Little Wisdom Tree* (小小智慧树, *Xiǎo Xiǎo Zhìhuì Shù*). Weekend blocks feature *Weekend Animation* (周末动画片, *Zhōumò Dònghuàpiàn*). These columns anchor daily curation for preschool and school-age viewers and reflect the channel's educational mission (CCTV 14 Children's Channel 2025).

Electronic program guides corroborate early starts and the placement of children's news and education strands in the first hours. Recent listings show openings around 05.55 with the national anthem and morning sequences that include *Big Pinwheel*, *Little Wisdom Tree* and *Animation Big Screening*, followed by family oriented slots later in the day and expanded animation on weekends. Titles and exact times vary and schedules remain subject to change (TVMao 2025; TVSou 2025).

The mix of domestic and imported content is curated rather than evenly distributed. Foreign series with high recognition are placed in designated slots, while domestic animation and factual entertainment form the backbone of the channel's identity. Live and on demand access are exposed on the network's digital properties, which present these strands as complementary components of the mandate to combine entertainment and learning for minors (CCTV 14 Children's Channel 2025; CCTV Live Portal 2025).

6.3.2 Children's Channels—Reconfiguring Audiences and Genres

The emergence of thematic children's channels in the mid 2000s reshaped the traditional distribution of animation in China by concentrating youth audiences around a small cluster of provincial satellite services and municipal broadcasters that aligned educational goals with market oriented branding. The early leadership of CCTV 14 (*CCTV Shào'ér* 少儿) created a template that other players adapted to local mandates and commercial strategies, yet over time the field consolidated around a handful of recognizable brands that continue to anchor broadcast visibility for domestic animation while coexisting with the expansion of digital platforms. This section considers that arc as a single trajectory rather than as a set of isolated case studies, using emblematic stations to illustrate structural change rather than to repeat institutional profiles in isolation. The core insight is that children's satellite channels grew out of policy support for national content and gradually became prestige gateways for domestic animation in an era when linear television no longer drives overall growth but still confers legitimacy and reach, especially outside first tier urban centers (CCTV 14 portal 2025; ICE 2023).

Among the earliest city based channels to generalize the CCTV model, Tianjin TV Children (天津电视台少儿频道, *Tiānjīn diànshìtái shào'ér píndào*) illustrates both the rapid build out of the period and the later retrenchment. Launched in 2004 within Tianjin Television, it offered a full schedule of animation and children's factual entertainment. The channel was discontinued on 31 October 2022 as part of a broader restructuring of the Tianjin broadcasting group, a decision that marks a clear difference between the expansive logic of the late 2000s and the current emphasis on fewer, stronger brands with wider carriage and simpler cost structures (Wikipedia 2025a, b, c, d, e, f, g).

By contrast, several provincial satellite channels have preserved and even reinforced their identities by pairing national coverage with a curated mix of domestic animation, studio magazines, and event television. Golden Eagle Cartoon (金鹰卡通卫视, *Jīnyīng kǎtōng wèishì*), affiliated with Hunan Broadcasting, began in 2004 as one of the first satellite animation services and later upgraded to high definition distribution with broad carriage on cable and IPTV networks. It continues to position itself as a nationwide family channel for viewers aged four to fourteen and expands brand recognition through seasonal spectaculars that combine children's performance with animated properties. In 2024 Hunan outlets announced a Global Children's Spring Festival Gala for the 2025 season, an example of how legacy broadcasters convert festive programming into networked cultural events that extend the station's symbolic role beyond linear transmission (Wikipedia 2025a, b, c, d, e, f, g; New Hunan 2024; Sohu 2024).

Beijing's *KAKU Children's Channel* (BRTV KAKU 少儿卫视, *KAKU Shào'ér Wèishì*), launched in 2004 and uplinked to satellite in 2007, has similarly stabilized its identity through a portfolio of named columns, editorial curation of domestic animation, and recurring seasonal events. It moved to widescreen and high definition in 2020, a technical upgrade that accompanied a refreshed brand presentation and a continued emphasis on education-oriented entertainment. The channel's official materials and schedules underscore a hybrid grid that alternates animation blocks with magazines, news for children, and weekend special screenings. Live portals and third-party electronic program guides consistently present early morning openings followed by rotating animation blocks and family-oriented strands through the day, which signals a durable broadcast grammar adapted to contemporary expectations of consistency and recognizability (Wikipedia 2025a, b, c, d, e, f, g; TVMao EPG 2025).

In Shanghai, the consolidation of *Xuàndòng Kǎtōng* (炫动卡通, *Xuàndòng Kǎtōng*) and *Hāhā Shào'ér* (哈哈少儿, *Hāhā Shào'ér*) into *Hāhā Xuàndòng Wèishì* (哈哈炫动卫视, *Hāhā Xuàndòng Wèishì*) in 2019 produced a unified children's channel that foregrounds the link between original animation, performance training, and arts education.

Official statements describe a schedule of roughly eighteen hours per day focused on preschool and school age viewers, a mix of domestic animated series and self produced cultural content, and a portfolio of original properties associated with Shanghai's youth arts ecosystem. This integration is a revealing sign of broadcast adaptation, since it rationalizes production resources while keeping a strong local brand that can still secure carriage nationwide via satellite and cable platforms (SMG 2022; TVMao EPG 2025).

Other regional satellite services play complementary roles within the same ecology. *Youman Cartoon* in Jiangsu (优漫卡通卫视, *Yōumàn Kǎtōng Wèishì*) presents itself as one of the five national satellite animation channels and emphasizes its specialization in high-volume children's programming. *Jiajia Cartoon* in Guangdong (嘉佳卡通, *Jiājiā Kǎtōng*), operating within the Guangdong Radio and Television Group, promotes children's variety shows and educational events alongside animation. These stations provide additional points of entry for domestic producers who seek television exposure and reinforce a national map of youth oriented broadcasting that balances central and provincial brands (JSTV Youman portal 2025; GRTN Jiajia channel 2025).

Across these channels, several continuities stand out. First, all of them articulate an explicitly pedagogical mandate and frame animation as part of a broader edutainment project. This is visible in the mission statements and stable columns on the official portals of CCTV 14 and KAKU and in Shanghai's description of Haha Xundong as a parent child and family channel. Such positioning aligns with national cultural policy and continues the long standing expectation that broadcast content for minors should integrate entertainment with moral and civic education, a requirement that has shaped both format selection and scheduling. Second, the channels cultivate prestige through live or televised gala events, seasonal blocks, and talent showcases that concentrate attention and drive promotional cycles, a strategy observable in Golden Eagle's Spring Festival plans and in KAKU's recurring Animation Spring Festival programming. Third, they maintain hybrid schedules in which foreign titles appear in curated slots while domestic animation remains the backbone of the offer. The CCTV animation portal, which aggregates listings from multiple children's channels, routinely shows rotations of popular domestic series across these stations, confirming that broadcast circulation still matters for national properties even as digital windows proliferate (CCTV 14 portal 2025; SMG 2022; New Hunan 2024; CCTV animation hub 2025).

At the same time, structural differences from the expansionary years of the late 2000s are apparent. Channel closures such as Tianjin's children's channel point to a narrower broadcast landscape in which national satellite brands and a few strong provincial services absorb attention and carriage. The economic logic has shifted from rapid multiplication of outlets to the cultivation of recognizable columns and stable franchises that can anchor advertising and sponsorship without requiring large capital outlays for new channel launches. Industry reporting on the overall television volume of animation also indicates a plateau. The most recent international market analysis available from the Italian Trade Agency estimates roughly four hundred fifty two thousand hours of animation broadcast on traditional television in 2023, a year on year increase of about 1%, which suggests that linearly scheduled animation remains a significant but no longer expanding driver of industry growth. Within this environment, children's satellite channels function less as engines of quantitative expansion and more as curatorial institutions that guarantee baseline visibility and cultural endorsement for domestic animation across the terrestrial and cable universe (ICE 2023).

The result is a dual configuration in which satellite children's channels retain symbolic and practical value within the traditional media system, while digital platforms have become the primary vector for audience growth among younger cohorts. For producers of animation, broadcast exposure on these channels still matters for reputation, for meeting regulatory expectations associated with children's programming, and for reaching households that rely on cable or terrestrial reception rather than high bandwidth streaming. For policymakers, the persistence of a curated broadcast layer ensures a nationally consistent framework for content aimed at minors and provides a stage for event television that foregrounds cultural heritage and educational themes. For viewers, the presence of familiar columns and seasonal specials sustains a sense of continuity with the broadcast culture of the 2000s even as consumption habits diversify. Thematic children's channels therefore remain a crucial part of the traditional distribution architecture of Chinese animation, reduced in number yet more coherent in brand identity, more explicit in mission, and more closely integrated with other provincial and national cultural institutions than during the expansionary years that followed the birth of CCTV 14 (CCTV 14 portal 2025; SMG 2022; JSTV Youman portal 2025; GRTN Jiajia channel 2025; Wikipedia 2025a, b, c, d, e, f, g).

6.4 Satellite Distribution—Lessons from the Japanese Model

Japanese satellite television offers a revealing benchmark for understanding how animation channels can scale across borders through brand consolidation and multi territory carriage. The most emblematic case is Animax, founded in 1998 as a twenty four hour anime network that quickly became the reference model for linear anime distribution and later a hybrid of satellite, cable, and streaming outlets. In its Japanese home market the channel began under Sony Pictures Entertainment Japan and assembled a shareholder base that included major studios. In 2024 Sony transferred Animax Broadcast Japan to Nojima's AK Entertainment, which now operates the service while the channel's identity as a dedicated anime network remains intact. The sale completed in April 2024 and marked Sony's strategic focus on global streaming assets consolidated under Crunchyroll, while the Japanese linear network continued under new ownership (Animax 2025; MarketScreener 2023, 2024).

Outside Japan the Animax brand has followed a different path. Sony sold its pan Asian channels business to KC Global Media in 2020, which now operates Animax Asia alongside AXN and GEM from its Singapore base. This move shifted control of the Southeast Asian and South Asian feeds away from Sony while preserving the channel's editorial profile as an anime specialist. Since 2023 and 2024 KC Global has added distribution through major Indian platforms including JioTV, Prime Video, Tata Play, and a free ad supported channel on Samsung TV Plus, which confirms a transition from exclusive pay television carriage to a mixed environment that includes direct to consumer apps and platform partnerships. Animax Asia's own materials and Wikipedia entries underline the channel's continued presence across Southeast Asian markets with the explicit exclusion of mainland China, where the brand does not hold carriage. The Vietnamese feed relaunched in 2020 and shut again in 2025, which illustrates the regulatory and market variability that regional channels navigate (Variety 2020; Animax Asian TV channel, 2025; Animax Asia 2025).

The evolution of Animax clarifies three structural features of satellite led anime distribution. First, a strong master brand can sustain a continuous flow of Japanese series across multiple territories even when ownership changes from a global studio to a regional operator. The Japanese parent network is now under Nojima, while the Asian feeds are under KC Global Media, yet both retain the Animax identity and a programming spine of subtitled and dubbed series timed to Japanese release windows where feasible. Second, carriage has diversified. The legacy satellite and cable footprint remains important for households that consume through electronic program guides, but new reach now comes from streaming and free ad supported channels integrated into domestic super apps and device based services. India is a case in point, where the linear channel exited in 2017 and returned through digital distribution beginning in 2023. Third, the brand's international map has contracted compared with the 2000s and early 2010s, when Animax operated in Europe and Latin America. In those regions linear services were replaced or discontinued by 2011 to 2016, while Asia has remained the brand's core, with South Korea now operated by a local company after a 2023 sale and Southeast Asia anchored in KC Global's portfolio (Animax 2025; Animax Asian TV channel, 2025).

This Japanese example is instructive for evaluating the export prospects of Chinese children's and animation channels. Chinese thematic channels such as KAKU Children's Channel in Beijing or Golden Eagle Cartoon in Hunan have strong domestic identities and robust brand recognition at home, yet they function primarily as national or provincial satellite services within China's regulated broadcast system. Unlike Animax, these outlets have not built sustained multi country linear footprints. The obstacles are structural and cultural rather than purely financial. They include regulatory asymmetries across markets, the requirement for extensive localization and editorial independence to reach older youth and adult anime publics, and the need for a transnational brand narrative that connects the channel name to a broad catalog of must watch series in multiple languages. The Animax story shows that distribution scale outside the home market requires either ownership by or partnership with a regional network operator that specializes in cross border carriage and platform deals. It also shows that the anime category travels across age groups in ways that animation for younger children does not always replicate on satellite and cable, especially when domestic policy prioritizes educational goals and prescriptive content standards. These dynamics partially explain why the linear internationalization of Chinese animation channels has been modest even as domestic viewership and production have grown. The Asian Animax feeds explicitly exclude mainland China, which underscores how regional anime distribution has developed largely outside China's broadcast ecosystem and instead interfaces with it through licensing and digital rights rather than through a shared satellite brand (Animax Asian TV channel 2025).

The historical association between satellite television and merchandise driven character economies remains relevant. Hello Kitty, created by Sanrio in 1974, offers a clear example of how character licensing, broadcast exposure, and event culture can reinforce one another over decades. The fiftieth anniversary cycle in 2024 and 2025 coincided with record financial results for Sanrio, driven by global licensing and brand collaborations. Company filings report sales of 144.9 billion yen and operating profit of 51.8 billion yen for the fiscal year ending March 2025. Press coverage places annual retail sales associated with Hello Kitty around three point one billion pounds, and the character continues to rank among the most valuable media franchises worldwide. The synergy between broadcast presence, consumer products, and themed events provides a yardstick for assessing how channel backed properties can accumulate value across markets when supported by consistent transmedia strategy. For Chinese producers the implication is that linear exposure on domestic satellite channels can legitimize properties, but sustained international recognition usually requires a branded distribution spine comparable to Animax and a licensing infrastructure of the kind perfected by Sanrio (Sanrio 2025; The Guardian 2024).

Taken together, the Japanese satellite model demonstrates that exportable identity arises from the combination of a clear genre promise, stable brand architecture, and flexible carriage that spans satellite, cable, and streaming environments. Animax began as a single purpose satellite network and then adapted its delivery to changing consumption while protecting the central promise of Japanese anime. In Japan the channel persists on satellite and cable under a new corporate parent. Across Asia it persists under a regional operator that has rebuilt distribution on a platform by platform basis and reentered markets through digital services where linear channels had closed. This mixture of persistence and adaptation is the central lesson for any attempt to build a cross border animation channel from China. The domestic prestige that accrues to broadcast exposure at home is necessary but not sufficient. What proved decisive for Animax was a recognizable pan regional brand that audiences could seek out regardless of platform and a catalog strategy that continually refreshed the schedule with anticipated titles. In practical terms, Chinese channels that aspire to travel will need to consolidate brands, coordinate with regional operators for multi market carriage, and pair linear presence with streaming availability and licensing campaigns centered on characters with cross cultural appeal. Without these elements satellite distribution alone is unlikely to deliver durable international growth, especially in a landscape where streaming discovery and platform partnerships now set the tempo for transnational anime circulation (Variety 2020; Animax 2025; Animax Asia 2025).

6.5 Cinema Distribution—Screens, Audiences, and Box Office Logics

China is now one of the most important cinema markets in the world. The national screen base continued to expand even during periods of box office volatility. Industry tallies indicate that in 2024 more than four thousand six hundred new screens were installed, lifting the total to about 91,000 and consolidating China's position as the largest screen network worldwide. The most recent overviews also show that domestic films accounted for close to four fifths of box office in 2024, which confirms the centrality of the local slate in sustaining admissions and shaping release calendars (China Daily 2025a, b, c).

The revenue cycle has been uneven but resilient. Official year end figures placed 2024 box office at 42.5 billion yuan, a contraction compared with the previous year but still a scale that keeps China among the top markets by global standards. Analysts linked the dip to fewer major releases, competition from short video platforms, and pressure on discretionary spending. The structural picture remains that of a very large market with a deep exhibition base and significant holiday peaks, a pattern visible again in the early months of 2025 when festival windows drew large family audiences back to theaters (China Daily 2025a, b, c).

Audience reception data indicates a shift in demographics. While animation was historically viewed by parents as a genre strictly for children, recent surveys (China Daily 2025a, b, c) suggest that the 'family viewing' model has evolved. Adult audiences, particularly 'Gen Z' consumers, increasingly treat animated blockbusters as event cinema, engaging in online discussions about plot complexity and visual fidelity rather than merely educational value. This reception shift has forced studios to layer narratives with themes that resonate across generations.

Animation plays a strategically visible role within this ecology because it addresses multigenerational audiences and aligns naturally with school calendars and national holidays. Hand drawn features and computer animated franchises have anchored peak seasons and helped stabilize attendance among family viewers. During the summer of 2025 the hand drawn feature *Nobody* set a new national benchmark for two dimensional animation and contributed to a season that exceeded the previous year on several indicators, including a single day record and higher cumulative admissions. These outcomes indicate that animated features now compete at the very top of the domestic box office and that the genre functions as event cinema for broad publics, especially during school breaks and the summer and winter holidays when family viewing is concentrated (Xinhua 2025a, b, c, d, e; Global Times 2025).

Given the focus of this chapter, it is sufficient to note in passing that *Nezha 2* set new records during the Lunar New Year period and has been widely reported as a landmark for domestic animation. We have discussed this case elsewhere, so here it serves simply as an emblem of the scale that animated franchises can now achieve in the national market (Reuters 2025a, b).

The social geography of exhibition also matters for animation. As high tier cities reached maturity, exhibitors extended coverage across county level cities and newly urbanized districts. Many of the newest screens are smaller and offer fewer premium large format auditoria, with lower average ticket prices and programming designed for local family audiences. This diffusion helps animated titles reach viewers who still rely on terrestrial or basic cable access and fosters repeated attendance through localized promotions and dubbed versions for younger viewers. The screen build out therefore complements the growth of online platforms rather than replacing them. Theatrical windows create moments of national attention, while digital circulation extends the life of titles and cultivates fan communities across regions (Omdia 2025).

The comparison with earlier decades underscores the speed of transformation. A little over 10 years ago the screen base was counted in the tens of thousands and China had just surpassed Japan to become the second largest market by box office. Today the country operates a screen network that approaches one hundred thousand and supports a domestic share that often exceeds 70%. This scale changes the production logic of animated features. Studios can now plan for multi week national runs, invest in more sophisticated visual design, and coordinate merchandise and publishing tie ins that depend on concentrated theatrical exposure. The cinema functions not only as a distribution channel but also as a stage for cultural visibility where domestic animation can present new mythological and historical narratives to a mass audience and negotiate the balance between creative ambition, market expectations, and regulatory frameworks. In this sense theatrical distribution remains an essential pillar of the animation economy in China and a key driver of the country's broader cultural influence (Wikipedia 2025a, b, c, d, e, f, g; China Daily 2025a, b, c).

Finally, it is important to recognize that animation's distinctive capacity to invite identification across cultural contexts does not depend on the physiognomic features of live performers. As scholars have noted, the adoption of anthropomorphic characters and stylized design can lower barriers to identification and allow stories to address universal themes through particular cultural symbols. This helps explain why animated features travel effectively across provinces and age cohorts within China and why they can appeal to international audiences when distribution allows. The case of Japanese anime is a well known precedent. The contemporary Chinese context suggests that when domestic animation combines recognizable character design with clear narrative identity and carefully timed release windows, it can mobilize large audiences in a market that is already among the most important globally.

6.6 The "Year of the Rabbit"—Shifting Landscapes of Circulation

The Year of the Rabbit in 2011 is widely remembered as a pivot because animation began drawing mass holiday audiences at an unprecedented scale. The clearest signal was the performance of *Kung Fu Panda 2* which set national records and showed exhibitors and producers that animated spectacle could anchor peak seasons for multiplexes across the country (The Guardian 2011).

What matters today is how that pivot matured into a stable exhibition pattern. After a volatile cycle in 2024 the official year end tally placed national box office at 42.5 billion yuan and trade coverage noted fewer major releases and pressure from short form video, yet the screen base kept expanding and theatrical windows retained their role as national events for families and youth (China Daily 2025a, b, c). The rebound was immediate at the start of 2025 when festival periods drew very large crowds and set new attendance highs, confirming that the market remains one of the most important globally despite year to year swings (China Daily 2025a, b, c).

Within this ecology animation functions as a reliable driver of seasonal peaks. Hand drawn and computer animated features have become event cinema for multigenerational audiences, especially during winter and summer holidays. In August 2025 the hand drawn feature *Nobody* crossed the one billion yuan mark and set a national record for two dimensional animation according to trade reports and official newswires, which indicates a broader acceptance of stylistic diversity in animated features and a stronger pipeline of locally developed properties (Cartoon Brew 2025; Xinhua 2025a, b, c, d, e).

For this chapter it is sufficient to note in passing that *Nezha 2* has been reported as the highest grossing film in Chinese history and the highest grossing animated film worldwide, a result achieved during the Lunar New Year window that illustrates the present capacity of domestic animation to scale to the very top of the market. A fuller discussion of the *Nezha* cycle follows later in the book, so here it serves only as a contemporary benchmark for the ceiling of the genre (Reuters 2025a, 2025b).

Current seasonal data underscore the strength of local slates. News coverage of the summer 2025 window reports that domestic films led the market and that cumulative summer grosses surpassed the previous year, while analytics cited in the press placed the domestic share above three quarters of the total. These snapshots confirm the consolidation of holiday programming as the organizing principle of theatrical distribution and the central role of animation within that cycle (Xinhua 2025a, b, c, d, e; Global Times 2025).

In sum, 2011 signaled that animation could command national attention. Today that mechanism has become routine. Theatrical animation activates family attendance, aligns with school calendars and festival weeks, and supports long tail revenue through merchandise and promotional tie ins. The market remains large in screens and admissions, resilient to short term fluctuations, and anchored by domestic properties that travel across age cohorts. This is the context within which subsequent case studies will be read, including the *Nezha* cycle which we address in a later section.

6.7 Beyond Traditional Circuits—Exhibitions and Festivals in China

Since 2011 the festival and exhibition circuit has become a central channel for the domestic circulation and the international projection of Chinese animation. Policy continues to encourage outward facing participation while local governments have scaled up state level platforms that mix public programming with professional markets. The clearest example is the *China International Cartoon and Animation Festival* (中国国际动漫节, *Zhōngguó Guójì Dòngmàn Jié*), held in Hangzhou, which has matured into a week that joins a mass-facing fair, an industry marketplace, curated screenings, and talent programs. The 2025 edition reported 1.46 million visits across five days and hosted 2573 companies and institutions from forty two countries and regions, with on site transactions and consumption of about 1.48 billion yuan, a scale that illustrates how a festival can function as both cultural showcase and trading floor (ehangzhou.gov.cn 2025).

CICAF is complemented by the International Animation and Game Business Conference iABC, a business to business forum embedded in the festival that frames itself as a global cooperation hub for animation and games and aligns its agenda with national digital culture priorities. The 2025 call described a focus on internationalization, specialization, and platform building in order to accelerate cross border partnerships and new productivity in the sector. This pairing of a mass festival with a professional market concentrates decision makers in a single calendar window and has become a stable route for domestic studios to meet broadcasters, streamers, and consumer product licensees (iABC 2025; CICAF, 2025a, 2025b).

Shanghai's China International Cartoon and Game Expo CCG Expo (中国国际动漫游戏博览会) shows the same hybrid logic with a different emphasis. It privileges consumer culture and direct fan engagement while keeping a visible industry presence. The 2025 edition gathered about 480 exhibitors and dedicated space to independent and tabletop games, which reveals how the animation economy interlocks with broader ACG practices and with small studio ecosystems. Media coverage by Xinhua and municipal sources highlighted the role of CCG Expo as the opening anchor of a citywide summer of animation and gaming events that spill into shopping districts and community venues (Xinhua 2025a, b, c, d, e; Shanghai Putuo Government 2025; JETRO J Messe 2025).

Beijing has reinforced its own platform mix. The *Beijing Animation Festival* (北京动画节, *Běijīng Dònghuà Jié*) returns in late September 2025 at the Beijing Exhibition Center with screenings, marketplace activities, and public interactive zones. The *Communication University of China* (中国传媒大学, *Zhōngguó Chuánméi Dàxué*) continues to operate *AniWow* (中国北京国际大学生动画节, *Zhōngguó Běijīng Guójì Dàxuéshēng Dònghuà Jié*) as a pipeline for student work and emerging talent. A distinct art-led strand has developed around *Feinaki Beijing Animation Week*, which sustains an auteur focus and international competition. Together these events tie education, industry exposure, and audience development into a metropolitan circuit that complements Hangzhou and Shanghai rather than competing with them (Beijing Municipal Government 2025a, b; FilmFreeway 2025; Animation Festivals 2025).

The trade fair ecosystem also matters. The *China International Fair for Trade in Services* (中国国际服务贸易交易会, *Zhōngguó Guójì Fúwù Màoyì Jiāoyì Huì*), or *CIFTIS*, has retained a cultural and tourism pavilion where animation and related digital content are promoted as exportable services. The 2025 edition at Shougang Park convened national and international delegations and continued the practice of bundling screenings, showcases, and signing ceremonies within a services trade narrative. Although CIFTIS is not an animation-only event, its prominence has given studios and regional clusters a neutral platform to pitch beyond the core fan public and to place animation alongside design, education, and technology services (Beijing Municipal Government 2025a, b; Xinhua 2025a, b, c, d, e).

Large-scale pop culture expositions further extend reach. *ChinaJoy* (中国国际数码互动娱乐展览会, *Zhōngguó Guójì Shùmǎ Hùdòng Yúlè Zhǎnlǎnhuì*) in Shanghai remains one of the country's largest interactive entertainment gatherings, with a long-running national cosplay league and a dense schedule of stage events.

The 2025 finals of the ChinaJoy Cosplay Super League were scheduled for August at the Shanghai New International Expo Center, confirming how cosplay has been institutionalized as a competitive and media friendly activity that intersects animation, gaming, and idol culture (ChinaJoy official X account 2025; China.com Tech 2025; SmartShanghai 2025).

Platform led showcases add a new layer. Bilibili World in Shanghai positions itself as an ACG carnival where platform creators, manufacturers, and international tech brands converge around animation fandom. Reports in July 2025 cited around three hundred thousand visitors over three days, with hundreds of exhibitors and extensive live streaming. This format captures how festivals now mediate between digital communities and physical retail, and how animation travels through creator economies and maker cultures as much as through broadcast and theatrical channels (City News Service 2025; Yicai 2025).

Museums provide continuity and heritage framing within this landscape. The *China Cartoon and Animation Museum* (中国动漫博物馆, *Zhōngguó Dòngmàn Bówùguǎn*) in Hangzhou opened to the public in 2021 and serves as a permanent anchor near the CICAF venues at Baima Lake. Official descriptions in 2025 emphasize a collection of more than twenty thousand items and frequent temporary exhibitions that place contemporary properties in dialogue with historical materials. This institutional infrastructure supports a year round pedagogy of animation and gives festivals a curatorial partner that can host retrospectives and craft based displays that exceed the temporal limits of a fair (CGTN 2025a, b; ehangzhou.gov.cn 2025).

Internationalization has also advanced through coordinated participation abroad. Chinese pavilions and delegations have maintained a visible presence at the Annecy International Animation Film Festival and its market, with showcases for features and shorts and with organized pitching events. Coverage in 2024 and 2025 noted Chinese industry showcases and a formal China Pavilion with partner sessions, while specific feature projects entered the competition lineup. These appearances illustrate the contemporary meaning of the going out strategy. Instead of a single export channel the model now combines overseas festival branding, market pavilions, and targeted co production pitches that link Chinese studios with European, Asian, and global partners (People's Daily Online 2024; CGTN 2025a, b; WorldScreenings 2025; PR Newswire 2025).

Cosplay deserves analytical attention within this ecology. Rather than a peripheral fan practice it has become a structured mode of participation that many events treat as a signature draw. CICAF's China Cosplay Super Show holds its national finals in Hangzhou each spring, while the ChinaJoy Cosplay Super League runs regional qualifiers that culminate in Shanghai. These competitions professionalize performance, costuming, and stage craft and in turn drive merchandise markets, prop making industries, and short video circulation. They also serve as recruitment channels for voice performance and for on site event staffing. The result is an integrated field in which cosplay operates as audience development, creative training, and experiential marketing wrapped into one practice (CICAF 2025a, b; China.com Tech 2025; ehangzhou.gov.cn 2025).

Taken together these festivals, fairs, and museum platforms perform three strategic functions for the diffusion of Chinese animation. They create dense contact zones where studios meet buyers, distributors, and technology vendors under highly visible public conditions. They translate fandom into measurable economic activity through ticketing, retail, and licensing while supplying a pedagogical frame that links contemporary content to national heritage. They provide outward facing stages that connect domestic brands to global industry calendars and to foreign publics. In this environment it is now common to see a property cycle through CICAF for visibility, negotiate at iABC for rights, court consumer engagement at CCG Expo or ChinaJoy, and then present abroad at Annecy's market. Brief reference to Nezha as a franchise is sufficient here since it is discussed later. Its presence as icon and merchandise at fairs, and its role in museum pedagogy, exemplify how large properties circulate within the festival economy without needing deep commentary in this section. What matters for the argument is that the festival circuit in China has become a structural pillar that complements television and theatrical distribution and that sustains both domestic consolidation and international outreach.

6.8 Case Study—*Ne Zha 2* and the Global Geography of Success

The phenomenal box office performance of *Ne Zha 2*, directed by Yang Yu (饺子, 杨宇, *Jiǎozi, Yáng Yǔ*) in 2025, can only be understood by situating the film within the longer history of the Nezha myth in Chinese literature and visual culture. Nezha is one of the most enduring characters of Chinese mythology, first appearing in the Yuan dynasty classic *The Investiture of the Gods* (封神演义, *Fēngshén Yǎnyì*). In the epic narrative, Nezha is born miraculously after his mother's long pregnancy and soon displays supernatural powers. The myth emphasizes his rebellious character, dramatized in episodes where he slays the Dragon King's son and defies his father, before committing suicide to protect his family and later being reborn with the help of his master. Nezha thus embodies tension between filial piety and personal destiny, themes that resonate deeply in Chinese cultural consciousness (Yang 2020).

The figure of Nezha has been repeatedly reinterpreted in modern Chinese animation. The most influential early adaptation was *Nezha Conquers the Dragon King* (哪吒闹海, *Nézhā Nào Hǎi*), produced by Shanghai Animation Film Studio in 1979. This feature combined Peking Opera performance styles with traditional ink painting aesthetics, marking a milestone in the golden age of Chinese animation (Lent and Ying 2013). It introduced Nezha as a heroic child who resists tyranny and injustice, aligning the myth with socialist values of resistance and collective identity. Later adaptations appeared across television and comics, yet none achieved comparable cultural impact until Yang Yu's *Ne Zha*, 2019. That film, known in English as *Nezha: Birth of the Demon Child*, radically reinterpreted the myth by portraying Nezha as a misunderstood outcast whose demonic appearance masks his heroic essence. The 2019 film grossed 742 million US dollars domestically, becoming at the time the highest-grossing animated film in Chinese history and opening the way for a sequel (Tartaglione 2019).

Ne Zha 2 expands this reinterpretation while retaining the thematic kernel of rebellion and transformation. Its narrative builds directly upon the 2019 film, situating Nezha within a universe that combines classical mythology with modern cinematic spectacle. The visual design emphasizes kinetic battle sequences, high-resolution textures, and a blend of fantasy and science fiction elements that depart from the restrained brushwork of the 1979 version. By embedding Nezha in a contemporary mythological cinematic universe, Yang Yu crafted a franchise model closer to Hollywood superhero films than to traditional standalone animated features.

The film's commercial trajectory is unprecedented. With a domestic gross of 15.44 billion yuan (2.13 billion US dollars) and 324 million admissions, *Ne Zha 2* is the highest grossing film in Chinese history and the most lucrative animated title in a single market worldwide (Xinhua 2025a, b, c, d, e). Its global tally surpassed two billion dollars, yet more than 95% of revenue originated in China, with North America contributing only about 23 million dollars (Reuters 2025a, b; Box Office Mojo 2025a, b). In contrast, DreamWorks' *Kung Fu Panda* series, long regarded as the archetype of Sinicized global animation, achieved worldwide totals between 500 and 700 million dollars each, distributed relatively evenly across international markets. The most recent installment, *Kung Fu Panda 4* (2024), earned 548 million dollars worldwide with a balanced distribution between North America and overseas territories (Box Office Mojo 2025a, b).

The comparison highlights divergent models of success. *Kung Fu Panda* became globally recognizable by translating Chinese cultural motifs into a framework easily consumable across borders. Its character design, celebrity voice cast, and comedic tone ensured cross-cultural portability, supported by DreamWorks' global marketing apparatus. By contrast, *Ne Zha 2* derives strength from cultural authenticity and national myth, achieving unprecedented resonance at home but failing to capture similar levels of recognition abroad. In effect, it is both the most successful animated film in the world and one of the least globally known among top earners.

Several structural factors account for this paradox. First, the film's release during the Lunar New Year capitalized on China's holiday exhibition infrastructure, where concentrated viewing periods can generate extraordinary box office peaks. Second, the myth of Nezha resonates with national audiences through its themes of defiance, reincarnation, and destiny, but it lacks the universal accessibility of anthropomorphic animals and broad humor that underpinned *Kung Fu Panda*. Third, the sequel strategy of *Ne Zha 2* prioritized building a domestic franchise before cultivating international audiences. Finally, the global distribution campaign was limited, with modest marketing outside China compared to DreamWorks' global rollouts.

The implications for the Chinese animation industry are critical. *Ne Zha 2* demonstrates that China now possesses the exhibition density, audience scale, and production capability to generate billion-dollar animation phenomena independently of Hollywood. Yet it also reveals the limitations of national blockbusters in securing transnational recognition without systematic localization, dubbing, merchandising, and cross-platform strategies. This divergence between scale and visibility suggests that future Chinese animated franchises must consciously design for both domestic and international audiences if they are to rival Hollywood in cultural as well as commercial terms (De Masi, 2025).

References

Animation Festivals. 2025. *Feinaki Beijing Animation Week*. Retrieved September 13, 2025, from https://www.animation-festivals.com/festivals/feinaki-beijing-animation-week/.

Animax. 2025. *Wikipedia*. Retrieved September 13, 2025, from https://en.wikipedia.org/wiki/Animax

Animax Asia. 2025. *Official site and schedule*. Retrieved September 13, 2025, from https://www.animax-asia.com/.

Animax Asian TV channel. 2025. *Wikipedia*. Retrieved September 13, 2025, from https://en.wikipedia.org/wiki/Animax_(Asian_TV_channel).

Beijing Municipal Government. 2025, August 13. *CIFTIS 2025 event advisory*. Retrieved September 13, 2025, from https://english.beijing.gov.cn/whatson/events/exhibition/202508/t20250813_4172039.html.

Beijing Municipal Government. 2025, September 12. *Beijing Animation Festival 2025*. Retrieved September 13, 2025, from https://english.beijing.gov.cn/whatson/events/consuming/202509/t20250912_4201047.html.

Blue Book 2011. Blue Book of Animation: Annual Report on Development of China's Animation Industry. Social Sciences Academic Press.

Box Office Mojo. 2025. *Kung Fu Panda 4 box office*. Retrieved September 13, 2025, from https://www.boxofficemojo.com/title/tt21692408/.

Box Office Mojo. 2025. *Ne Zha 2 box office detail*. Retrieved September 13, 2025, from https://www.boxofficemojo.com/title/tt34956443/.

Cartoon Brew. 2025, August 18. *Nobody crosses 1 billion yuan and sets a China 2D animation record*. Retrieved September 13, 2025, from https://www.cartoonbrew.com/box-office-report/china-nobody-1-billion-yuan-2d-box-office-252083.html.

CCTV 14 Children's Channel. 2025. *Official channel homepage and hot columns*. Retrieved September 13, 2025, from https://tv.cctv.com/cctv14/.

CCTV animation hub. 2025. *Animation channel listings and schedules*. Retrieved September 13, 2025, from https://donghua.cctv.com/.

CCTV Live Portal. 2025. *CCTV 14 Children's Channel live and replay pages*. Retrieved September 13, 2025, from https://tv.cctv.com/live/cctvchild/.

CGTN. 2025, June 2. *China Cartoon and Animation Museum tracing China's animation legacy*. Retrieved September 13, 2025, from https://news.cgtn.com/news/2025-06-02/China-Cartoon-and-Animation-Museum-Tracing-China-s-animation-legacy-1DSn1pCJzBC/p.html.

CGTN. 2025, June 10. *Chinese animated film competes at Annecy*. Retrieved September 13, 2025, from https://news.cgtn.com/news/2025-06-10/Chinese-animated-film-competes-at-Cannes-of-animation--1E5oLTRZISQ/p.html.

CICAF. 2024–2025. *China International Cartoon and Animation Festival official site*. Retrieved September 13, 2025, from https://www.cicaf-en.com/.

CICAF. 2025. *China Cosplay Super Show overview*. Retrieved September 13, 2025, from https://www.cicaf-en.com/detail/160.html.

China.com Tech. 2025, March 23. *2025 ChinaJoy North China division launches, national Cosplay Super League finals set for August*. Retrieved September 13, 2025, from https://m.tech.china.com/hea/articles/20250323/202503231651531.html.

China Daily. 2025a, January 1. *China's box office revenue totals 42.5 billion yuan in 2024*. Retrieved September 13, 2025, from https://global.chinadaily.com.cn/a/202501/01/WS6774c2b9a310f1265a1d8689.html.

China Daily. 2025b, January 8. *Chinese cinema tries new plots and innovation to sharpen its edge*. Retrieved September 13, 2025, from https://www.chinadailyhk.com/hk/article/601935.

China Daily. 2025c, January 9. *Chinese cinema tries new plots, innovation to sharpen its edge*. Retrieved September 13, 2025, from https://www.chinadaily.com.cn/a/202501/09/WS677efe10a310f1265a1d9bf6.html.

ChinaJoy official account. 2025. *Event dates and updates*. Retrieved September 13, 2025, from https://x.com/chinajoy10.

City News Service. 2025, July 13. *Bilibili World transforms Shanghai into a mecca for gaming fans and AI innovation*. Retrieved September 13, 2025, from https://www.citynewsservice.cn/news/Bilibili-World-transforms-Shanghai-into-a-mecca-for-gaming-fans-and-AI-innovation-dmjb7b6n.

De Masi, V. 2025. *Ne Zha 2 Breaking Records and Redefining Chinese Animation*. Retrieved September 13, 2025, from https://www.academia.edu/127835780/Ne_Zha_2_Breaking_Records_and_Redefining_Chinese_Animation.

ehangzhou.gov.cn. 2025, May 29–June 6. *China International Cartoon and Animation Festival opens and closes with strong results*. Retrieved September 13, 2025, from https://www.ehangzhou.gov.cn/2025-05/29/c_293816.htm.

FilmFreeway. 2025. *Aniwow China Beijing International Student Animation Festival*. Retrieved September 13, 2025, from https://filmfreeway.com/Aniwow2025DiErShiJieZhongGuoBeiJingGuoJiDaXueShengDongHuaJie.

GRTN. 2025. *Jiajia Cartoon channel page*. Retrieved September 13, 2025, from https://www.gdtv.cn/tvChannelDetail/66.

Global Times. 2025, September 1. *China's summer box office reaches almost 12 billion yuan*. Retrieved September 13, 2025, from https://www.globaltimes.cn/page/202509/1342325.shtml.

iABC. 2025. *International Animation and Game Business Conference*. Retrieved September 13, 2025, from https://iabc.cicaf.com/home.html?lang=en.

ICE Italian Trade Agency. 2023. *Market research on the Chinese audio-visual industry 2023*. Retrieved September 13, 2025, from https://www.ice.it/it/sites/default/files/inline-files/Market%20Research%20on%20Chinese%20Audiovisual%202023_Intro_0.pdf.

JETRO J Messe. 2025, July 16. *CCG Expo 2025 overview*. Retrieved September 13, 2025, from https://www.jetro.go.jp/en/database/j-messe/tradefair/detail/156086.

JSTV. 2025. *Youman Cartoon satellite channel portal*. Retrieved September 13, 2025, from https://tv.jstv.com/ymkt/.

Lent, J. A., and X. Ying. 2013. Chinese animation: A historical and contemporary analysis. *Journal of Chinese Cinemas* 7(2): 109–124.

Lexology. 2025, June 3. *Media law and regulation in China.* Retrieved September 13, 2025, from https://www.lexology.com/library/detail.aspx?g=11e350e8-1f54-4948-a52d-9e6c013d768a.

Lu, B., Niu, X., and Zheng, Y. 2011. Blue Book of Animation: Annual Report on Development of China's Animation Industry. *Social Sciences Academic Press.*

Lu, B., Niu, X., and Zheng, Y. 2012. Blue Book of Animation: Annual Report on Development of China's Animation Industry. *Social Sciences Academic Press.*

MarketScreener. 2023, December 18. *Nojima Corporation agreed to acquire Animax Broadcast Japan Inc. and Kids Station Inc. from Sony Pictures Entertainment (Japan) Inc.* Retrieved September 13, 2025, from https://www.marketscreener.com/quote/stock/NOJIMA-CORPORATION-14116129/news/Nojima-Corporation-agreed-to-acquire-Animax-Broadcast-Japan-Inc-and-Kids-Station-Inc-from-Sony-Pict-45664084/.

MarketScreener. 2024, April 29. *Nojima Corporation completed the acquisition of Animax Broadcast Japan Inc. and Kids Station Inc.* Retrieved September 13, 2025, from https://www.marketscreener.com/quote/stock/NOJIMA-CORPORATION-14116129/news/Nojima-Corporation-completed-the-acquisition-of-Animax-Broadcast-Japan-Inc-and-Kids-Station-Inc-fro-49718049/.

New Hunan. 2024, October 5. *Global Children's Spring Festival Gala announced for 2025.* Retrieved September 13, 2025, from https://m.voc.com.cn/xhn/news/202410/20785982.html.

Omdia. 2025, February 13. *Cinema in China. The ups and downs of a rollercoaster ride.* Retrieved September 13, 2025, from https://omdia.tech.informa.com/om128522/cinema-in-china-the-ups-and-downs-of-a-rollercoaster-ride.

People's Daily Online. 2024, June 13. *Outstanding Chinese animation showcased in France.* Retrieved September 13, 2025, from http://en.people.cn/n3/2024/0613/c90000-20180880.html.

PR Newswire. 2025. *China Pavilion set for Annecy showcase.* Retrieved September 13, 2025, from https://www.prnewswire.com/news-releases/china-pavilion-set-for-annecy-showcase-302567898.html.

Qing, X. 2006. An Economic Research of China's Animation Industry (中国动画片的产业经济学研究). China Market Press.

Reuters. 2025a, February 6. *'Nezha 2' becomes China's highest grossing film amid Lunar New Year boom.* Retrieved September 13, 2025, from https://www.reuters.com/world/china/chinese-movie-nezha-2-becomes-highest-grossing-film-country-2025-02-06/.

Reuters. 2025b, February 18. *Chinese film 'Nezha 2' becomes highest grossing animated film globally.* Retrieved September 13, 2025, from https://www.reuters.com/lifestyle/chinese-film-nezha-2-becomes-highest-grossing-animated-film-globally-2025-02-18/.

Sanrio. 2025. *Message from the Executive Officer in Charge of Finance [FY3/2025 results].* Retrieved September 13, 2025, from https://corporate.sanrio.co.jp/en/ir/about/financial_strategy/.

Shanghai Media Group. 2022. *Haha Xundong channel profile.* Retrieved September 13, 2025, from https://www.smg.cn/review/202211/0164836.html.

Shanghai Putuo District Government. 2025, July 8. *Animation and Game Carnival Month opens with CCG Expo.* Retrieved September 13, 2025, from https://english.shpt.gov.cn/news/news/3526.shtml.

SmartShanghai. 2025. *ChinaJoy 2025.* Retrieved September 13, 2025, from https://www.smartshanghai.com/event/78244.

Sohu. 2024, September 29. *Golden Eagle Cartoon to launch a 2025 Global Children's Gala.* Retrieved September 13, 2025, from https://www.sohu.com/a/812810113_121924583.

Tan, L., and Yin, J. 2006. Animation Industry (动漫产业). Sichuan University Press.

Tartaglione, N. 2019, August 4. *'Ne Zha' Becomes China's Biggest Animated Film Of All Time At $742M*. Deadline. Retrieved September 13, 2025, from https://deadline.com/2019/08/china-ne-zha-box-office-record-742m-1202660984/.

The Guardian. 2011, June 6. *Kung Fu Panda 2 smashes China's box office records.* Retrieved September 13, 2025, from https://www.theguardian.com/film/2024/nov/01/global-phenomenon-hello-kitty-celebrates-50th-birthday.

The Guardian. 2024, November 1. *As Hello Kitty turns 50 her cuteness is still earning £3.1bn a year*. Retrieved September 13, 2025, from https://www.theguardian.com/artanddesign/2024/nov/01/global-phenomenon-hello-kitty-celebrates-50th-birthday.

TVMao. 2025. *Program listings for Haha Xundong and KAKU Children's Channel*. Retrieved September 13, 2025, from https://mtmadm.tvmao.com/program_satellite/TOONMAX1-w1.html.

TVSou. 2025. *CCTV 14 schedule and weekly EPG*. Retrieved September 13, 2025, from https://t1.tvsou.com/epg/yangshi/6fff4f43_w3/.

Variety. 2020, January 7. *Sony Pictures sells Asia channels to former executives Andy Kaplan and George Chien*. Retrieved September 13, 2025, from https://variety.com/2020/tv/asia/sony-pictures-sells-asia-channels-andy-kaplan-george-chien-1203459292/.

Wikipedia. 2025a. *Beijing Animation Festival*. Retrieved September 13, 2025, from https://en.wikipedia.org/wiki/Beijing_Animation_Festival.

Wikipedia. 2025b. *BRTV KAKU Children's Channel*. Retrieved September 13, 2025, from https://zh.wikipedia.org/wiki/%E5%8D%A1%E9%85%B7%E5%B0%91%E5%84%BF%E5%8D%AB%E8%A7%86.

Wikipedia. 2025c. *CCTV-14*. Retrieved September 13, 2025, from https://en.wikipedia.org/wiki/CCTV-14.

Wikipedia. 2025d. *Cinema of China*. Retrieved September 13, 2025, from https://en.wikipedia.org/wiki/Cinema_of_China.

Wikipedia. 2025e. *Golden Eagle Cartoon Satellite TV*. Retrieved September 13, 2025, from https://zh.wikipedia.org/zh-hans/%E9%87%91%E9%B9%B0%E5%8D%A1%E9%80%9A%E5%8D%AB%E8%A7%86.

Wikipedia. 2025f. *Haha Xundong Satellite TV*. Retrieved September 13, 2025, from https://zh.wikipedia.org/wiki/%E5%93%88%E5%93%88%E7%82%AB%E5%8A%A8%E5%8D%AB%E8%A7%86.

Wikipedia. 2025g. *Tianjin Radio and Television Station*. Retrieved September 13, 2025, from https://zh.wikipedia.org/wiki/%E5%A4%A9%E6%B4%A5%E5%B9%BF%E6%92%AD%E7%94%B5%E8%A7%86%E5%8F%B0.

WorldScreenings. 2025, June. *China Pavilion set for Annecy showcase*. Retrieved September 13, 2025, from https://worldscreenings.com/showcase/crossing-animation-boundaries-china-pavilion-set-for-dazzling-annecy-debut/.

Xinhua. 2025a, August 29. *China's 2025 summer box office surpasses 2024 as hand drawn feature sets a new record*. Retrieved September 13, 2025, from https://english.news.cn/20250829/6c6112a6e4df48c89c921fd39c408bd2/c.html.

Xinhua. 2025b, June 30. *Ne Zha 2 ends record-breaking China run with 2.13 billion US dollars*. Retrieved September 13, 2025, from https://english.news.cn/20250630/74574b4e9823406fb2da565b750fa4a7/c.html.

Xinhua. 2025c, July 4. *CCG Expo 2025 kicks off in Shanghai*. Retrieved September 13, 2025, from https://english.news.cn/20250704/eb09e6f986f543559fe61c12bdb540ae/c.html.

Xinhua. 2025d, September 1. *China's summer box office reaches almost 12 billion yuan*. Retrieved September 13, 2025, from https://english.news.cn/20250901/fa4ff2de327947d085faaf9d52e3aa04/c.html.

Xinhua. 2025e, September 13. *CIFTIS opens to the public in Beijing*. Retrieved September 13, 2025, from https://www.xinhuanet.com/english/20250913/311db0a3390c42419276f627025d3c9d/c.html.

Yicai. 2025, July 10. *Hundreds of thousands flock to Shanghai for Bilibili World 2025*. Retrieved September 13, 2025, from https://www.yicaiglobal.com/news/hundreds-of-thousands-of-comic-and-gaming-fans-flock-to-shanghai-for-bilibili-world-2025.

Yang, L. 2020. Mythological archetypes in Chinese animation: Nezha and the problem of cultural translation. *Animation Studies 15*(1): 88–104.

Wang, Y. 2011. The Market Positioning Study of Animation Consumer Product (动漫衍生产品研发的市场定位研究). In Blue Book of Animation (动漫蓝皮书). Social Sciences Academic Press.

Chapter 7
New Media Diffusion and Digital Convergence

Abstract This chapter examines how the diffusion of Chinese animation has been transformed by the rise of New Media and digital convergence. It begins with the rapid expansion of internet connectivity and mobile technologies, which positioned video consumption at the center of Chinese digital culture. The chapter traces the emergence of web-based and mobile animation, noting the early popularity of Flash works and the gradual rise of online platforms that enabled short-form, serialized, and user-generated content. Platforms such as Bilibili, Youku, Tencent Video, and Douyin reshaped the circulation of animation by combining distribution, fan participation, and monetization. Case studies, including *Miss Puff*, illustrate how independent creators leveraged the web to reach audiences outside state-controlled frameworks, while the growth of fan networks and grassroots practices expanded participatory cultures. The chapter also addresses mobile-first design, distributed animation (Màn dònghuà), and the integration of comics, games, and short videos into convergent ecosystems. By the mid-2020s, Chinese animation was embedded in a consolidated digital economy where streaming platforms, interactive formats, and e-commerce defined consumption. These dynamics demonstrate that New Media not only broadened access and accelerated circulation but also reconfigured the industrial and aesthetic boundaries of Chinese animation.

Keywords Bilibili · Youku · Tencent Video · Douyin · Miss Puff · Distributed animation · Màn dònghuà

7.1 Digital Networks—New Ecologies of Circulation

By the mid 2020s China had become one of the most highly connected countries in the world, with nearly 1.10 billion internet users and a penetration rate of about 78% of the total population (CNNIC 2024). Almost all of these users, 99.7%, accessed the internet primarily through mobile phones. The number of cellular connections reached approximately 1.76 billion in 2024, which is higher than the total population and shows that many people use more than one device (DataReportal 2024). Video

© The Author(s), under exclusive license to Springer Nature Switzerland AG 2026
V. De Masi, *A Critical Analysis of China's Animation Industry*, Numanities - Arts and Humanities in Progress 37, https://doi.org/10.1007/978-3-032-18656-0_7

consumption has become nearly universal. In June 2024 about 1.068 billion people in China were online video users, representing 97.1% of all internet users, while 1.050 billion consumed short video content, equivalent to 95.5% of netizens (CNNIC 2024). These figures highlight the centrality of video to Chinese digital culture and provide the backdrop against which the diffusion of animation through New Media must be understood.

At the beginning of the twenty first century the Chinese government had already identified digital technologies as strategic instruments for cultural and industrial growth. Policy initiatives encouraged the modernization of creative industries and their integration with new communication technologies in order to expand the distribution of cultural products (Tan 2006). The notion of New Media referred to mass communication channels transformed by the spread of information technology. It encompassed both digitized forms of traditional media and new devices such as mobile phones, tablets, laptops, gaming consoles, and e-book readers. Their defining characteristic was convergence, which allowed content to circulate across platforms and to be consumed at any time and place (Dedney 2006).

Animation was among the first creative sectors to take advantage of these dynamics. Digital platforms not only facilitated the distribution of existing content but also encouraged the creation of works specifically designed for mobile and online environments. Flash animation, in particular, emerged as a popular form in the early 2000s. Supported by the spread of broadband and the expansion of 3G networks, it provided models for web-based distribution that later influenced on-demand systems for both comics and animation. By 2010 a growing market for mobile and online animation had already taken shape in China.

Japan provided a key comparative model. By 2010 around 80% of its population, nearly 100 million people, enjoyed 3G coverage with the transition toward 4G already underway. High-definition screens on mobile devices and consoles made animated content more immediate and accessible, stimulating a rapid expansion of the digital animation market (Blue Book, 2012). In China, however, digital animation and mobile games accounted for only about 30% of services, underscoring the gap with neighboring countries such as Japan and South Korea, both of which had invested heavily in communication infrastructures and creative content development.

Despite this slower start, the growth of mobile networks and e-commerce soon transformed the Chinese animation market. New forms of commercial activity included derivative products such as ringtones, animated MMS, short films, specialized magazines, online games, applications, and *Manhua*. These models shortened sales cycles and allowed consumers to purchase merchandise directly online, reinforcing the profitability of the sector (Ruilan 2011). The emergence of fan-based forums and blogs, such as *Greed Continent* (贪婪大陆, *Tānlán dàlù*), signaled the rise of participatory communities that played a vital role in circulation and promotion.

The 2010s and early 2020s witnessed the consolidation of major platforms such as Bilibili (哔哩哔哩), which originated in 2009 as a fan site and later became one of the most important ecosystems for anime, comics, games, and original programming. By 2022 Bilibili had over 330 million monthly active users, including nearly 30 million paying subscribers, demonstrating how New Media reshaped the circulation of animation and derivative content (Market Report Analytics 2025).

More recently the growth of short-form, mobile-first content has influenced the creative landscape in profound ways. The *duanju* (短剧) phenomenon, short vertical dramas distributed on platforms such as Douyin and Kuaishou, generated revenues of more than ¥50 billion in 2024, surpassing the national film box office and providing employment for more than 600,000 people (Wikipedia 2025). While not exclusively animated, this industrial model of mobile-optimized short content has affected how animation is conceived and monetized.

The expansion of the fan economy has further intensified the role of New Media. Companies increasingly integrate fan practices into creative and marketing strategies, and participatory engagement has become central to platform activity. Studies highlight how fandom now operates not only as a cultural force but also as a commercial driver in China's ACG sector (Jiang, 2024; Cui and Wu 2024). This integration has reinforced the vitality of digital distribution and the importance of derivative markets, particularly for younger consumers (Global Times 2024).

From the early experiments with Flash animation in the 2000s to the establishment of 2010 as a reference point for mobile expansion and into the platform ecosystems of the 2020s, the trajectory of Chinese animation illustrates how New Media have transformed its modes of diffusion. Digital infrastructures and participatory cultures have redefined not only the distribution of content but also the commercial models that sustain the industry, positioning animation as one of the most dynamic components of China's creative economy.

7.2 The Web as Infrastructure—Platforms and Audiences

The web has become the most important platform for the distribution of animation in China. The earliest efforts of major broadcasters such as CCTV, which launched online streaming services in 2009 through China Network Television (CNTV), illustrate how the internet was initially used to provide on-demand access to existing television programming, including animation. These initiatives served as the foundation for the rapid expansion of online video, marking the first stage in a process that would fundamentally transform media consumption (Cunningham 2012).

Since then the industry has evolved into one of the largest streaming markets in the world. By mid 2024 China counted 1.10 billion internet users, with 1.068 billion consuming online video, representing more than 97% of all users (CNNIC 2024). Within this landscape, online video platforms have become dominant cultural intermediaries. Companies such as iQIYI, Tencent Video, Youku, and Bilibili now provide comprehensive libraries of animation, from classic series to new productions, often combining free access supported by advertising with subscription models. These services increasingly target segmented audiences, offering youth-oriented animation, adult animated dramas, and derivative products linked to popular franchises.

The scale of online video revenues illustrates the sector's economic significance. According to Market Research Future (2025), China's entertainment and media market reached over USD 500 billion in 2023 and is projected to grow to USD 650 billion by 2028. Online video represents one of the most dynamic components of this growth. Platforms are investing heavily in exclusive animated series, feature-length films, and adaptations of popular *Manhua* and online novels. For instance, Bilibili, originally launched as an anime, comics, and games site, reported over 330 million monthly active users and nearly 30 million paying subscribers by 2022. It has since expanded into international co-productions and original programming, positioning animation at the core of its brand identity.

An important feature of web-based animation is the integration of participatory culture. User comments, live chat features known as *danmu* (弹幕), and fan-made edits are central to the experience of platforms like Bilibili. These forms of interactivity not only reinforce community ties but also influence production strategies. Studies confirm that animation companies increasingly integrate fan preferences and practices into their commercial models, resulting in a feedback loop between audiences and producers (Jiang 2024; Cui and Wu 2024).

The contemporary landscape is also shaped by regulatory frameworks. While state agencies such as the National Radio and Television Administration (NRTA, formerly SARFT) continue to enforce content guidelines, the diversification of distribution has complicated traditional censorship mechanisms. Web-based animation has given rise to independent productions, often created by small studios or individual artists, that circulate online with limited resources but significant cultural impact. Some of these works address social realities and everyday life in China, offering perspectives rarely visible on state-controlled television. Although subject to potential removal, their visibility reflects how the web has expanded the space for creative experimentation.

Another major development is the synergy between animation and e-commerce. Platforms such as iQIYI and Tencent Video integrate merchandising directly into their interfaces, allowing users to purchase derivative products while watching. This convergence of streaming and online retail reinforces the commercial viability of animation, turning it into a central driver of China's broader digital economy.

Historically, the absence of Western platforms such as YouTube, which remain blocked in China, created a protected environment for domestic companies. This lack of external competition enabled Chinese platforms to consolidate quickly and dominate the domestic market. By 2025, the ecosystem of Chinese streaming platforms not only replaced international competitors but also developed distinctive business models tailored to local consumption habits, particularly the prevalence of mobile-first viewing and the near-universal popularity of short videos.

In summary, the diffusion of animation on the web in China reflects both continuity and transformation. The early experiments of broadcasters in the late 2000s provided a historical foundation. However, the decisive shift occurred in the 2010s and 2020s, when streaming platforms, fan participation, e-commerce integration, and regulatory negotiation turned online video into the central hub for animation consumption. Today animation is not only one of the most widely accessed cultural products on

Chinese streaming platforms but also a vital component of the country's digital creative economy.

7.3 Video-Sharing Platforms—Bilibili, Youku, and Beyond

The evolution of Chinese video sharing platforms reflects both the global rise of online video in the 2000s and the particular regulatory and industrial conditions of China. In their early stages these platforms resembled YouTube and were dominated by user uploads without copyright. Pirated films, television dramas, and animations circulated widely, attracting enormous audiences but limiting the incentives for professional production. This environment played a decisive role in creating habits of online consumption, yet it also exposed structural weaknesses. From the early 2010s a combination of state regulation, market consolidation, and technological innovation reshaped the sector. The industry moved from informal piracy-driven growth to structured ecosystems based on licensing, original content, subscriptions, and integrated e-commerce.

Youku.com (优酷, *Yōukù*), founded in 2006, rapidly became China's most visible video-sharing platform. In its first years it operated much like YouTube, relying heavily on user uploads, but it soon began to acquire licenses and expand into professional programming. By the early 2010s Youku had secured more than 1500 licenses for films, television, and animation (Jarboe 2011). The company also invested in original production and launched *Youku Dongman* (优酷动漫, *Yōukù Dòngmàn*), a dedicated animation section. It provided visibility to independent works such as *One Hundred Thousand Bad Jokes* (十万个冷笑话, *Shíwàn gè Lěng Xiàohuà*), *Kuang Kuang* (狂狂, *Kuáng Kuáng*), and *Zombie Brother* (尸兄, *Shī Xiōng*). These titles demonstrated how online platforms could incubate creative projects that later entered the mainstream market. Youku's 2012 acquisition of Tudou marked a turning point in the consolidation of the sector. Although its market share has declined in the face of new competitors, Youku remains an important reference point, particularly for long-form video and licensed content.

Tencent Video (腾讯视频, *Téngxùn Shìpín*), launched in 2011, leveraged Tencent's wider digital ecosystem of WeChat, QQ, and online gaming. It quickly established itself as a leader in the streaming market by acquiring exclusive rights to Japanese anime and investing in original domestic productions. By 2023 it reported hundreds of millions of active users and significant revenues from advertising and subscription models. Animation is central to Tencent's strategy, with sections dedicated to both imported series and new Chinese works.

iQIYI (爱奇艺, *Àiqíyì*), founded in 2010 and backed by Baidu, also became a dominant platform. From the mid-2010s it emerged as one of the most globally ambitious Chinese streaming services, producing original animated series and adapting *manhua* and online novels. It integrated streaming with e-commerce and merchandising, turning animation into a multi-revenue driver. Despite financial challenges linked to the high cost of production, iQIYI remains one of the top three platforms in the country, with animation as a major source of engagement, particularly among younger audiences.

Bilibili (哔哩哔哩, *Bīlībīlī*), created in 2009, represents the platform most directly associated with anime, comics, and games (ACG) culture. Unlike Youku, Tencent Video, and iQIYI, which evolved from general video sharing into professional streaming, Bilibili was designed from the beginning as a community space for fans of Japanese and Chinese animation. It introduced distinctive features such as *danmu* (弹幕, *dànmù*), real-time comments overlaid on videos, which created highly participatory viewing experiences.

By 2022 Bilibili reported more than 330 million monthly active users and nearly 30 million paying subscribers. It has expanded into original production, co-productions with global studios, and live events such as its annual New Year's Eve animation gala. For younger generations, Bilibili has become the central hub for discovering, discussing, and consuming animation, while also shaping trends in fan culture and derivative markets.

Douyin (抖音, *Dǒuyīn*), the domestic version of TikTok, has transformed the landscape of video consumption in China since its launch in 2016. While primarily known for short-form vertical videos, Douyin has become increasingly significant for animation distribution and promotion. Short animated clips, adaptations of *Manhua*, and fan-edited sequences circulate widely on the platform, reaching audiences that traditional streaming services often fail to capture. In 2024 the *duanju* (短剧) phenomenon, short dramas optimized for mobile viewing, generated more than ¥50 billion in revenue, surpassing the national box office (Wikipedia 2025). Although not all *duanju* are animated, their industrial model of rapid production and mobile monetization has strongly influenced the distribution and consumption of animated content. Douyin integrates social interaction, commerce, and micro-payment systems, turning short videos into powerful marketing and distribution channels for animation.

By 2025 the Chinese streaming market is dominated by four pillars, Tencent Video, iQIYI, Youku, and Bilibili, alongside Douyin, which operates in a different but complementary segment. Together they account for the vast majority of online video consumption. According to Market Research Future (2025), the Chinese entertainment and media market exceeded USD 500 billion in 2023 and is expected to reach USD 650 billion by 2028, with online video representing one of the fastest-growing sectors. Animation occupies a central role across these platforms, benefiting from the convergence of streaming, e-commerce, fan participation, and mobile-first formats.

The trajectory of Chinese video sharing platforms shows how the industry evolved from a fragmented and piracy-driven environment in the 2000s to a consolidated ecosystem of powerful corporate actors in the 2020s. Animation has been at the heart of this transformation, both as a cultural product and as a commercial asset that continues to drive innovation in the digital economy.

7.3.1 Audience Reception and Everyday Uses of Chinese Animation

The shift from linear television to digital platforms has profoundly altered how Chinese audiences integrate animation into their everyday lives (The Business of Fashion 2021). While industry reports often focus on click-through rates and box office returns, the lived experience of viewers reveals a complex negotiation between state narratives, market entertainment, and personal identity (Chen 2018).

For younger demographics, particularly Gen Z and millennials, consuming domestic animation (*guochuang*) has become a performative act of cultural pride (Dao Insights 2020). Unlike previous generations who grew up viewing Japanese anime as the standard of quality, contemporary viewers increasingly treat high-end Chinese productions like *The King's Avatar* or *Fog Hill of Five Elements* as markers of national technological progress (Radii 2018). On platforms like Bilibili, the use of *danmu* (bullet comments) transforms viewing into a communal ritual, where audiences do not merely watch but actively annotate content, policing moral values or celebrating visual fidelity in real-time (Chen 2018). This participatory reception creates a feedback loop where "word-of-mouth" (*koubei*) can make or break a series within hours of release (Dao Insights 2020).

However, reception outside these fan circles presents a different dynamic, particularly within the family unit. For Chinese parents, animation is frequently utilized as a tool for "electronic babysitting," yet it is simultaneously scrutinized through a lens of educational utility (Dong 2019). The "educational imperative" - the expectation that animation must instruct rather than merely entertain - remains a dominant filter for parental reception (Dong 2019). This dynamic was visibly demonstrated during the controversies surrounding *Pleasant Goat and Big Big Wolf*, where parental complaints regarding on-screen violence forced regulatory intervention (BBC News 2013). Consequently, the everyday use of animation in households often involves a negotiation between children's desire for entertainment and parents' demand for safe, moralizing content (Dong 2019).

Furthermore, the "everydayness" of animation has expanded through mobile technology. The rise of short-form video apps has fragmented consumption into "micro-moments"—watching a 3-min *duanju* episode during a subway commute or a lunch break (Naavik 2024). This mode of reception privileges fast-paced, high-stimulus narratives over the slow-burn storytelling of traditional cinema, fundamentally reshaping audience attention spans and narrative expectations in the post-2020 era (ThinkChina 2025).

7.4 New Creators in the Digital Age—The Case of *Miss Puff*

In the last 15 years Chinese animation has witnessed the rise of a new generation of authors who have used the web as their privileged space of production and circulation. The rapid expansion of digital platforms, together with the popularity of video sharing sites and the diffusion of mobile connectivity, has enabled independent directors and small studios to propose narratives that differed from those promoted by state broadcasters and commercial giants. In the early 2000s the environment was characterized by the uncontrolled circulation of content without copyright protection, with platforms resembling YouTube that offered entire pirated libraries. This situation, although problematic from a legal and ethical standpoint, contributed to the formation of habits of online consumption and created the conditions for later experimentation. By the beginning of the 2010s platforms entered a phase of consolidation, accompanied by tighter regulation and increasing professionalization of content. It was in this context that *Miss Puff* emerged as one of the first cases of original animation designed exclusively for the web, quickly becoming both a cultural phenomenon and a commercial success.

The author of *Miss Puff*, Pi San (皮三, *Pí Sān*, real name Wei Bo), stands as a central figure in the transition between traditional media and digital innovation. Having previously collaborated with CCTV in series such as *The Station of Happiness* (快乐驿站, *Kuàilè yìzhàn*) in 2004, he later decided to found his own independent studio in Beijing's 798 Art Zone, a district that had become a symbol of urban creativity. From this environment came projects such as *Kuang Kuang*, an animated series with critical and satirical content that did not hesitate to address sensitive political and social issues. Some episodes, like the one dedicated to the 2008 scandal of contaminated infant formula, were censored, yet they revealed an innovative use of animation as a language of critique and reflection. Pi San's ambition was to use animation as a new form of communication that went beyond traditional boundaries and reflected the anxieties and daily experiences of ordinary citizens.

With *Miss Puff* (泡芙小姐, *Pào fú xiǎojiě*), launched in 2011 as a *Youku Original*, Pi San found a formula that combined narrative experimentation, contemporary aesthetics, and economic viability. The series told the story of a young woman navigating urban life, work, and romantic relationships, approaching these themes with irony and realism. Its direct language, metropolitan setting, and focus on everyday issues resonated strongly with young urban audiences, especially women, who recognized their own struggles and aspirations in the animated episodes. The use of product placement and the creation of an active online community transformed *Miss Puff* into a landmark cultural and commercial project. From the very first season the episodes reached tens of millions of views, and over time the franchise surpassed one billion aggregated views, eventually spanning eight seasons and more than one hundred episodes. The later release of a film adaptation in 2018 confirmed its vitality, demonstrating that a product born on the web could evolve into a transmedia franchise.

The significance of *Miss Puff* becomes clearer when examined alongside other cases that marked the development of Chinese web animation. *One Hundred Thousand Bad Jokes* (十万个冷笑话, *Shí wàn gè lěng xiàohuà*), also initiated as an online animation, was later adapted into a feature film funded through crowdfunding in 2014, showing how fan engagement could be mobilized into financial support. *The Legend of Hei* (罗小黑战记, *Luō Xiǎohēi Zhàn Jì*), which began as a web series and later became a successful 2019 film followed by a 2025 sequel, demonstrated the potential of online-born works to develop complex narrative universes capable of competing in global markets. Similarly *All Saints Street* (万圣街, *Wànshèng Jiē*), which originated as a webcomic before being adapted into an animated series distributed by Tencent Video and Bilibili, shows the continuum between digital comics, fan communities, and serialized animation.

Taken together, these examples indicate that the web has provided fertile ground for the emergence of an ecosystem where independent or semi-independent creators can tell unconventional stories and engage directly with audiences. Yet this model is not without limitations. The weak enforcement of copyright in the early years fostered rapid circulation but raised questions of sustainability and legality. As state authorities tightened regulation, obtaining proper licenses and complying with censorship requirements became necessary, creating new constraints for independent voices. Preventive censorship remains a structural limitation, as series overtly critical of the government or addressing politically sensitive themes are often blocked or modified. Even creators who, like Pi San, focus on social and urban issues must navigate implicit boundaries of moral and ideological acceptability. Economic sustainability also represents a challenge, since high-quality animation requires considerable resources, and only works that achieve strong popularity can sustain themselves through advertising, merchandising, or product placement.

The legacy of *Miss Puff* and the works that followed is twofold. On the one hand they demonstrated that original web animation could develop into viable cultural products capable of competing with traditional television, supported by innovative distribution models and strong fan communities. On the other hand they highlighted the fragility of independent studios in a market increasingly dominated by corporate conglomerates and shaped by regulatory oversight. Despite these challenges, the contribution of new Chinese authors has been to expand the expressive possibilities of animation, introducing contemporary themes, hybrid aesthetics, and a more intimate dialogue with younger generations.

Today *Miss Puff* is not only remembered as an early success but also as a model that continues to influence the production of online animation in China. The experience of Pi San illustrates that even in a system characterized by heavy regulation and industrial concentration there is space for independent narratives that reflect the concerns of their audiences. At the same time, more recent cases confirm that the vitality of Chinese animation depends on the capacity to balance creativity with sustainability, narrative innovation with institutional constraints. The path opened by *Miss Puff* remains central to understanding the ongoing renewal of Chinese animation, which increasingly combines local creativity, global ambitions, and the digital platforms that connect them.

7.4.1 The Technical and Artistic Analysis of Miss Puff

The technical and artistic analysis of *Miss Puff* can be approached through the theoretical frameworks outlined by David Bordwell and Kristin Thompson in *Film Art: An Introduction*, which defines essential principles of lighting, narration, color, framing, and editing (Bordwell & Thompson 2013). While the series was created using Flash animation, Pi San decided to experiment with a hybrid form by combining animated characters with live-action footage of real urban spaces. This choice was not entirely new in animation history, but in this case it served two specific functions: to lower production time and costs, and to project the image of a modern and realistic China.

Jill Nelmes in *An Introduction to Film Studies* highlights how the use of live-action backgrounds transforms animation into a representation of reality, capturing what is "tangible and concrete" (Nelmes 2012). This strategy was used in *Miss Puff* both to increase audience immersion and to enable extensive product placement. The animated protagonists interact with real consumer goods such as cars, mobile phones, and laptops, offering Youku the advertising revenues necessary to sustain the production. The choice of handheld camera techniques in the live-action segments enhanced this realism by producing less stable yet more intense imagery. Careful photographic design allowed backgrounds and animated characters to blend smoothly, with lighting and colors calibrated to create continuity between the animated figures and the filmed environment. In several sequences the merging of animated elements and live-action backgrounds was so fluid that it became difficult to discern whether certain shots contained real or artificial components.

The narrative strategy of the first five episodes reinforces this hybridization. The city depicted is presented as a "non-place," a concept theorized by Marc Augé (1995) to describe anonymous, ahistorical, and transitory spaces such as airports, multiplex cinemas, and international hotel chains. The apartments, offices, and leisure sites in *Miss Puff* resemble Western consumerist environments, from IKEA-style interiors to Apple products and European football broadcasts. Such choices deliberately positioned the series in a global cultural framework. Scholars such as Moscon (2010) and Cucco (2009) have emphasized the connection between non-places and blockbusters, noting how cultural hybridity and the absence of strong national markers are often used to maximize international appeal. *Miss Puff* fits within this logic, offering a world that is both globally recognizable and locally ambiguous.

Pi San himself confirmed this strategy in a 2012 interview, stating that at the beginning he did not want to situate the story in a clearly Chinese city but rather in a modern metropolis without explicit national references. Only after the series gained popularity did the creators begin to insert more identifiable markers of Beijing, from peripheral neighborhoods to the new CCTV building. By the eighth episode the audience could clearly identify the setting as the Chinese capital. This gradual transition from a globalized non-place to a recognizable cityscape reflects a deliberate narrative evolution, aimed at attracting broad audiences before narrowing the cultural focus.

The intertextual dimension of *Miss Puff* further reinforces its hybrid identity. References to Japanese video games such as *Super Mario* and *Street Fighter*, echoes of Japanese television dramas like *Train Man* (電車男, *Densha Otoko*), and soundtracks inspired by Western cinema all contribute to its cosmopolitan profile (Cohn 2012). Yet from the fifth episode onward the show increasingly incorporated elements of contemporary Chinese culture, situating Miss Puff's experiences in recognizable neighborhoods, presenting real social issues such as the housing crisis, and even showing maps of Beijing.

The representation of housing difficulties is particularly significant. In one episode Miss Puff searches for a new apartment, a storyline that resonated with young viewers familiar with the phenomenon of the "Bei Piao," migrants striving to make a living in Beijing, and the so-called "Ant Tribe" of overqualified yet underpaid graduates struggling with urban housing (Shi 2010). These storylines anchored the series in the lived experiences of urban youth, blending aspirational lifestyles with realistic social challenges. Pi San himself admitted that the visual inspiration for Miss Puff came from the singer and actress Wang Fei (王菲), while the personality was based on his wife, a mixture that created a protagonist who was glamorous yet relatable.

The artistic choices of *Miss Puff* thus reveal its dual ambition: to capture the modernized and globalized identity of China while also reflecting the specific social and cultural dynamics of Beijing. Scholars such as Gates (2006) have connected this approach to China's broader strategies of cultural soft power, which aim to construct a modern, attractive, and internationally legible image of the nation. *Miss Puff* can therefore be understood not only as a pioneering web animation but also as a cultural experiment that negotiated between global aesthetics, local realities, and market imperatives.

7.5 Mobile Media—Animation in the App Economy

China's mobile environment has transformed the production, circulation, and reception of animation. The 2010s remain the decisive historical phase in which smartphones, app ecosystems, and 3G–4G networks turned "online video" into an everyday habit, while platforms adapted catalogues and interfaces to mobile-first viewing. That decade also consolidated audience expectations for short, serialized, highly shareable content. Against this historical backdrop, the current landscape is defined by near-universal mobile access and by video use that has become almost coterminous with being online. By December 2024, China counted about 1.07 billion online video users, equivalent to 96.6% of all netizens, and short-video users reached roughly 1.04 billion, or 93.8% (CNNIC 2025). Earlier in mid-2024, CNNIC reported a similar scale and underscored the rapid rise of micro-drama audiences, confirming that the dominant behaviors established in the 2010s now structure everyday mobile media consumption (CNNIC 2024). Mobile connectivity underpins this universality. At the start of 2025, the number of mobile connections had increased by more than one hundred million year-on-year and, according to GSMA Intelligence as summarized by DataReportal, essentially all active connections in China are now broadband class, meaning 3G, 4G, or 5G (DataReportal 2025). Administrative data further indicate the deep penetration of 5G: by late 2024 the Ministry of Industry and Information Technology reported more than one billion 5G handset subscriptions across operators (Marbridge Consulting 2024).

These figures clarify a structural shift. In 2013, historical benchmarks still captured an ecosystem in transition, with hundreds of millions accessing video on handhelds and a strong share of youth usage. Today the device is the default screen and video the default format. The audience profile has broadened beyond the under-25 demographic described in early surveys (Zhang Zhaole 2011), and short video has become a near-universal behavior across age cohorts. The rise of *duanju* micro-dramas on mobile platforms demonstrates how mobile time, portrait orientation, and recommendation algorithms now shape content design, pacing, and editorial choices in ways that also influence animation commissioning and marketing (CNNIC 2025).

Aesthetics and craft have evolved with the screen. The constraints identified in the early 2010s for "anima-mobile" remain relevant, yet are now formalized in platform playbooks: compositions tend to privilege close and medium shots to maintain legibility on small displays; color palettes and line weight favor clarity; timing compresses narrative payoffs into markedly shorter arcs than broadcast series; and episode lengths frequently sit well below the twenty-minute ceiling once considered optimal. These parameters interact with discovery systems. Because swipes and feeds determine survival in the first seconds, opening beats carry a disproportionate share of narrative load, while character design favors silhouettes and facial features that are instantly recognizable in miniature. Such choices echo earlier Flash-based web practices but are now conditioned by high-resolution screens, high-bitrate delivery, and social metrics that reward retention curves and rewatchability rather than linear scheduling (Bordwell & Thompson 2013; Nelmes 2012).

Industrial organization has followed the screens. The large streaming services that built their scale in the 2010s redesigned their mobile apps around low-friction access, mini-programs, and in-app commerce. Their animation catalogues straddle three pipelines: licensed imports, domestic long-form series, and mobile-native shorts that function as feeders to larger intellectual-property plays. In parallel, short-video platforms have become systemic gateways for animation discovery. Clips, motion-comics, animatics, and micro-episodes circulate as promotional vanguards that drive audiences toward longer seasons, theatrical releases, or merchandise drops. The funnel between short-video feeds and subscription hubs is now a standard route to scale, refining earlier, more experimental models of the 2010s that relied on portal front pages and manually curated carousels.

The economics of mobile diffusion have also matured. A decade ago, market commentary emphasized advertising growth tied to 3G adoption and the hurried creation of apps for Apple, Android, and Java devices (Ruilan 2011). Today revenue mixes are more diversified. Subscription video remains important on the major platforms, while mobile-native monetization has expanded through brand integrations, live commerce, tipping, and season-pass micro-payments. Product placement first systematized in early web hits carries over to mobile, but is now complemented by shoppable interfaces, QR-linked campaigns, and social commerce pathways aligned with mobile payment ubiquity. CNNIC's 2024–2025 data on online payment users, which exceed one billion, frame this shift toward seamless conversion from viewing to transaction within the same app environment (CNNIC 2025).

For animation specifically, mobile access has lowered barriers to entry for both audiences and producers. The historical experiments of the 2010s, such as Golden Eagle's early mobile-tailored series and festival circuits dedicated to original mobile works, anticipated today's layered model in which a short mobile format can serve as proof-of-concept, audience test, and marketing engine for longer arcs. Case studies from that period demonstrate how mobile-first production aligned with policy initiatives and industrial promotion, including recognition by state agencies for innovative children's formats and the development of derivative goods portfolios around characters, from books and games to apparel and toys. The current system preserves that logic but with greater scale and tighter integration, supported by mature data stacks, recommendation systems, and cross-platform analytics that inform commissioning and renewal decisions.

Regulation remains a decisive variable. Preventive content oversight, present since the 2010s, is now adapted to mobile interfaces, short-form formats, and algorithmic circulation. The earlier absence of rigorous copyright enforcement that fueled rapid audience accumulation has been replaced by stricter licensing regimes and platform compliance frameworks. This transition reduced blatant infringement while encouraging investment in original IP and formal co-production agreements, yet it also concentrates bargaining power within a handful of platforms and studios, raising the bar for independent creators whose breakout strategies once depended on looser ecosystems (Hauben 1997). The result is a paradox familiar since the 2010s: mobile diffusion expands reach and precision, but also tightens industrial and regulatory coordination.

Audience behavior illustrates the continuity between historical and current phases. The convenience of always-on, socially embedded, mobile video sustains exceptionally high adoption rates across genres. Animation benefits because it is modular, easily excerpted, and visually legible at small scales. The portability that once differentiated "mobile video" from "web video" has collapsed into a single dominant modality in which mobile is the web for most users. Updated national statistics reinforce this point. In January 2024 China had roughly 1.09 billion internet users and an internet penetration rate over three quarters of the population, and by early 2025 the country had added more than one hundred million mobile connections compared with the previous year (DataReportal 2024, 2025). Combined with CNNIC's accounting of short-video and micro-drama adoption in 2024, these indicators substantiate the claim that mobile diffusion is not a subset of online circulation but its principal driver (CNNIC 2024, 2025).

From a design perspective, the implications for creative practice are clear. Story worlds are conceived with multiplatform agility, characters are engineered for instant recognition in portrait orientation, and narrative arcs are planned with both episodic bingeability and clip-ability in mind. The compactness, clarity, and immediacy that once defined the best mobile pieces in the early 2010s have become baseline expectations for all animation intended for contemporary Chinese audiences. At the same time, the longer traditions of cinematic craft remain relevant, especially where hybrid techniques and live-action integration seek to anchor animation in recognizable urban realities. In this sense, the technical lessons codified in film-studies handbooks about framing, color, and continuity find renewed purpose on the smallest screen, where perceptual thresholds are unforgiving and viewer attention is wholly contingent (Bordwell & Thompson 2013; Nelmes 2012).

Historically, then, the 2010s established the social habits, industrial infrastructures, and regulatory templates that made mobile diffusion central to the animation economy. The most recent data confirm that the trend has reached saturation in terms of user adoption, but it continues to evolve in format logics, monetization pathways, and cross-platform orchestration. What began as an ancillary screen is now the default horizon of consumption and the primary arena in which Chinese animation competes for attention, loyalty, and revenue.

7.6 Distributed Animation—Grassroots Practices and Fan Networks

The term *Màn dònghuà* (漫动画), literally "comic-moving," was introduced around 2011 to describe a hybrid form distinct from both traditional comics and mainstream television animation. It designates digital products that merge comics, animation, audio and video, interactive features, and multi-touch graphics, distributed primarily through mobile devices and online platforms. Such works extend the expressive power of traditional comics by integrating animation and interactivity, creating an enhanced relationship between product and audience (Liu 2012). For this reason, the notion of "distributed animation" is more suitable than "moving comic" when referring to these multimedia formats.

From the late 2000s onward, Chinese authorities supported the development of this new field. The Ministry of Culture, the General Administration of Press, and SARFT invested significant resources in promoting original animation, digital publishing, and mobile formats. Song Xiaohong of the China Publishing Group emphasized that *Màn dònghuà* represented a new type of art rooted in New Media, highlighting the opportunities created by mobile internet and smart terminals. According to Song, traditional comics needed to evolve into electronic formats capable of combining narrative strength, interactive design, and innovative modes of publication (Lu 2011).

The economic rationale was also evident. Traditional animation involves long production cycles and high costs, with relatively passive audience participation. Distributed animation, by contrast, offers lower costs, shorter production times, more rapid returns on investment, and compatibility with multiple platforms. Its interactive character makes it especially appealing for commercialization and user engagement (Cheng 2012). Already in the early 2010s, companies such as China Publishing

Group Digital Media (2012) began digitizing archives and experimenting with interactive comic apps like *Rabbit Diary* (达兔日记, *Dá tù rìjì*), *Lafeng Tu* (拉风兔, *Lā fēng tù*), and *Red Classic* (红色经典, *Hóngsè jīngdiǎn*), often released for both Apple and Android systems. National contests like the First Distributed Animation Competition in 2012 encouraged young creators to combine comic traditions with interactive innovation.

The Tianjin Spirit World Comics company became another early leader, digitizing hundreds of thousands of pages and developing interactive adaptations such as *Romance of the Three Kingdoms—Battle of Red Cliff* (三国演义之赤壁之战, *Sānguó yǎnyì zhī chìbì zhī zhàn*), which won awards for originality and innovation in national competitions. Works like *The Legend of Ji Gong* (村人画趣, *Cūnrén huà qù*) were successfully distributed internationally, first in Japan and later in the United States, confirming the potential of this new format (Du 2011).

In the 2020s, distributed animation has become a structural component of the Chinese cultural industries. Major platforms such as Kuaikan Comics, Tencent Comics, and NetEase Comics host millions of users and publish thousands of serialized works. Successful cases illustrate how a distributed comic can evolve into a cross-media property. *Biao Ren: Blades of the Guardians* (镖人), for example, began as a digital manhua read over two billion times across dozens of platforms before being adapted into a popular donghua released on Tencent Video in 2023 (Wikipedia 2024). The trajectory from online serialization to animated adaptation, merchandising, and transmedia franchising exemplifies the industrial logics that distributed animation makes possible.

Recent industry reports confirm that the webcomics and digital comics sector, closely linked with distributed animation, has grown into a global market valued at USD 7.63 billion in 2024 and projected to exceed USD 8.17 billion in 2025, with China playing a central role (Fortune Business Insights 2024). In this environment, the boundaries between webcomics, digital animation, short videos, and interactive media are increasingly fluid. Other phenomena such as *duanju* (短剧), or short vertical dramas, though not themselves animated, exert influence on storytelling formats and audience expectations in mobile environments.

Technically, distributed animation has consolidated an aesthetic optimized for mobile screens. Characters are often presented in close or medium shots to ensure legibility, colors and line work are designed for clarity, and episodes are structured in short, modular arcs. The hybrid use of live-action backdrops, photographic layers, or video integration, practices experimented with since the 2010s, remains common. Monetization models have expanded from advertising and product placement to include subscriptions, micropayments, tipping systems, and integration with e-commerce. Platforms encourage seamless shifts between reading, watching, and purchasing, supported by widespread mobile payment adoption.

Regulation has tightened over the years, with stricter copyright enforcement and licensing requirements replacing the permissive environments of the early 2010s when unauthorized distribution was common. While this professionalization has encouraged investment in original IP, it has also raised barriers for independent creators. Yet despite these challenges, distributed animation has proven to be a promising creative industry segment, bridging comics and animation, tradition and innovation, and domestic and international markets.

In summary, what began as experimental attempts to animate comics for mobile devices in the early 2010s has, by the mid-2020s, become an established field of cultural production. Distributed animation reflects the convergence of technologies, industries, and audiences in contemporary China, and its trajectory highlights the capacity of new media forms to reshape not only the aesthetics of animation but also its economic and cultural significance.

7.7 Emerging Technologies—Experimentation and Convergence

The evolution of digital technology in China's animation industry has made it among the most significant sectors of the creative economy in the twenty-first century because it intersects with many traditional industries and derivative markets. During the 2010s the introduction of 3D animation began reshaping production pipelines. New professional roles emerged capable of producing content of very high visual quality for a global audience. Animation in three dimensions found applications not only in films and series but also within video games, advertising, virtual tourism, architectural visualization and other design fields. As the real estate and architectural sectors in China continued expanding, demand for 3D modelling and visualization rose sharply. Though in the early 2010s the number of professionals was limited and still forming (Zhou 2008), today there are many specialists in 3D modelling, lighting, rendering, and virtual environment design working across studios of various sizes.

Recent years have seen further technological advances accelerate innovation. Real-time rendering engines such as Unreal Engine and Unity have become widely adopted in Chinese animation studios, allowing creators to preview scenes live, adjust lighting and camera movement in real time, and reduce iteration cycles. These tools enhance productivity and allow more immersive or interactive projects to be feasible. In addition, artificial intelligence (AI) is now being integrated into many parts of the pipeline. One study shows that with AI-assisted virtual reality technology, the time to produce a 3D animation clip was nearly halved compared with traditional methods, with cost per lens reduced significantly, improvements in visual effects, fluidity of movement, and viewer immersion (Hong 2025). Edge intelligence and large-model based systems are also being explored for animation design to manage data, speed workflow, and enable rendering on mobile or decentralized platforms (Zhu et al. 2024).

Facial modelling technologies and neural rendering methods have also improved rapidly. Gaussian splatting and other novel representations now permit real-time rendering of facial expressions and head avatars even on mobile hardware at high resolutions. For example PSAvatar (Zhao et al. 2024) uses point-based shape models combined with 3D Gaussian techniques to achieve high fidelity rendering and expressive body and face motion in real time. Similar developments are visible in real-time portrait animation frameworks, where audio-driven motion generation allows talking heads or virtual presenters with natural expression and timing (Dingcheng Zhen et al. 2025).

Such technological improvements enable production for multiple platforms with lower cost, shorter turnaround times, and greater flexibility. Studios now plan for multiplatform release (TV, streaming, mobile, VR/AR) from the earliest design stages. Animations are optimized for mobile viewing, for example by using simplified shaders, efficient rendering workflows, scalable assets, and adaptive lighting. Because mobile devices now have more computational power and better bandwidth, streaming of 4K or high frame rate animation is becoming more common, even on smartphones, under favorable network conditions.

The economic implications are considerable. Lower costs and faster production mean that content creators can test new ideas more quickly and afford riskier, more experimental works. Monetization models that combine subscription, advertising, product placement, live commerce and interactive features are supported by technology that tracks audience metrics and enables personalized recommendations. AI tools help in automating lip-sync, inbetweening, background generation or rigging, reducing labor intensity.

Nonetheless there remain challenges. Highly polished 3D animation still requires large initial investment in skilled artists, software, hardware and rendering infrastructure. Independent creators may struggle to access these resources. Furthermore, state regulations on content, especially when using AI-generated or procedurally generated visuals, are still evolving. There is also the risk of homogenization: as many studios adopt similar tools and asset libraries, differences in style may reduce, making originality harder to achieve.

Historically the 2010s established the foundations—introduction of 3D, early adoption of digital tools, and rising internet/mobile infrastructure. The early experiments with Flash and 2D hybrids set precedents in cost efficiency and distribution strategies. Today the convergence of real-time rendering, AI-assisted design, mobile capable hardware, and hybrid media forms means technology is not simply enabling but shaping animators' creative choices. New technologies are thus not only improving production quality but redefining what animation can be: more interactive, more responsive, more distributed, and more globally competitive.

7.8 The Expanding Video Game Market in China

The video game industry in China has always been closely related to animation by virtue of shared skills in character design, visual storytelling, interactivity, and digital graphics. During the 2010s many animation graduates preferred to enter game development because the game sector was seen as more dynamic, with faster feedback loops and more stable income, compared to the long production cycles typical of animation content. The government recognized this overlap and supported game development through policy, subsidies, and licensing reforms, especially after the decision in January 2014 to reopen the market to foreign video game consoles following more than a decade of bans.

Today the Chinese video game market is among the largest in the world and continues to grow strongly. In the first half of 2025 revenue from domestic game sales reached approximately 168 billion yuan, an increase of about 14% year over year. Mobile games accounted for the majority of that revenue, contributing 125.3 billion yuan, or roughly 75% of the total, while mini-games also grew rapidly at over 40%. Console game revenues rebounded nearly 30% in the same period (Caixin Global 2025).

Chinese personally-developed games gained substantial ground overseas. In 2025 overseas revenue from domestic mobile games exceeded 9.5 billion U.S. dollars, up about 11% year over year (Caixin Global 2025).

A notable case illustrating recent trends is *Black Myth: Wukong*, developed by Game Science. It achieved tremendous global impact following its release, both in terms of sales and reputation. *Black Myth: Wukong* sold more than ten million units within the first few days and earned over one billion U.S. dollars, setting a benchmark for high-budget, high-quality Chinese game production imbued with cultural elements, refined art direction, and advanced technical infrastructure (Financial Times 2025).

Major companies remain dominant players in the ecosystem. Tencent has reported strong growth in its gaming division, with domestic revenue growth of more than 20% in recent quarters driven by well-performing titles, while regulatory easing has helped revive revenue streams after stricter controls in previous years (Reuters 2025).

Despite these successes, the industry still faces structural challenges. Game approval processes, content regulation, limits on play time for minors, and restrictions on monetization methods have periodically tightened, affecting both domestic developers and foreign publishers. Independent studios often struggle to compete on production scale, and high development costs for AAA-style titles remain a barrier. However, the rising economic scale, growing international recognition, and increasing output quality suggest strong momentum.

In sum, compared to the 2010s when the Chinese video game sector was expanding, professionalizing, and reopening to foreign hardware, the current stage in 2024–2025 is one of maturation. Revenue is larger, mobile remains the primary vector of growth, overseas markets are more significant, and technical ambition is greater. The convergence between game technology, animation, storytelling, and regulatory oversight continues to define how the market expands and what kinds of content succeed.

References

Augé, M. 1995. *Non-lieux: Introduction à une anthropologie de la surmodernité*. Seuil.
BBC News. 2013. Chinese TV cartoon blamed for child injuries. https://www.bbc.com/news/entertainment-arts-25447851.
Blue Book. 2012. Blue Book of Animation: Annual Report on Development of China's Animation Industry (2012) (动漫蓝皮书:中国动漫产业发展报告(2012)). 2012. Social Sciences Academic Press.
Bordwell, D., and K. Thompson. 2013. *Film art: An introduction*, 10th ed. McGraw-Hill.
Caixin Global. 2025, August 1. *China's domestic gaming market generated 168 billion yuan in revenue, with mobile games accounting for most of the growth*. Retrieved from https://www.caixinglobal.com/2025-08-01/china-proves-a-winner-in-the-gaming-market-as-growth-hits-a-five-year-high-102347448.html.
Chen, Z.T. 2018. Poetic prosumption of animation, comic, game and novel in a post-socialist China: A case of a popular video-sharing social media Bilibili as heterotopia. *Journal of Consumer Culture* 21 (2): 257–277. https://doi.org/10.1177/1469540518787574 (Original work published 2021).
China Publishing Group Digital Media. 2012. *Rabbit Diary (达兔日记, Dá tù rìjì)*. Beijing: China Publishing Group.
CNNIC (China Internet Network Information Center). 2024. *The 54th Statistical Report on China's Internet Development*. Retrieved from https://www.cnnic.com.cn/IDR/ReportDownloads/202411/P020241101318428715781.pdf.
CNNIC (China Internet Network Information Center). 2025. *The 55th Statistical Report on China's Internet Development*. Retrieved from https://www.cnnic.com.cn/IDR/ReportDownloads/202505/P020250514564119130448.pdf.
Cohn, J. 2012. *Anime and cultural translation in contemporary media*. Routledge.
Cucco, M. 2009. Blockbusters and global cinema: Cultural hybridity in transnational markets. *Cinema e Storia* 1 (2): 45–60.
Cui, D., and F. Wu. 2024. *Toward an operationality perspective on fandom: Exploring Chinese fans' emerging practices in platform-mediated environments*. Retrieved from https://www.researchgate.net/publication/384991382_Toward_an_operationality_perspective_on_fandom_Exploring_Chinese_fans%27_emerging_practices_in_platform-mediated_environments.
Dao Insights. 2020. Bilibili grows from niche anime audience to powerful Gen Z platform. https://daoinsights.com/works/bilibili-grows-from-niche-anime-audience-to-powerful-gen-z-platform/.
DataReportal. 2024. *Digital 2024: China*. Retrieved from https://datareportal.com/reports/digital-2024-china.
DataReportal. 2025. *Digital 2025: China*. Retrieved from https://datareportal.com/reports/digital-2025-china.
Dedney, A. 2006. *New media and convergence*. In *Media Studies Journal*.
Dingcheng Zhen, S., S. Yin, S. Qin, Y. Hou, Z. Zhang, S. Liu, Q. Gan, and M. Tao. 2025. *Teller: Real-Time streaming audio-driven portrait animation with autoregressive motion generation*. Retrieved from https://arxiv.org/abs/2503.18429.
Dong, D. 2019. Chinese cartoons and animated shows for kids. Medium. https://medium.com/@daniel.wdong111/chinese-cartoons-and-animated-shows-for-kids-8125b76a62a4
Du, Y. 2011. Mobile comics and international circulation: The case of The Legend of Ji Gong. *Asian Comics Review* 2 (1): 45–58.

Financial Times. (2025, January 3). *China's video game industry is poised for more blockbuster releases in 2025 following global success of Black Myth: Wukong*. Retrieved from https://www.ft.com/content/24d330fe-6f82-4571-85ec-8e1d429d6da1.

Fortune Business Insights. 2024. *Webcomics market size, share, growth & trends 2025–2032*. Retrieved from https://www.fortunebusinessinsights.com/webcomics-market-105731.

Gates, H. 2006. Cultural strategy and Chinese soft power. *The China Quarterly* 186: 285–302.

Global Times. 2024, December 24. *2024 Yearender: China's Gen Z embracing anime, comic and game culture*. Retrieved from https://www.globaltimes.cn/page/202412/1325689.shtml.

Hauben, M. 1997. *The Net and Netizens: The impact the net has had on People's Lives*. IEEE Computer Society.

Jarboe, G. 2011. *YouTube and video marketing: An hour a day*. Wiley.

Jiang, Z. 2024. *Strategic insights into China's fan economy: Synergizing fandom and commerce*. Retrieved from https://www.ewadirect.com/proceedings/aemps/article/view/18264.

Liu, X. 2012. Interactive animation and the rise of Màn dònghuà. *Publishing Research* 8: 55–60.

Lu, Y. 2011. Policies supporting original Chinese animation in the digital age. *Cultural Development Studies* 3 (2): 14–21.

Marbridge Consulting. (2024, December 23). *MIIT: China's mobile subscriber base up 1.7M in November 2024*. Retrieved from https://www.marbridgeconsulting.com/marbridgedaily/archive/article/115190/miit_chinas_mobile_subscriber_base_up_17_mln_in_november_2024.

Market Research Future. 2025. *China Entertainment & Media Market Report 2025–2035*. Retrieved from https://www.marketresearchfuture.com/reports/china-entertainment-media-market-43835.

Market Report Analytics. 2025. *Emerging China Media and entertainment market trends and forecasts 2023–2028*. Retrieved from https://www.marketreportanalytics.com/reports/china-media-and-entertainment-market-4745.

Moscon, V. 2010. Non-places and the multiplex: Cinema spaces in global culture. *Journal of Film and Media Studies* 5 (1): 23–40.

Naavik. 2024. Microdramas: China's new craze goes global. https://naavik.co/digest/microdramas-chinas-new-craze/.

Nelmes, J. 2012. *An introduction to film studies*, 5th ed. Routledge.

Radii. 2018. China's Gen Z anime fans rejoice as Bilibili goes public in US. https://radii.co/article/chinas-gen-z-anime-fans-rejoice-as-bilibili-goes-public-in-us.

Reuters. 2025, March 19. *Tencent posts strong Q4 as gaming business rebounds*. Retrieved from https://www.reuters.com/technology/chinas-tencent-q4-revenue-exceeds-estimates-2025-03-19/.

Ruilan, Z. 2011. Mobile animation and the rise of digital comics. *China Publishing Journal* 4: 23–29.

Shi, T. 2010. Ant Tribe: Housing struggles of Beijing's youth. *Beijing Social Sciences Journal* 4 (3): 33–48.

Tan, Z. 2006. *Animation industry in China: Policies and practices*. Beijing: China Broadcasting Press.

The Business of Fashion. 2021. A guide to Bilibili, China's Gen-Z hangout. https://www.businessoffashion.com/articles/china/a-guide-to-bilibili-chinas-gen-z-hangout/.

ThinkChina. 2025. 'Brainless' but satisfying: How Chinese micro-dramas are taking over our screens. https://www.thinkchina.sg/society/brainless-satisfying-how-chinese-micro-dramas-are-taking-over-our-screens.

Wikipedia. 2024. *Biao Ren*. Retrieved from https://en.wikipedia.org/wiki/Biao_Ren.

Wikipedia. 2025. *Duanju*. Retrieved from https://en.wikipedia.org/wiki/Duanju.

Hong, Z. 2025. *Application of virtual reality technology based on artificial intelligence for 3D animation storyboards*. Retrieved from https://link.springer.com/article/10.1007/s10791-025-09670-7.

Zhao, Z., Bao, Z., Li, Q., et al. 2024. Real-Time Head Avatar Animation with 3D Gaussian Splatting. *arXiv preprint*. https://arxiv.org/abs/2401.12900

Zhou, Y. 2008. 3D animation and the transformation of Chinese studios. *China Animation Studies* 2 (1): 44–59.

Zhu, J., et al. 2024. *Edge intelligence-assisted animation design with large models.* Journal of Cloud Computing, *13*, Article 127. Retrieved from https://journalofcloudcomputing.springeropen.com/articles/10.1186/s13677-024-00601-3.

Chapter 8
Competing Geographies of Animation

Abstract This chapter situates Chinese animation within the wider East Asian and global landscape by comparing it with the industrial models of Taiwan, South Korea, North Korea, and Japan. The analysis begins with Taiwan, where the animation sector developed both as a service provider for international studios and as a laboratory of hybrid cultural forms, particularly through glove puppetry and the internationally recognized Pili series. South Korea is examined as a dynamic hub where comics and animation converged, supported by state policies that fostered exports and technological modernization, allowing the country to become a major subcontractor for global media corporations. In contrast, North Korea represents a system in which animation is tightly controlled by the state, serving primarily ideological functions and producing content that reflects authoritarian priorities. Japan, finally, is presented as the most influential regional competitor, with anime shaping global cultural imagination and providing a reference point for Chinese producers. By comparing these different geographies, the chapter highlights how regional proximity, cultural exchange, and industrial competition have influenced China's strategies, reinforcing both the challenges and opportunities of positioning Chinese animation within a highly competitive and interconnected global market.

Keywords Taiwan animation · Pili puppetry · South Korea animation · North Korea propaganda · Japanese anime · East Asian media industries

8.1 Comparative Industrial Models—Taiwan and the Animated Market

When discussing Asian animation, attention is usually directed immediately to Japan and China. Nevertheless, other countries such as Taiwan and South Korea have succeeded in developing distinctive styles and productive industrial chains that have often been taken as models in the formulation of Chinese industrial policies in recent years. In order to better contextualize the trajectory of the Chinese animation sector, it is useful to examine first the competing markets of its geographically and culturally

© The Author(s), under exclusive license to Springer Nature Switzerland AG 2026
V. De Masi, *A Critical Analysis of China's Animation Industry*, Numanities - Arts and Humanities in Progress 37, https://doi.org/10.1007/978-3-032-18656-0_8

proximate neighbors. The following analysis therefore considers the development of animation in Taiwan, then South Korea, and finally Japan, which continues to be perceived as the most formidable competitor.

Although each of these countries has cultivated its own industrial and commercial configuration, it is important to recognize that the broader East Asian region has consistently been shaped by the influence of Japanese animation. This chapter also includes a critical examination of different schools of animation and of specific case studies such as the Taiwanese *Pili* series, which provide significant insights into alternative forms of development that may inform the evolution of Chinese animation.

The Taiwanese animation industry occupies a distinctive position in the East Asian media landscape, shaped by its dual role as both a service provider for international studios and a laboratory of hybrid cultural forms that integrate traditional performance practices with digital technologies. While mainland China focuses on massive scale, Taiwan's industry offers a contrasting model of high-specialization, particularly in its capacity to service Western co-productions (such as those with French or Canadian studios) requiring complex 3D integration, a niche that Chinese mainland studios are only recently beginning to dominate. According to the Ministry of Economic Affairs report published in 2013 through the Digital Content Industry Promotion Office, the sector is divided into several core components including animated films, television animation, new media animation, and the related copyright and merchandising markets (MoEA 2013). Computer-generated animation has been at the center of industrial expansion, with the market registering a growth rate of 14.77% in 2012 compared with 2011, reaching an estimated value of 128 million euros or 176 million dollars (MoEA 2012). Much of this expansion was driven by international outsourcing, which allowed Taiwanese studios to provide cost-effective and high-quality services to global corporations, particularly from the United States and Japan. In 2011 outsourcing alone grew by 10.1%, while animation for new media recorded a growth of 4.6% due to the rise of smartphone-based content and applications for Android and Apple systems (MoEA 2012).

Despite the relatively small domestic market of just over 23 million inhabitants, Taiwanese companies have pursued strategies of internationalization to expand their digital content industries into neighboring territories such as mainland China, Hong Kong, Japan, and South Korea. Geographic and cultural proximity facilitated this process, and several enterprises successfully established subsidiaries abroad. Notable examples include SoftWorld International Corporation (智冠科技股份有限公司, *Zhì guān kējì gǔfèn yǒuxiàn gōngsī*), with branches across Southeast Asia, and Gamania Digital Entertainment (遊戲橘子數位科技股份有限公司, *Yóuxì jú zǐ shùwèi kējì gǔfèn yǒuxiàn gōngsī*), which opened offices in Tokyo, Beijing, Shanghai, Hong Kong, and Seoul. XPEC Entertainment (樂陞科技, *Lè shēng kējì*) represents another successful case, operating subsidiaries not only in Asia but also in the United States, where it has collaborated with leading American and Japanese corporations on large-scale productions (Chiu 2012). These companies illustrate the ways in which Taiwan leveraged its flexible, export-oriented economy to gain visibility in the global animation and gaming sectors.

The Taiwanese government has historically played an active role in supporting international distribution and market access for local animation and video game producers. Public institutions have promoted participation in festivals, fairs, and exhibitions abroad, often providing financial support to companies and encouraging executives to visit leading studios in order to build transnational partnerships (Chiu 2012). This strategy has yielded notable results, with Taiwanese firms establishing collaborations with global giants such as Sony, Microsoft, and Nintendo, thereby reinforcing the country's image as a reliable production hub. Domestically, however, the distribution of original animation has remained limited. Of the 215 million minutes of animation broadcast annually, only about 4000 min are locally produced. Nevertheless, the situation has improved with the emergence of thematic channels, public television initiatives, and children's programming networks such as YoYo TV, which have created new spaces for homegrown animation. A crucial difference compared with the Chinese mainland is that Taiwanese audiences tend to prefer local productions, which they often perceive as superior in narrative structure and visual quality. Ministry of Economic Affairs surveys from 2007 already indicated that such preferences stimulated continuous growth in original productions since 2003 (MoEA 2007).

The historical development of the industry underscores the transitional role of outsourcing. Taiwanese animation initially developed through subcontracting for Western studios, particularly in the late 1970s and 1980s. Wang Film Productions, also known as Hong Guang (宏廣), founded in 1978 by James Wang (王中元), became the most prominent outsourcing studio in the world. Originally established to work on six projects for Hanna-Barbera, it quickly expanded to serve virtually all major American and European studios. Wang Film contributed to feature films such as *Balto II: Wolf Quest* (2002) and *Balto III: Wings of Change* (2004) for Universal Cartoon Studios, *Mulan II* for Disney, and *Scooby-Doo and the Monster of Mexico* for Warner Bros. Its portfolio also included influential television series such as *Garfield and Friends* (1993–1995), *Teenage Mutant Ninja Turtles* (1987–1996), *Batman: The Animated Series* (1992–1995), and even the Italian franchise *Winx Club*. Wang's international expansion, with branches across Asia, consolidated Taiwan's reputation as an indispensable node in the global animation supply chain.

Over time, Taiwanese animation evolved beyond subcontracting into a sphere of original creation, often blending local culture with innovative techniques. One of the most remarkable contributions has been the revival of puppet animation, or glove puppetry, which originated in Fujian province in southeastern China and flourished in Taiwan as a popular theatrical form. While most other countries abandoned puppet animation with the rise of computer-generated imagery, Taiwan transformed it into a sophisticated television and film genre. The best-known example is the long-running *Pili* series, produced by Pili International Multimedia Inc., which has generated more than 1600 episodes and an extensive range of derivative products. The franchise expanded into cinema with *The Legend of the Sacred Stone* (2000) and later entered the digital age with three-dimensional productions and online streaming adaptations. *Pili Fantasy: War of Dragons*, released internationally on Netflix in 2019, marked an unprecedented moment in which Taiwanese glove puppetry reached global audiences, demonstrating the possibility of combining traditional craftsmanship with international media distribution.

The success of *Pili* illustrates how Taiwan has managed to convert traditional art forms into viable media commodities while resisting the homogenization often associated with computer-generated production. Puppet animation's revival also highlights the cultural capital embedded in Taiwanese animation, offering a stark contrast to the fate of glove puppetry in mainland China, where it had been promoted during the Cultural Revolution for ideological purposes but was subsequently abandoned. In Taiwan, on the other hand, puppet animation was institutionalized, taught in specialized schools, and supported by multimedia corporations that recognized its potential as a cultural export. The integration of digital visual effects and computer graphics into puppet performances created a hybrid aesthetic that appealed to both domestic audiences and global niche markets interested in non-Western forms of animation.

Recent developments confirm the resilience of Taiwan's animated sector despite its structural limitations. The 2020s witnessed the acceleration of digital platforms and streaming services that provided new channels for Taiwanese content. Governmental initiatives such as the Taiwan Creative Content Agency (established in 2019) further reinforced the state's role in supporting local media production, encouraging co-productions with Japan and South Korea, and offering grants for projects with international distribution potential. The agency has explicitly identified animation and gaming as priority industries, recognizing their capacity to promote Taiwan's cultural identity abroad while stimulating domestic employment in creative fields. Between 2019 and 2023, the Taiwanese animation industry increasingly participated in cross-border collaborations, particularly with Japanese studios, which saw Taiwanese firms not merely as subcontractors but as partners in co-producing original works.

At the same time, the Taiwanese animation sector faces ongoing challenges, including competition from South Korea's K-animation wave, which has achieved considerable success on global streaming platforms, and from the dominant Japanese industry that continues to dictate aesthetic and narrative standards in the region. Taiwan's comparative advantage lies less in scale and more in its ability to fuse tradition with innovation, offering narratives rooted in local folklore and practices that resonate with cultural authenticity. This balance allows Taiwan to maintain visibility in a highly competitive regional environment while differentiating its productions from the standardized outputs of larger industries.

The trajectory of Taiwanese animation therefore reveals a paradox: while the domestic market remains modest in size, the sector has consistently demonstrated resilience through adaptation, outsourcing, and cultural reinvention. By capitalizing on international subcontracting, investing in digital technologies, and valorizing traditional puppet animation as a vehicle for contemporary storytelling, Taiwan has carved out a distinctive position in the East Asian media ecology. Its experience demonstrates that small markets can nonetheless play a significant role in global cultural industries when they succeed in combining historical continuity with technological innovation. Looking ahead, the ability of Taiwan to sustain and expand this dual strategy will determine whether its animation industry can further consolidate its place not only as a subcontractor but also as a recognized source of original creative content in the global arena.

8.2 Glove Puppetry and the Pili Phenomenon—Tradition Meets Modern Media

Glove puppetry, known in Southern Min as *pò-tē-hì* and in Chinese as *budaixi* (布袋戏, *Bùdàixì*), has deep roots in Chinese cultural history. Scholars usually place its mature form in the seventeenth century, especially in Quanzhou (泉州, *Quánzhōu*) and Zhangzhou (漳州, *Zhāngzhōu*) in Fujian (福建, *Fújiàn*), and in Chaozhou (潮州, *Cháozhōu*) in Guangdong (广东, *Guǎngdōng*). Some sources trace its origins even earlier, to the Song dynasty, while folklore links it to the story of an official who, after losing his position, invented a puppet show to make a living. Whatever its precise beginnings, the art spread from Fujian to Taiwan during major waves of migration. There, it found fertile ground and became part of the island's evolving cultural identity.

For more than two centuries Taiwan developed a rich ecosystem of popular theatre in which glove puppetry thrived. Families of performers created schools that passed down knowledge from one generation to the next. Among them, the Huang family is the most influential. Huang Haidai (黄海岱, *Huáng Hǎidài*) is remembered as the great master of *pò-tē-hì*. He introduced martial arts and popular music into the shows, which gave the performances new energy and appeal. His innovations laid the foundation for the modern style of glove puppetry that would later evolve into the television series *Pili* (霹雳, *Pīlì*).

The art was transmitted through successive generations. Huang Junxiong (黄俊雄, *Huáng Jùnxióng*) brought glove puppetry to television, marking a turning point in its history. Later, the third generation, represented by artists like Huang Qianghua (黄强华, *Huáng Qiánghuá*), expanded the reach of the family's tradition. According to interviews, the move from theatre to television began almost by accident, when a producer from Taiwan's public broadcaster attended a live puppet performance and proposed an adaptation for studio recording. The broadcast was a huge success, reaching an audience share of 97%. This response encouraged Huang Junxiong to transform traditional stage plays into serialized television dramas. The productions combined puppetry with new techniques such as cinematic camera angles and, later, digital effects.

The success of the early series convinced the Huang family to expand. Chris and Vincent Huang created a satellite channel devoted entirely to *Pili* content. They also produced the feature film *The Legend of the Sacred Stone* (圣石传说, *Shèng Shí Chuánshuō*) in 2000, which achieved box office success in Taiwan.

This film blended traditional puppetry with computer graphics and proved that glove puppetry could work as a modern cinematic form. The international impact grew further when Warner Bros collaborated on *Wulin Warriors* (2006), which aired on Cartoon Network in the United States. Although the series had a short run, it was significant as the only Chinese animated property purchased by the network at that time (Chang 2011).

From these beginnings, *Pili* evolved into a multimedia phenomenon. The integration of digital effects and the use of advanced cinematography gave puppet figures a sense of weight and realism. Their design also changed. The early puppets were about thirty centimeters tall, with fixed painted eyes and simplified limbs. Today, they reach ninety centimeters in height and feature glass eyes, natural hair, and articulated joints modeled on the ball-jointed doll system. These changes make it possible for puppets to wield heavy weapons, perform acrobatic moves, and appear more lifelike on screen. Backgrounds also developed from flat scenic cloths into miniature sets enhanced with 3D computer graphics. These advances created a hybrid aesthetic that combines the tactility of handcrafted puppets with the visual dynamism of digital animation (Wu 2023).

Music played a central role in the transformation of glove puppetry. Early television series used *Nanguan* 南管 and Chaozhou opera 潮剧 melodies, which linked the shows to their temple roots. Over time, composers introduced music from Beijing opera, Taiwanese folk songs, and even Western popular genres. By the late 1980s, soundtracks included synthesizers, pop ballads, and rock elements. The Huang family also collaborated with Taiwanese pop artists, creating opening themes and insert songs that resembled the strategies of Japanese anime. This musical evolution made the series more appealing to younger audiences while still retaining a connection to tradition. The result was a soundscape that combined ritual depth with contemporary energy, a balance that contributed greatly to the franchise's popularity (Arts Foundation 2004).

Narrative design further distinguished *Pili*. Each season told an independent story, yet the overarching plot developed through recurring characters, most notably Su Huanzhen (素还真, *Sù Huánzhēn*). He became the central hero of the saga, embodying intelligence, restraint, and moral ambiguity. His presence linked the many arcs together and gave coherence to the series. The scripts drew on Confucian, Daoist, and Buddhist traditions, but also incorporated allegories of Taiwanese politics and current affairs. This flexibility allowed the franchise to remain relevant across decades. Viewers were captivated by the mixture of myth, philosophy, and topical references.

Another factor in *Pili*'s success was performance. Huang Qianghua (黄强华, *Huáng Qiánghuá*), known as the "Eight Voices Talent" (八音才子, *Bā Yīn Cáizǐ*), provided voices for thousands of characters.

His ability to shift between registers gave the series a unique vocal identity. Combined with sophisticated scripts and detailed visuals, the vocal performance reinforced the immersive quality of the stories.

Commercially, *Pili* developed into a diversified media empire. By 2012 the company had broadcast more than 1700 episodes, each lasting around one hour. Revenue came not only from television but also from DVDs, soundtrack albums, figurines, and branded merchandise. The characters appeared on credit cards, in supermarket promotions, and in election campaign advertisements. This commercialization turned *Pili* into a cultural icon in Taiwan. The brand became deeply embedded in popular life, and glove puppetry moved from the temple stage to the heart of the creative industries.

The expansion continued in the digital era. With the rise of streaming platforms, *Pili* found new audiences abroad. *Pili Fantasy: War of Dragons* appeared on Netflix in 2019, making glove puppetry visible to global viewers for the first time on a major platform (Pili International Multimedia 2019; Tsai 2020). The international release confirmed that audiences outside Taiwan were receptive to this hybrid form of animation. The show's success encouraged Taiwanese policymakers to view glove puppetry not only as cultural heritage but also as a strategic export.

The establishment of the Taiwan Creative Content Agency (TAICCA) in 2019 further reinforced this perspective. TAICCA identified animation and gaming as priority sectors and provided funding, training, and international promotion for projects with strong cultural identity (TAICCA 2019, 2021). *Pili* benefited from these initiatives, gaining support for international distribution and co-production. Scholars have noted that the case of *Pili* demonstrates how digital tools can extend traditional practices rather than replace them, creating a living heritage that speaks to both domestic pride and global curiosity (Wu 2023).

The Taiwanese model contrasts with the situation in mainland China. There, puppet animation was heavily promoted during the Cultural Revolution for ideological purposes, but it lost relevance in the digital era. Taiwan instead revitalized glove puppetry by combining heritage with modern media. The success of *Pili* shows that audiences can embrace subtitles, stylized movement, and hybrid aesthetics if the storytelling is coherent and the craftsmanship is visible. It suggests that preserving cultural specificity can be a competitive advantage in global media markets.

The history of glove puppetry and its reinvention through *Pili* demonstrates the dynamic relationship between tradition and innovation. Hand-carved puppets and digital effects coexist in a single frame. Ancient melodies and pop songs share the same soundtrack. Classical heroes and contemporary allegories meet in the same scripts. This hybrid quality makes *Pili* both a guardian of heritage and a vehicle for creative experimentation. It also explains why the franchise has remained vital for decades, producing weekly episodes, feature films, and spin-off products while continuing to train new generations of performers and technicians.

For Taiwan, glove puppetry has become more than entertainment. It is a cultural symbol, a commercial brand, and an example of how small markets can shape global cultural flows. For China, it represents an alternative path in animation, one that values continuity with tradition as much as technological progress. The case of *Pili* shows that animation can be both deeply local and internationally relevant, an achievement that positions Taiwan as an important player in East Asian creative industries.

8.3 South Korea—Animation and Comics in a Regional and Global Frame

Among the main competitors and at the same time models for China, South Korea occupies a particularly important place. In only a few decades the country developed a strong industrial chain in animation and comics. Today this sector is considered a pillar of both national culture and creative industries. From the beginning, the South Korean government treated animation as a strategic domain. It promoted the industry with consistent policies that protected intellectual property, created incentives for investment, and connected local studios with international partners. In many respects China followed a similar path, yet its adoption of these policies came almost 20 years later and under very different technological conditions (Tang 2006).

The Korean term *manhwa* (만화, 漫畫, *manhwa*) is significant. It refers to both comics and animated productions, mirroring the Chinese term *manhua* (漫画, *mànhuà*). The similarity of terminology reflects not only linguistic proximity but also comparable trajectories in which comics and animation have developed as interconnected media sectors (Netcomics 2008).

The history of Korean animation began with modest experiments. The first animated short was a commercial for a soft drink, *OBsinalko* (OB시날코, *OB Sinalko*), broadcast on HLKZ TV in 1956 and lasting only a few seconds (Yihangru 2004). A decade later the first feature film appeared: *Hong Gildong* (홍길동, *Hong Gildong*), 1967. The film was based on a classic novel from the Joseon dynasty, *Tale of Hong Gildong* (홍길동전, 洪吉童传, *Hong Gildong-jeon*), written in the fifteenth century. The story of a nobleman's illegitimate son who becomes a righteous outlaw resonated strongly with audiences and established a tradition of drawing upon national literature for animated narratives.

During the 1970s and 1980s Korean animation went through a decisive phase. Like Taiwan, Korea initially built its industry through outsourcing work for American and European studios. Series such as *The Simpsons* and *Family Guy* included production segments handled in Korean studios, which developed expertise in large-scale animation pipelines. Yet the country's trajectory was also marked by a unique political decision. Between the early 1970s and the late 1980s, the Korean government banned the import of Japanese cultural products. The prohibition covered films, television programs, magazines, anime, and manga. This measure, rooted in anti-Japanese sentiment from the colonial period, forced local studios to turn toward domestic stories and original creations (Dator 2006; Lent 1999).

The ban had paradoxical effects. On one hand, it limited exposure to Japanese cultural trends. On the other hand, it encouraged Korean studios to invent their own characters and stories. By the late 1980s more than 120 studios were active, producing not only for foreign clients but also for Korean television and cinema. Many works from this period drew inspiration from Korean folklore and history. The animated series *Taoist Mutul* (머털 도사, 1989) is a clear example. It combined Taoist legends with animation techniques borrowed from both Japan and the United States.

The period also saw the rise of imitation and adaptation. Studios often created unlicensed versions of Japanese anime that were already popular with Korean audiences. *Robot Taekwon V* (로보트 태권 V, *Roboteu Taegwon V*), 1976, was strikingly similar to *Mazinger Z* (マジンガーZ, *Mazingā Zetto*), 1972, while *Space Gundam V* (스페이스 간담브이, *Seupeiseu Gandam Bui*), 1982, echoed *Macross* (マクロス, *Makurosu*). These productions, directed by Kim Cheong-gi (김청기, 金青基, *Gim Cheonggi*), became milestones of modern Korean animation. Despite their derivative origins, they found international markets, with some sold to the United States, Canada, and Europe. Kim Cheong-gi became an iconic figure because he managed to turn adaptation into a springboard for national creativity. His film *Golden Wing 123* (황금 날개 123, *Hwanggeum Nalgae 123*), 1978, was co-produced with American partners Frank and Ahmed Agrama, which gave the Korean industry valuable experience in international collaboration.

Robot Taekwon V became a national symbol. Although inspired by Japanese models, the robot embodied a specifically Korean hero. It fought using the martial art of Taekwondo, directly linking the narrative to national identity. The film's success generated multiple sequels and established a local tradition of robot stories that appealed strongly to young audiences. Unlike China, where outsourcing rarely translated into recognizable domestic franchises, Korea succeeded in transforming international subcontracting into a platform for local creativity.

Other hits soon followed, such as *Fly Super Board* (날아라 슈퍼보드, *Nalara Syupeobodeu*), 1990, *Baby Dinosaur Dooly* (아기공룡 둘리, *Agi Gongnyong Dooly*), 1987, and *Kkobi Kkobi* (꼬비꼬비, *Kkobi Kkobi*), 1997. These titles consolidated a popular culture that blended imported techniques with original storytelling.

The growth of animation was accompanied by equally important developments in comics. *Manhwa* evolved from serialized print magazines into digital formats, particularly with the rise of online platforms in the 2000s. Webtoons became a distinctive Korean innovation, using vertical scrolling formats adapted to smartphones. By the mid-2010s webtoons had become a global phenomenon, exported to Japan, China, and Western markets. They also fed back into animation, as many successful webtoons were adapted into animated series. This cycle created a sustainable ecosystem linking comics, animation, and transmedia production.

A decisive boost came from government intervention. In 1999 the "Basic Law for the Promotion of Cultural Industries" established a legal framework for supporting creative sectors, with animation as a central focus. The state introduced fiscal incentives, direct subsidies, and special funds for risky projects. If a project succeeded, profits were shared between government and company. Stronger copyright protection was also introduced. In 2001 the criminal code was amended to include harsher penalties for copyright infringement (Tan 2006a, b). These measures protected intellectual property and encouraged investment, something China only achieved more recently.

The government also built infrastructure. New centers such as the Bucheon Cartoon Information Data Center and the Seoul Cartoon Information Data Center opened in 1999. Institutions like the Korean Cartoon Museum and the Cartoon &

Animation Society in Korea provided platforms for research, archiving, and exhibitions (Tang 2006). Numerous associations were created, including the Korean Cartoonist Association, the Korean Women Cartoonist Association, and the Korean Society of Cartoon & Animation Studies. These organizations nurtured professional networks and fostered recognition of animation as a serious cultural practice.

Education was another key component. By 2004 Korea had already established 114 university programs in animation, producing more than 5000 graduates annually (Qin 2006). The link between academia and industry ensured a steady supply of skilled labor. Students were also encouraged to study abroad and often returned to Korea with advanced training and international contacts. This return flow contrasted with the Chinese case, where many students trained abroad did not return. The effect was to strengthen Korea's global network while consolidating the domestic industry.

By the early 2010s Korea hosted around 500 animation studios employing about 86,000 professionals (Research and Markets 2013). The industry produced more than 178,000 min of animation in 2013, placing the country third in the world after China and Japan. Around 90% of production was outsourced work for foreign clients in North America, Europe, and Japan. Yet Korea also built a reputation for original productions and distinctive aesthetics.

Unlike Chinese animation, which historically targeted mainly children, Korean animation addressed a wider demographic. Following the example of Japanese anime, Korean series explored social themes, romance, and complex emotional narratives. This broader scope helped the industry appeal to both domestic and international audiences. By the mid-2010s animation was recognized as one of the six most important creative sectors of the Korean economy, with an annual growth rate of 8–10%. Including derivatives and spin-offs, the market reached an estimated value of 4.85 billion euros (Research and Markets 2013).

In recent years Korean animation has continued to expand in global visibility. Collaborations with streaming platforms such as Netflix have introduced new audiences to Korean animated works. At the same time, the international success of Korean popular culture, known as the Korean Wave or Hallyu—has created synergies between K-pop, drama, gaming, webtoons, and animation. Animated adaptations of popular webtoons such as *Tower of God* (2020) and *Noblesse* (2020) have been distributed internationally, proving that Korea's digital-first approach can produce transmedia properties that resonate worldwide. The industry now exports not only labor but also intellectual property, moving beyond its earlier dependence on outsourcing.

The Korean case therefore illustrates how a small domestic market can build global influence through strategic policy, investment in education, and protection of intellectual property. For China, Korea represents both a competitor and a model. While China has adopted similar policies, it has done so with delay and under different political constraints. Korea's success shows that sustained state support, combined with creativity rooted in local identity, can transform a national animation sector into a global industry.

8.4 North Korea—Ideological Control and Animation Under Authoritarianism

North Korea has often been perceived as an isolated country, yet its animation industry has played a surprisingly strategic role in the international market. For decades, foreign studios relied on North Korean labor for large-scale outsourcing projects. One of the most frequently cited examples is the claim that animators in Pyongyang contributed to Disney's *The Lion King* (1994). Although the details remain debated, the episode illustrates how global corporations occasionally turned to North Korea for cost-effective labor despite political sanctions and trade restrictions. Reports also suggest that several feature-length animated films were produced in North Korea for the American market, even during periods of official embargo (Schönherr 2012).

The central link between North Korean animation and global media industries has been the South Korean company *AKOM Production* (애이콤프로덕션, *Aeikom Peurodeoksyeon*, "Animation KOrea Movie"). Founded by Nelson Shin (신능균, *Shin Neung-kyun*), a Korean-born animator with a long career in the United States, AKOM quickly became one of the most important subcontractors for international television. The studio gained prestige by animating global hits such as the first two seasons of *The Simpsons*, as well as *X-Men*, *Transformers*, and other series.

Shin himself established close ties with North Korea, where he had been born, and he maintained a working relationship with the country's main animation powerhouse: the *April 26 Children's Film Studio*, more commonly known as *SEK Studio* (조선4·26 아동영화촬영소, *Chosŏn 4·26 Adong Yŏnghwa Ch'waryŏngso*).

SEK was originally founded to produce ideological propaganda for domestic consumption. Its mandate was to educate children in socialist values and promote loyalty to the ruling regime. Over time, however, SEK transformed into one of the world's most productive outsourcing studios. Employing approximately 1500 artists, many trained at top institutions such as Kim Il Sung University, the studio developed the technical and organizational capacity to deliver animation for dozens of foreign companies. By the 2000s SEK was working with around seventy international clients (Kitchens 2003).

Europe became the primary destination for North Korean animation. Italian and French studios in particular established strong ties with Pyongyang. According to Dominique Boischot, president of the French company Les Films de la Perrine, SEK offered high-quality animation at a fraction of European costs. Producing the same content in France could be six times more expensive. Boischot noted, however, that contractual arrangements with North Korea were highly controlled. All agreements had to be signed by the studios as institutions, and direct communication with individual animators was not permitted. Emails and phone calls with artists were forbidden, ensuring that interaction remained strictly between companies (Kitchens 2003).

Italy's Mondo TV S.p.A. became SEK's most consistent partner. Founded in 1964 by Orlando Corradi, Mondo TV had already specialized in acquiring Japanese animated series for European distribution. From the mid-1980s the company began to produce its own shows and turned to North Korea for affordable outsourcing. Together, Mondo TV and SEK produced a large number of series and films. Among the most notable was *Sandokan: The Tiger of Malaysia*, a 26-episode series co-produced with RAI in Italy, Taurus Film in Russia, and TF1 in France. Later, in 2006, SEK and Mondo TV co-produced a ninety-minute animated feature about Padre Pio, which illustrated how religious and cultural narratives could be adapted for global markets through North Korean labor.

SEK's artists became recognized for their ability to adapt to a wide range of styles, from children's cartoons to action-oriented series. The studio's most celebrated achievement was *Empress Chung* (왕후 심청, Wanghu Simcheong). Directed by Nelson Shin and released in 2005, the film was a co-production between North and South Korea. Remarkably, it premiered simultaneously in both countries on August 12, 2005. The story, based on a Korean folktale about filial piety and sacrifice, carried symbolic meaning for inter-Korean relations. The project was hailed as an unprecedented cultural bridge across the peninsula's political divide.

International recognition also followed. According to *Animation Career Review* (2021), SEK ranked eighty-fifth among the one hundred most influential animation studios of all time. This classification reflected not only its volume of work but also the consistent quality of its productions, which often matched or surpassed that of more expensive studios in other regions.

The paradox of North Korean animation lies in its dual nature. Domestically, animation serves primarily as propaganda, with stories emphasizing loyalty, collectivism, and anti-Western themes. Internationally, the same studios provide commercial services for capitalist markets, often working on children's entertainment that has little or nothing to do with socialist ideology. This duality illustrates the complex ways in which North Korea engages with globalization. On one hand, the regime maintains strict control over content at home. On the other hand, it opens carefully managed channels to the outside world in order to generate foreign currency and technological know-how.

The reliance of European studios on SEK during the 1980s and 1990s also raises questions about ethical responsibility. Outsourcing to Pyongyang meant benefiting from low labor costs under an authoritarian regime. Yet many companies, particularly in Italy and France, considered the arrangement purely in economic terms. For them, SEK offered skilled animators at a price unmatched elsewhere. In some cases, the ideological implications were simply ignored.

In recent years, however, the global landscape has shifted. The expansion of South Korea's webtoon and animation industries, the rise of digital platforms, and the spread of cheaper computer graphics across Asia have reduced the competitive advantage of North Korean studios. Western sanctions have also tightened, making direct contracts more difficult to sustain. Nonetheless, SEK continues to operate and remains attractive for some European producers who seek affordable alternatives.

For China, the case of North Korea offers an interesting comparison. While the Chinese industry also built part of its capacity through outsourcing, it combined this with strong domestic policies to promote original content. North Korea, by contrast, remains largely dependent on foreign contracts. Its most notable original projects, such as *Empress Chung*, are exceptions rather than the rule. Yet the example of SEK demonstrates that even a highly isolated country can insert itself into global creative networks when cost structures and technical skills align with international demand.

Looking toward the future, it remains uncertain how North Korean animation will evolve. If international sanctions continue, the ability of SEK to work openly with foreign partners may decline. At the same time, the global demand for low-cost animation has not disappeared, particularly for educational projects and smaller television series. It is therefore likely that SEK will remain part of the global supply chain, even if in a more limited and less visible capacity.

North Korea's place in the history of animation is thus paradoxical but significant. It shows how a cultural industry born as propaganda can adapt to global markets. It reveals the importance of outsourcing networks that cross even the most rigid political boundaries. And it highlights how cultural production, even in closed societies, can become a tool of economic survival and limited international cooperation.

8.5 Japan—Anime and the Global Cultural Imagination

Japanese anime is widely recognized as both a cultural driver and an economic powerhouse. In 2023 the industry generated a record 22 billion US dollars in revenue, marking a 14% increase from the previous year, with overseas markets surpassing domestic takings for the first time (Screendaily 2024).

Overseas revenues alone reached 1.72 trillion yen, equivalent to 11.2 billion US dollars, while the domestic sector relied heavily on merchandise, which continued to account for nearly half of the market value (Animenomics 2023). These developments confirm that anime has moved from being a national cultural product with limited exports to a global cultural industry with international income exceeding domestic performance.

The industry's long-term stability has relied on the enduring popularity of series such as *Sazae-san* (サザエさん, *Sazae-san*), first broadcast in 1969, and *Anpanman* (アンパンマン, *Anpanman*), which since 1988 has remained the most beloved show among children in Japan. Such properties sustain financial stability through their merchandise and media spin-offs, enabling studios to experiment with new productions. The longevity of these titles is an industrial strategy rather than a cultural anomaly, ensuring that risks associated with new projects are balanced by the steady income of long-running series.

The historical turning point was 1963, when Fuji TV broadcast *Astro Boy* (鉄腕アトム, *Tetsuwan Atomu*) by Osamu Tezuka. This series set the template for the Japanese approach to animation: economical production, emotionally compelling stories, and a clear synergy with the publishing industry. The cycle linking *manga*, *anime*, and merchandise created an ecology that reinforced itself across media. Japanese anime thus became deeply integrated into the popular imagination, and soon also into global consumption.

In 2023 the Japanese anime market was valued at 12.72 billion US dollars, with analysts projecting a compound annual growth rate of 3.9% until 2030 (Grand View Research 2024). Streaming platforms are driving this expansion, while physical home video formats continue to decline. At the same time, the industry faces challenges: a Teikoku Databank survey reported that although the market value for anime production reached 2.45 billion US dollars in 2024, nearly 60% of studios were experiencing declining profits due to labor shortages, rising costs, and longer production times (Economic Times 2024). This paradox of growth accompanied by internal fragility is one of the structural tensions of the Japanese model.

Cultural specificity remains central to anime's global success. Japanese productions draw inspiration from daily life, folklore, and history, even when set in futuristic or fantastical scenarios. Robots and mecha echo the ethos of the samurai, while school life or neighborhood settings create relatable frames. This balance between local particularity and universal emotional storytelling explains why anime has consistently found acceptance abroad (Pellitteri 2008). The evolution of aesthetics during the 1980s, especially through the spread of *kawaii* (かわいい, *kawaii*) as a cultural sensibility, reinforced this capacity by blending cuteness and familiarity with sophistication in design. *Kawaii* became a national and global code, influencing not only anime but also urban spaces, advertising, and even public institutions. Police stations or train platforms decorated with anime mascots exemplify how deeply the medium permeates Japanese everyday life.

The government has long recognized anime as a cultural and economic asset, even though the sector is largely driven by private companies. Policies have focused less on direct financing of productions and more on creating favorable conditions for global circulation. Regional administrations present anime as a green industry, encouraging tourism and branding areas as Anime Towns (Naizhen 2012). Nationally, soft power strategies have been institutionalized since the 2000s. One example is the allocation of around 190 million euros in 2005 to distribute anime freely in emerging markets, where young viewers might develop lifelong attachments to Japanese cultural products (Tan 2006a, b). The Ministry of Foreign Affairs has also promoted characters as cultural ambassadors, reinforcing anime's role in diplomacy and trade.

Recent commentary highlights how anime exports have become almost as significant as traditional goods such as steel or semiconductors in Japan's trade profile, contributing directly to soft power and international image (Semafor 2024). Scholars studying the "Cool Japan" initiative suggest that the future of this strategy depends on maintaining a balance between global appeal and cultural authenticity, while also addressing domestic challenges such as labor exploitation and creative sustainability (ResearchGate 2024).

The global performance of Japanese franchises illustrates these dynamics. *Demon Slayer: Kimetsu no Yaiba – Infinity Castle* became the second highest-grossing film in Japanese history in 2024, overtaking *Spirited Away* within two months (India Times 2024). Such results show that anime is not only a television and streaming phenomenon but also a theatrical powerhouse.

Forecasts confirm the expansion: the global anime market is expected to grow from 32.3 billion US dollars in 2024 to 68.6 billion by 2033, at an annual growth rate of 8.73% (MarketDataForecast 2025). Japan remains central in this geography, though competition from Korea and China is intensifying.

For China, the Japanese model offers several lessons. Export markets are crucial, merchandising remains the backbone of financial stability, and cultural specificity enhances rather than diminishes global reach. At the same time, sustainability challenges in Japan warn against assuming that growth alone ensures stability. Japan demonstrates that creative ecosystems thrive when cultural identity, industrial discipline, and global ambition are carefully balanced.

References

Animenomics. 2023. *Anime market outside Japan grew 11 percent in 2022*. Retrieved from https://news.animenomics.com/p/anime-market-outside-japan-grew-11-percent-2022.

Animation Career Review. 2021. *Top 100 animation schools and colleges in the world*. Retrieved from https://www.animationcareerreview.com/articles/top-100-animation-schools-and-colleges-world.

Arts Foundation. 2004. *Traditional music and performance in Taiwan*. Taipei: Arts Foundation Press.

Chang, J. 2011. *Taiwanese glove puppetry and media transformation*. Taipei: National Taiwan University Press.

Chiu, C. 2012. *Taiwan's animation industry: Internationalization and cultural policy*. Taipei: Ministry of Economic Affairs.

Dator, J. 2006. Korea as the wave of a future: The emerging dream society of icons and aesthetic experience. *Journal of Futures Studies* 10 (1): 31–44.

Economic Times. 2024. *Anime industry hits $2.45 billion, yet 60 percent of studios see declining profits*. Retrieved from https://m.economictimes.com/news/international/us/anime-industry-hits-2-45-billion-yet-60-per-cent-of-studios-see-declining-profits-what-does-it-mean-for-fans/articleshow/123499850.cms.

Grand View Research. 2024. *Japan anime market size & trends report, 2023–2030*. Retrieved from https://www.grandviewresearch.com/industry-analysis/japan-anime-market-report.

India Times. 2024. *Demon Slayer Infinity Castle overtakes Spirited Away*. Retrieved from https://indiatimes.com/trending/demon-slayer-infinity-castle-overtakes-spirited-away-becomes-japans-2nd-highest-grossing-film-after-mugen-train-669737.html.

Kitchens, S. 2003. Outsourcing and secrecy in North Korean animation. *Animation Journal* 11 (2): 55–69.

Lent, J. A. 1999. *Animation in Asia and the Pacific*. Bloomington: Indiana University Press.

MarketDataForecast. 2025. *Global anime market forecast 2024–2033*. Retrieved from https://www.marketdataforecast.com/market-reports/anime-market-report.

Ministry of Economic Affairs (MoEA). 2012. *Annual report on Taiwan's animation industry*. Taipei: Digital Content Industry Promotion Office.

Ministry of Economic Affairs (MoEA). 2013. *Annual report on Taiwan's animation industry*. Taipei: Digital Content Industry Promotion Office.

Ministry of Economic Affairs (MoEA). 2007. *Survey on Taiwan's animation industry*. Taipei: Digital Content Industry Promotion Office.

Naizhen, C. 2012. Cultural policy and the international circulation of Japanese animation. *Journal of Asian Cultural Studies* 5 (2): 77–95.

Netcomics. 2008. *The history of manhwa*. Seoul: Netcomics.

Pellitteri, M. 2008. *The Japanese imagery in Europe*. Latina: Tunué.

Pili International Multimedia. 2019. *Pili Fantasy: War of Dragons* [TV series]. Netflix.

Qin, X. 2006. *Animation education and industry linkages in Korea*. Seoul: Korean Educational Development Association.

Research and Markets. 2013. *Animation industry in South Korea: Analysis and forecasts*. Dublin: Research and Markets.

ResearchGate. 2024. *An analysis of the evolution and influence of Japan's Cool Japan strategy on national image and soft power*. Retrieved from https://www.researchgate.net/publication/391771464_An_Analysis_of_The_Evolution_and_Influence_of_Japans_Cool_Japan_Strategy_on_National_Image_and_Soft_Power.

Screendaily. 2024. *Japanese anime industry generated record $22bn in 2023*. Retrieved from https://www.screendaily.com/news/japanese-anime-industry-generated-record-22bn-in-2023-with-overseas-surpassing-local-takings/5198698.article.

Semafor. 2024. *Growing anime industry boosts Japan's soft power*. Retrieved from https://www.semafor.com/article/10/22/2024/growing-anime-industry-boosts-japans-soft-power.

Schönherr, J. 2012. *North Korean cinema: A history*. Jefferson, NC: McFarland.

Tan, H. 2006a. *Copyright law and cultural industries in South Korea*. Singapore: Asian Media Law Journal.

Tan, H. 2006b. Soft power and media export strategies in East Asia. *Asian Communication Research* 5 (3): 55–72.

Tang, M. 2006. *Comparative policies in Chinese and Korean animation industries*. Beijing: Communication University Press.

Taiwan Creative Content Agency (TAICCA). 2019. *Establishment and policy framework*. Taipei: TAICCA.

Taiwan Creative Content Agency (TAICCA). 2021. *Annual report on Taiwan's cultural content industries*. Taipei: TAICCA.

Tsai, E. 2020. Taiwan glove puppetry goes global: The case of Pili Fantasy on Netflix. *International Journal of Cultural Studies* 23 (6): 847–862. Retrieved from https://doi.org/10.1177/1367877920921104.

Wu, C.J. 2023. Tradition meets digital innovation: The evolution of puppet animation in Taiwan. *Journal of Asian Cinema* 34 (1): 45–61. Retrieved from https://doi.org/10.1386/jac_00057_1.

Yihangru. 2004. *The first steps of Korean animation*. Seoul: Media History Publishing.

Chapter 9
Concluding Reflections

Abstract This concluding chapter synthesizes the historical, industrial, and cultural trajectories of Chinese animation, drawing together the themes explored throughout the book. It begins by addressing the paradox at the heart of the industry: while Chinese studios have long been indispensable to global production pipelines through outsourcing and post-production work, original domestic properties struggled for international recognition. The so-called gold rush of the 2000s and 2010s, fueled by subsidies and speculative investment, expanded capacity but often prioritized short-term returns over sustainable creativity. Subsequent reforms and tighter oversight sought to correct these imbalances, yet structural fragilities remained. The chapter also highlights the cultural and economic value of animation as both a market commodity and a tool of soft power, while underlining the centrality of labor, collaboration, and creative resilience. Finally, it considers the future, where artificial intelligence, streaming platforms, and the rise of micro-dramas are reshaping industrial logics and audience expectations. These developments signal both opportunities and contradictions: innovation may expand global influence, but long-term success will depend on balancing cultural authenticity with economic efficiency in an increasingly competitive and convergent media landscape.

Keywords Outsourcing · Gold rush · Subsidies · Cultural value · Soft power · Artificial intelligence · Micro-dramas

9.1 The Gold Rush—Speculation, Capital, and Industrial Growth

The central question that motivates this study is whether Chinese animation possesses the capabilities required to scale in global markets. An immediate answer emerges from the persistent reliance of many international studios on Chinese labor and post production capacity for execution, where Chinese teams supply the industrial discipline and technical skills that sustain global pipelines. The cost of this model is visible in the relative fragility of fully original Chinese properties, which for a

© The Author(s), under exclusive license to Springer Nature Switzerland AG 2026

V. De Masi, *A Critical Analysis of China's Animation Industry*, Numanities - Arts and Humanities in Progress 37, https://doi.org/10.1007/978-3-032-18656-0_9

long time lagged behind service work despite sustained state efforts to structure the industry. The asymmetry between world class execution for others and modest international traction for domestic originals has been the defining paradox of the field, although recent hits and new formats indicate partial rebalancing.

The expansion of animation capacity in the 2000s and early 2010s created an investment environment often described as a gold rush. Subsidies and preferential policies at the central and local levels, together with expectations of rapid market growth, drew capital from firms with little prior cultural expertise. In many localities funds were allocated through opaque clientelist channels that privileged speed of capacity building over coherent industrial strategy, which produced a crowded field of small studios with thin development pipelines and limited narrative ambition. Over time central authorities tightened eligibility and oversight, yet local dispersion of incentives continued to generate uneven outcomes and short termism that prioritized broadcast placement over sustainable intellectual property development. The result was a disorderly system in which television delivery and quota fulfillment trumped world building, derivative markets, and long tail monetization, leaving many studios trapped in low margin production with little leverage in domestic broadcasting negotiations.

The current cycle modifies rather than erases those structural legacies. Demand has diversified and a large share of growth now arises from platform centered ecosystems where animation interlocks with games, livestream commerce, and short video. Bilibili's continued investments in anime and donghua 动画 production and acquisitions, documented in its 2023 annual filings, reveal a strategy that internalizes content capability to expand a proprietary library and capture merchandising and licensing revenue streams that were previously external to the platform core (Bilibili 2024). At the same time, the explosive rise of micro dramas duanju 短剧 has shifted attention toward high velocity, mobile first serialization. Industry reporting in 2024 and 2025 places the micro drama economy in the multibillion dollar range with rapid international spillovers through apps that repurpose Chinese production know how for global audiences, a trajectory that both competes with and complements animation by training viewers to accept short form narrative units and rapid release cadences while normalizing algorithmic commissioning and tight cost control (Reuters 2024; Wired 2025). Platforms now experiment with animated micro dramas and creator programs that promise tens of millions of renminbi in monthly revenue, which channels capital toward formats where turnaround speed and audience analytics dominate greenlighting decisions (Tech in Asia 2025).

Policy remains a constitutive force. The 2025 Measures for the labeling of AI generated synthetic content set a compliance framework for watermarking and disclosure that directly touches animation and visual effects pipelines and that will come into force on 1 September 2025. The measures clarify platform and provider responsibilities, seek traceability, and aim to stabilize an ecosystem where generative video and image tools are entering production at scale. For animation studios this encourages adoption with accountability while discouraging low quality flooding and opaque authorship, a balance that may raise average standards yet add new compliance costs for smaller firms (China Law Translate 2025; Reuters 2025a, b; Inside

Privacy 2025; Loeb 2025). In parallel, state media pilots have already validated AI assisted workflows, signaling that innovation is desirable so long as it aligns with cultural governance and disclosure norms.

The strengths of the sector are concentrated in market scale, infrastructure, and technical learning curves. The domestic market can now generate unprecedented single territory outcomes, as recent box office cycles demonstrate, which reduces dependence on foreign underwriting and affirms that animation can succeed as a mainstream entertainment form rather than a niche for children only. Platform integration accelerates feedback between audience data and commissioning and supports mid tier studios that master delivery for digital ecosystems. The maturation of service capacity into original development is visible in improved production values and in the emergence of studios that manage both execution and intellectual property growth. Scholarly analysis of the post pandemic period identifies these political and technological conditions as facilitators of sustainable strategies when paired with better chain coordination and attention to cultural specificity that reads as authentic rather than imitative (Feng 2024).

The weaknesses remain significant. International recognition still lags behind domestic scale and many titles that dominate at home remain nearly invisible abroad. Local protectionism at the broadcaster level has diminished but not disappeared and historical reliance on low cost formats trained buyers to expect volume over depth. Rights enforcement has improved but piracy and informal distribution continue to erode value in secondary and tertiary markets. Human capital gaps persist in writing, showrunning, and music direction, the very roles that convert technical competence into emotionally durable franchises. The gold rush mentality has not fully receded in municipal policy, where announcements of parks and zones can still precede credible talent and pipeline strategies. Research based estimates of sector size differ widely, which reflects opacity in accounting and the coexistence of high value box office winners with long tails of undercapitalized series whose economics hinge on a single broadcast sale or a short window of in app monetization. Without sustained investment in development culture, cross departmental craft, and rights management, the sector risks replicating earlier cycles where capacity grows faster than creative distinctiveness.

The path forward is visible in the convergence of three trajectories. First, platforms and leading studios are internalizing parts of the value chain, from development to licensing, which stabilizes financing and encourages iterative world building. Second, regulatory clarity around AI supported production and synthetic media labels creates a compliance corridor in which innovation can scale transparently, strengthening trust with audiences and buyers. Third, the normalization of mobile first serialization alters consumption habits in ways that animation can leverage through short cycle specials, micro series, and spin offs that feed into feature projects and games. If these trajectories are aligned with stronger writers' rooms, long term character bibles, and international localization strategies, Chinese animation can transform the old gold rush into a consistent pipeline for exportable properties while sustaining the domestic scale that already distinguishes the market.

9.2 The Cultural and Economic Value of Animation

The value of Chinese animation resides in the completeness of its emerging value chain from upstream story development and visual design to midstream production and downstream licensing and platform distribution. During the earlier expansion many studios optimized for delivery to broadcasters which privileged volume over durable intellectual property. The present cycle shows a deliberate reweighting toward character franchises, licensing, and platform centered monetization. Industry trackers estimate the Chinese anime market at roughly 2.24 billion US dollars in 2024 with merchandising as the largest revenue segment and internet distribution as the fastest growing channel which confirms that value capture increasingly occurs beyond the first screen window through e commerce and live services linked to platforms and fan communities (Grand View Research 2025). This platform logic is visible in the evolution of Bilibili which integrates commissioning, community tools, and rights management in a single environment and reports a steady rise in revenue diversification across advertising, value added services, and licensing that reduces reliance on any single income stream while increasing bargaining power with studios and suppliers (Bilibili 2025a, b). The licensing ecosystem has expanded in parallel as retail sales of licensed merchandise and services in China reached an estimated 13.77 billion US dollars in 2023 which signals that character and brand strategies can sustain downstream revenue even when theatrical attendance softens (Licensing Expo China 2024).

The comparative lens clarifies the stakes of chain coordination. Japan's manga to anime pipeline continues to offer a reference model in which audience validation in print precedes animation greenlights and creates predictable derivative paths in games music and retail. Korea's experience demonstrates how state backed coordination through agencies and export programs supported upgrading from subcontracting to original co production and global partnerships which enabled firms to move from low margin execution to higher value governance positions within global value chains (Lee 2011; UNCTAD 2023). China converges toward a hybrid of these paths. The domestic market is large enough to finance originals at scale while platform integration shortens feedback loops between early audience response and commissioning. Yet the literary feeder of manga style serial publication is less central and the regulatory environment conditions content choices and windowing. These differences require Chinese studios to design their own path to predictable franchise development with attention to longer development cycles strong writers' rooms and cross media planning that preserves cultural specificity while facilitating translation.

Rights and enforcement remain decisive. The 2021 amendments to the Copyright Law introduced higher statutory damages more explicit recognition of certain rights and stronger tools for civil and criminal action which improved the legal baseline for creative industries. Practice still varies by locality and administrative enforcement remains most effective for straightforward trademark and counterfeiting cases while complex and persistent infringements benefit from civil litigation or coordinated criminal referrals. Rights holders continue to report opacity and uneven capacity among provincial authorities even as headline campaigns and model cases proceed. The result is a mixed picture where the legal framework has strengthened but the transaction costs of enforcement can still erode value for small and mid sized studios and can discourage early investments in development and music rights which are key to international sales and long tail monetization (NPC 2021; USPTO 2024; IIPA 2024).

Macroeconomic context complicates valuation. The theatrical market contracted by nearly a quarter in 2024 which reflected both cyclical softness and a shift in consumption toward mobile streaming and short form serials. The same year and into 2025 domestic hits and festival season releases still produced outlier outcomes that validate the potential of local originals but the average title faces more competition for attention and tighter marketing budgets. For animation the implication is clear. Value capture must rely on multi window strategies that treat theatrical as one component among streaming licensing merchandising events and live commerce while targeting age segments beyond children. Platforms have responded with creator funds for animated microdramas and with internal studios that pilot short cycles tied to merchandising drops and game integrations which aligns production calendars with moments of peak online traffic and offers an alternative to the old broadcaster gatekeeping model (Financial Times 2025; Tech in Asia 2025).

Strengths and weaknesses follow from these conditions. The strengths include a market that can amortize high production values domestically integration of community and monetization within platforms that operate at national scale and growing competence in art direction effects and pipeline management. Weaknesses persist in the uneven depth of story development the scarcity of globally portable franchises and gaps in music direction showrunning and localization that limit export potential. Enforcement frictions remain a drag on small studios that cannot afford sustained legal strategies and that therefore struggle to protect designs and characters once they leave the initial release window. Where Japan converts manga validation into predictable derivative revenue and where Korea leverages coordinated export policy Chinese firms must compensate through stronger development culture and tighter platform studio coordination that turns first season success into long tail licensing.

Policy can accelerate this transition if it continues to move from capacity building to value chain discipline. The recent labeling measures for synthetic media which enter into force in late 2025 represent an adjacent development. They create a compliance corridor for the integration of AI assisted workflows across animation and visual effects with transparent labeling and platform obligations. This does not directly increase licensing income but it encourages trust and reduces reputational risk which supports brands and rights holders in markets where disclosure and authenticity concerns can affect downstream merchandise sales and international broadcast deals. Studios that adopt clear provenance and disclosure practices are likely to find it easier to negotiate with platforms distributors and advertisers in the coming cycle and to protect their characters across retail channels that are sensitive to rights and quality signals (Reuters 2025a, b; China Law Translate 2025; Inside Privacy 2025; Loeb and Loeb 2025).

In sum the value of Chinese animation is shifting from broadcast dependent revenue toward diversified chains in which platforms function as hubs for development community building and monetization. The legal framework is more supportive than a decade ago yet enforcement practice still imposes costs that fall most heavily on smaller firms. The comparative evidence suggests that sustainable growth will require disciplined chain coordination and a renewed emphasis on original storytelling and music which are the levers that convert technical excellence and platform scale into franchises with durable cultural and commercial value at home and abroad.

9.3 Practices of Creation—Labor, Collaboration, and Innovation

The core bottleneck remains creative development. For more than a decade studios have excelled as service providers to foreign productions, yet the domestic pipeline from concept to screenplay to greenlight has been thin and uneven. Recent scholarship converges on the same prescription. Sustainable growth requires shifting from a build first manage later approach to a system in which content creation is the nucleus, technology is a driver, talent is the foundation, and an integrated industrial chain is the backbone (Feng and Yang 2024). Earlier strategic work reached similar conclusions and emphasized resource integration, chain improvement, enterprise upgrading, legal protection, and external talent training as preconditions for quality storytelling that travels beyond the children's segment (Fan and Feng 2021).

Signs of a healthier development culture are visible. Platforms sponsor screenwriting showcases and creator programs that elevate writers for film, series, and animation. iQIYI's Golden Screenwriters Night has become a recurring mechanism to identify and reward new talent, while the company couples events with broader IP development and monetization plans that keep writers closer to commercial decision making (iQIYI 2024; iQIYI 2025a, b). Bilibili's Awakening Program for animated short dramas targets the fast growing microseries form and offers structured support to small studios and independent creators, which expands the pool of tested concepts before large budget commitments are made (Tech in Asia 2025). These interventions do not replace the writers room model that dominates in Japan and the United States, yet they function as upstream development filters that reduce execution risk and gradually normalize iterative script work in Chinese animation.

Production craft has advanced sharply, especially in art direction and compositing. Deep Sea by Tian Xiaopeng 田晓鹏 blends painterly techniques inspired by Chinese ink with high end 3D rendering to stage an emotionally legible world of water and light. International critics highlighted the film's unique visual language, even when they found the narrative uneven, which is precisely the kind of constructive feedback that helps future projects tighten story architecture without abandoning stylistic ambition (The Guardian 2024). Light Chaser Animation's New Gods cycle under director Zhao Ji 赵霁 demonstrates a parallel path. It reimagines foundational myths in contemporary idioms and positions mythic IP for serial expansion, a strategy that builds recognizability while leaving room for tonal experimentation across installments (Animation Magazine 2023).

The length and complexity of the feature pipeline still pressure narrative discipline. Case studies of leading studios note that a single animated feature can span 3–5 years from development to delivery, with high demands on asset accuracy and rendering, and with multiple teams coordinating across layout, effects, and color timing. That calendar raises the cost of script indecision and magnifies the value of early table reads, animatics, and small scale audience tests that lock character arcs before full asset build (Light Chaser case study, c. 2023). As Chinese film schools and media universities expand animation and screenwriting programs and curate student festivals, the talent base for story editors, dramaturgs, and production managers is slowly widening, which can shorten revision loops and improve institutional memory across shows (CUC Aniwow 2024).

There has also been a recalibration of target audiences. Works such as Thirty Thousand Miles from Chang'an leveraged literary heritage to reach family and adult viewers, showing that domestic animation can sustain historical drama, not only preschool comedy. The film's local box office run illustrated strong home market appetite for culturally specific themes and high craft, and industry coverage identified it as a benchmark for Light Chaser's new cultural series strategy, as articulated by producer Yu Zhou 于洲 (Cartoon Brew 2023; China News Service 2024). The lesson for development is that cultural specificity can be a market asset when wedded to clear emotional stakes and genre clarity.

Music and sound design are a continuing frontier. Deep Sea's soundscape and original songs supported its interior emotional logic and showed that carefully authored music can carry thematic weight in animation aimed beyond children, echoing long standing Japanese practices in which original scores and theme songs are planned as brand assets from the outset (The Guardian 2024; Tribeca 2023). Building stronger music supervision and post sound capacity would align Chinese pipelines with this integrative approach to audience affect.

Finally, tool adoption is reshaping how teams create without displacing authorship. Studios report using AI as a previsualization companion for mood boards, style frames, and rough blocking, while platforms run competitions that channel experimentation into short form outputs where risk is bounded. Used this way, AI reduces iteration costs in early development and frees artist time for character psychology and scene rhythm. The operational rule is simple. Human authored story comes first. Generative tools follow as support for pre production and technical polish. Public initiatives such as iQIYI's AI Short Film Competition formalize this sandbox and help establish norms that distinguish craft enablement from content substitution (iQIYI 2025a, b).

In sum, the creative constraint is no longer purely technical capacity. It is the institutionalization of narrative development habits that keep writers, directors, editors, and producers in sustained dialogue from premise to final mix. Where that dialogue is protected and resourced, recent Chinese features have matched international best practice in visual invention and are closing the gap in story economy and character voice. The path forward is clear. Invest in writers and story editors, treat development artifacts as decision tools rather than deliverables, connect schools and studios through juried showcases, and protect the time needed for scripts to become films. The industry literature and the best recent films point in the same direction. Creativity is the system's flywheel, not its afterthought (Feng and Yang 2024; Fan and Feng 2021).

9.4 Futures of Chinese Animation—Contradictions, Innovation, and the AI Horizon

Chinese animation enters its next cycle with a clear contradiction at its core. The sector now commands extraordinary domestic scale and technical capability while its original properties still struggle to convert national resonance into stable global familiarity. The case of *Ne Zha 2* directed by Yang Yu Jiaozi 杨宇 shows how a locally rooted myth can generate world beating numbers almost entirely within a single market, a feat that demonstrates industrial maturity at home but also reveals limited diffusion abroad when compared with long running Hollywood franchises whose revenues are spread across many territories (Reuters 2025a, b; Xinhua 2025). This asymmetry will remain the strategic test for the coming decade, since durable global presence requires not only spectacle and craft but also long term localization, distribution alliances, and a repertoire of characters designed for multilingual audiences.

Market conditions sharpen the stakes. Theatrical revenue contracted in 2024 as audiences shifted toward streaming and mobile first formats, even as outliers proved that domestic blockbusters can still carry seasons. The rebound of early 2025 was propelled by local hits rather than imported titles. In this environment platforms function as multipurpose hubs for commissioning, community building, and monetization, and they increasingly internalize parts of the value chain that once sat with broadcasters and third party distributors (Financial Times 2025; Bilibili 2025a, b). The platform turn offers resilience for studios that can pair visual excellence with data informed development, yet it also raises the bar for narrative distinctiveness since algorithmic feeds reward volume and velocity more than careful world building unless editorial discipline is protected inside the commissioning loop.

The international benchmark remains instructive. *Kung Fu Panda 4* closed with a balanced split between North America and the rest of the world near 548 million dollars worldwide, a pattern consistent with global brands that depend on diversified territories rather than one dominant base. The comparison underscores that Chinese animation already exceeds individual Hollywood entries in domestic scale yet still trails them in the breadth of international recognition. The lesson is not imitation but design for portability that respects cultural specificity while planning dialogue, music, and humor for multilingual performance (Box Office Mojo 2025).

Creative infrastructure has progressed. Recent features display advances in art direction, lighting, and compositing that match international best practice. The persistent constraint has been story economy, character voice, and music supervision. These are precisely the roles that transform technique into lasting franchises. The emergence of writers showcases, creator funds, and microseries labs on major platforms indicates that upstream development is slowly institutionalizing. If these programs evolve toward robust writers rooms and long term character bibles, the pipeline can shift from single project bursts to serial world building with predictable derivatives and licensing. Evidence from platform disclosures shows revenue diversification across advertising, value added services, mobile games, and intellectual property derivatives, which strengthens the incentive to invest in development rather than only delivery (Bilibili 2025a, b).

The rise of short form micro dramas duanju 短剧 is both competitor and complement. This format trains audiences to accept compressed story beats and rapid release cadences and it puts pressure on animation to deliver frequent touchpoints between features. The same production logic can be harnessed for animated microseries that keep characters present in the feed between films and games, provided quality control prevents a race to the bottom. Industry reporting places the micro drama economy in the multibillion dollar range and documents its expanding international spillovers, a reminder that Chinese narrative formats now travel outward through platforms as well as through theatrical exports (Reuters 2024).

The AI horizon now crosses the entire field. Chinese research groups and platforms have released competitive video generation systems including Kling from Kuaishou, HunyuanVideo from Tencent, and the anime focused AniSora from Bilibili. These models integrate into creator ecosystems and begin to support industrial workflows from previsualization to reference guided motion. At the same time Vidu from ShengShu Technology and Tsinghua University demonstrates cross border collaboration through a planned short form science fiction series with a United States based studio, which positions Chinese models not only as domestic tools but as international co production infrastructure. The opportunity is efficiency with creative control if studios treat generative systems as assistants for design exploration and layout while keeping human authored narrative and direction at the center (Kuaishou IR 2024; Kuaishou IR 2025; Tencent GitHub 2024; Bilibili GitHub 2025; SCMP 2025).

Governance has moved in tandem. The 2025 measures for labeling AI generated synthetic content require explicit and implicit identifiers and clarify responsibilities for platforms and providers, with effect from 1 September 2025. This framework normalizes disclosure and provenance across images, audio, and video and directly touches animation and visual effects pipelines. Clear labeling can raise trust among audiences and buyers and supports rights management in downstream retail and licensing. Compliance will add workflow costs, yet it should also reduce reputational risk and discourage low quality flooding, which ultimately benefits studios that compete on craft and originality (China Law Translate 2025; Reuters 2025a, b; Inside Privacy 2025).

A plausible strategic path emerges from these conditions. First, double down on writers rooms, music direction, and editorial leadership since these functions convert technical proficiency and platform scale into emotionally durable properties. Second, build international presence through early localization and festival strategies that are planned alongside domestic campaigns rather than appended after release. Third, use AI to compress preproduction cycles while maintaining human authorship of story and performance and disclose use in line with the new measures to strengthen brand trust. Fourth, deepen partnerships between platforms and studios so that microseries, features, and games share worlds and art direction and so that merchandising and licensing strategies are designed from the premise stage. If the sector executes on these principles, it can reconcile the current contradiction between domestic dominance and global obscurity and can turn the AI horizon from a source of uncertainty into a catalyst for creative renewal.

References

Animation Magazine. 2023, January 15. *New Gods: Yang Jian interview with Ji Zhao on conjuring a cutting-edge epic fantasy*. https://www.animationmagazine.net/2023/01/new-gods-yang-jian-director-ji-zhao-on-conjuring-a-cutting-edge-epic-fantasy/.

Bilibili. 2024, March 27. *2023 annual report* [PDF]. https://ir.bilibili.com/media/lvrofkwj/bilibili-inc-2023-annual-report.pdf.

Bilibili. 2025a, March 25. *2024 annual report*. https://ir.bilibili.com/media/jesfytmo/bilibili-inc-2024-annual-report.pdf.

Bilibili. 2025b, August 21. *Report of foreign issuer Q2 2025 highlights*. https://ir.bilibili.com/media/4lxmb0mo/report-of-foreign-issuer-rules-13a-16-and-15d-16-2.pdf.

Bilibili GitHub. 2025. *AniSora repository*. https://github.com/bilibili/Index-anisora.

Box Office Mojo. 2025. *Kung Fu Panda 4 box office*. https://www.boxofficemojo.com/title/tt21692408/.

Cartoon Brew. 2023, August 10. *Chang'an becomes a top Chinese animated hit*. https://www.cartoonbrew.com/feature-film/chang-an-chinese-box-office-mutant-mayhem-231456.html.

China Law Translate. 2025, March 14. *Measures for labeling of AI-generated synthetic content* [English translation]. https://www.chinalawtranslate.com/en/ai-labeling/.

China News Service. 2024, August 28. *Yu Zhou 于洲 on Light Chaser's cultural series*. https://www.chinanews.com.cn/sh/2024/08-28/10276224.shtml.

Communication University of China. 2024. *Aniwow international student animation festival collaborators*. https://aniwow.cuc.edu.cn/en_aniwow/202410/14/c8850a244066/page.htm.

Fan, K.K., and T.T. Feng. 2021. Sustainable development strategy of Chinese animation industry. *Sustainability* 13 (13): 7235. https://www.mdpi.com/2071-1050/13/13/7235.

Feng, T.T. 2024. A case study of the animation industry in China. *Sustainability* 16 (22): 9796. https://www.mdpi.com/2071-1050/16/22/9796.

Feng, T.T., and L.F. Yang. 2024. Sustainable development of the cultural and creative industries in the post-pandemic era. *Sustainability* 16 (22): 9796. https://www.mdpi.com/2071-1050/16/22/9796.

Financial Times. 2025, January 17. *China's box office takings drop by a quarter as viewers turn to streaming*. https://www.ft.com/content/e2c04590-cb4f-43cc-85dc-786377fb5cb2.

Grand View Research. 2025. *China anime market size and outlook 2024–2030*. https://www.grandviewresearch.com/horizon/outlook/anime-market/china.

Inside Privacy. 2025, March 18. *China releases new labeling requirements for AI-generated content*. https://www.insideprivacy.com/international/china/china-releases-new-labeling-requirements-for-ai-generated-content/.

International Intellectual Property Alliance (IIPA). 2024, September 10. *China's WTO compliance submission*. https://www.iipa.org/files/uploads/2024/09/2024-IIPA-Chinas-WTO-Compliance-Submission-FINAL.pdf.

iQIYI. 2024. *Golden Screenwriters Night champions creative excellence*. https://www.prnewswire.com/news-releases/iqiyi-celebrates-fourth-annual-golden-screenwriters-night-championing-young-talent-and-creative-excellence-302166939.html.

iQIYI. 2025a. *AI short film competition*. https://aic.iq.com/.

iQIYI. 2025b. *Fifth Golden Screenwriters Night honors sixty-two writers*. https://finance.yahoo.com/news/iqiyi-celebrates-fifth-annual-golden-080800502.html.

Kuaishou. 2024. *Kling AI global beta announcement*. https://ir.kuaishou.com/news-releases/news-release-details/kuaishou-launches-full-beta-testing-kling-ai-global-users-0.

Kuaishou. 2025. *Kling AI multi-image reference feature*. https://ir.kuaishou.com/news-releases/news-release-details/kuaishou-kling-ai-unveils-multi-image-reference-feature-further.

Lee, J.Y. 2011. *Animating globalization and development* (Doctoral dissertation). Duke University. https://dukespace.lib.duke.edu/bitstreams/1a612c86-eb1a-4030-b895-c510e384e880/download.

Licensing Expo China. 2024, September. *Empowering China's licensing market* [Post-show report]. https://en.licensingexpochina.com/wp-content/uploads/2024/09/%E8%8B%B1%E6%96%87-24%E5%B1%95%E5%90%8E%E6%8A%A5%E5%91%8A.pdf.

Light Chaser Animation. c. 2023. *Case study on pipeline and collaboration*. https://www.splashtop.com/api/assets/4nY1C7ISj8CWAHnS7p3l0H/Light-Chaser-Case-Study.pdf.

Loeb and Loeb. 2025, March 24. *China's AI labeling measures and mandatory national standards take effect September 1*. https://www.loeb.com/en/insights/publications/2025/03/chinas-ai-labeling-measures-and-mandatory-national-standards-take-effect-september-1.

National People's Congress (NPC). 2021, September 18. *Translation of the amended Copyright Law*. https://www.chinaiplawupdate.com/2021/09/chinas-national-peoples-congress-releases-translation-of-the-amended-copyright-law/.

Reuters. 2024, September 21. *Low-brow and vulgar micro-dramas shake up China's film industry*. https://www.reuters.com/world/china/low-brow-vulgar-micro-dramas-shake-up-chinas-film-industry-aim-hollywood-2024-09-21/.

Reuters. 2025a, February 18. *Chinese film Ne Zha 2 becomes highest-grossing animated film globally*. https://www.reuters.com/lifestyle/chinese-film-nezha-2-becomes-highest-grossing-animated-film-globally-2025-02-18/.

Reuters. 2025b, March 14. *Chinese regulators issue requirements for labeling AI-generated content*. https://www.reuters.com/world/asia-pacific/chinese-regulators-issue-requirements-labeling-ai-generated-content-2025-03-14/.

SCMP (South China Morning Post). 2025, March 18. *China's Sora-like Vidu breaks into Hollywood with deal to produce GenAI anime series*. https://www.scmp.com/tech/tech-trends/article/3302808/chinas-sora-vidu-breaks-hollywood-deal-produce-genai-anime-series.

Tech in Asia. 2025, June 19. *Bilibili unveils support program for animated microdramas*. https://www.techinasia.com/news/bilibili-unveils-support-program-animated-microdramas.

The Guardian. 2024, June 3. *Deep Sea review*. https://www.theguardian.com/film/article/2024/jun/03/deep-sea-review-underwater-restaurant-yarn-cooks-up-dazzlingly-psychedelic-images.

Tribeca Film Festival. 2023. *Deep Sea program note*. https://tribecafilm.com/films/deep-sea-2023.

UNCTAD (United Nations Conference on Trade and Development). 2023. *K-content goes global*. https://unctad.org/system/files/official-document/ditctsce2023d3_en.pdf.

USPTO (United States Patent and Trademark Office). 2024. *Administrative enforcement of intellectual property rights in China*. https://www.uspto.gov/sites/default/files/documents/china-admin-enforcement-2024.pdf.

Wired. 2025, August 7. *Americans are obsessed with watching short video dramas from China*. https://www.wired.com/story/china-reel-short-dramas-video-social-media.

Xinhua. 2025, June 30. *Ne Zha 2 ends record-breaking China run with 2.13 billion US dollars*. https://english.news.cn/20250630/74574b4e9823406fb2da565b750fa4a7/c.html.

The manufacturer's authorised representative in the EU is Springer Nature Customer Service Centre GmbH, Europaplatz 3, 69115 Heidelberg, Germany. If you have any concerns regarding our products, please contact ProductSafety@springernature.com

Printed and bound by CPI Group (UK) Ltd, Croydon, CR0 4YY
16/09/2026
02217791-0002